Home Cooking

CONTENTS

COOK WITH THE BEST

America's Best Homemade Recipes!

CONTENTS	PAGE
Appetizers To Savor	3
Beverages To Drink	4
Breads To Make	5
Brunch Fare	16
Cakes To Bake	21
Casseroles Creative	37
Cookies & Bars	39
Cooking For Two	51
Desserts Delicious	54
Foreign & Exotic	65
Fruits Fantastic	69
Meat Dishes	70
Micro-Magic	83
Party Fare	86
Pies To Bake	88
Salad Bowl	97
Salad Dressings	103
Sauces & Toppings	104
Soups & Stews	105
Vegetables Delight	109
Home Cooking Index	122

OVER 600 FAMILY-PROVEN RECIPES!

WOMEN'S CIRCLE
Home Cooking

EDITOR
JUDI MERKEL

ART DIRECTOR
VICKI MACY

GRAPHIC ART
RONDA BOLLENBACHER
CAROL DAILEY

PHOTOGRAPHY
RHONDA DAVIS
NANCY SHARP
MARY JOYNT

Published by
The House of White Birches, Inc.
306 East Parr Road
Berne, Indiana 46711

PUBLISHERS
CARL H. MUSELMAN
ARTHUR K. MUSELMAN

CHIEF EXECUTIVE OFFICER
JOHN ROBINSON

MARKETING DIRECTOR
SCOTT MOSS

CREATIVE DIRECTOR / MAGAZINES
DAN KRANER

CIRCULATION MANAGER
CAROLE BUTLER

PRODUCTION
SANDRA RIDGWAY

ADVERTISING DIRECTOR
JANET PRICE-GLICK

DISPLAY ADVERTISING
LAUREL SMITH

CLASSIFIED ADVERTISING
SHARYL BERRY

(219) 589-8741
Fax: (219) 589-8093

Women's Circle Home Cooking cookbook is a collection of recipes obtained from *Women's Circle Home Cooking* magazine which is published by The House of White Birches, 306 East Parr Road, Berne, Indiana 46711.

RETAILERS: If you are not presently being provided House of White Birches magazine copies by your area newsstand wholesaler, contact the House of White Birches (219) 589-8741 in Berne to set up a direct account.

CONTRIBUTORS: We welcome your articles with or without photos–please send manuscript and editorial materials to *Home Cooking*, 306 East Parr Road, Berne, IN 46711. Every effort is made to return submissions if accompanied by return postage. Publisher not responsible for loss or damage, so please keep a copy for your files.

Printed in U.S.A.

Exclusively distributed by:

P.S.I. & Associates, Inc.
13322 S.W. 128th St.
Miami, Florida 33186
(305) 255-7959

Appetizers
TO SAVOR

CANNOLI SHELLS AND FILLINGS

4 cups flour (sifted)
1 tablespoon sugar
1/4 teaspoon cinnamon
3/4 cup wine (Italian red)
Egg white for sealing

Sift flour, sugar, and cinnamon together onto a bread board or table top. Make a well in center, and fill with wine. With a fork, gradually blend flour into wine. Knead dough until smooth and stiff, about 15 minutes. If dough is too dry, add a little more wine. Cover dough and let stand for 2 hours in the refrigerator. Then roll 1/3 of dough to paper thinness, making a 16-inch round. Cut into eight, 5-inch circles. Wrap circles loosely around a 6-inch long cannoli form or dowels, 1 inch in diameter. Seal with egg white, and fry 2 cannoli at a time in deep fat for 1 minute or until brown on both sides. Lift out gently with a slotted spoon or tongs, drain on paper towels to cool. Remove forms *gently.* Continue until all dough is used. Then fill with Ricotta Filling or Cream Filling.

Ricotta Filling:
3 pounds Italian Ricotta
1-3/4 cups confectioners' sugar
1/2 teaspoon cinnamon
2 tablespoons citron (chopped)
1/4 cup chocolate bits (semi-sweet)

Beat Ricotta cheese in a large bowl for 1 minute. Add sugar and beat until very light and creamy, about 5 minutes. Add cinnamon, citron and chocolate bits and mix until thoroughly blended.

Cream Filling:

1 gallon milk
1 box cornstarch
4 cups sugar
1/4 cup chocolate chips (semisweet)
1 stick cinnamon (remove later)

Cook milk on a low heat and mix all ingredients except chocolate bits. Cook slowly until mixture thickens. Cool, then add chocolate bits and put filling into cannoli shells.
Leona Teodori, Warren, Mich.

MACARONI PIZZA
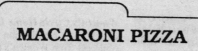
Serves 6

2 cups uncooked macaroni
15-1/2-ounce jar spaghetti sauce
1 egg
1/2 teaspoon salt
1/2 cup milk
3 tablespoons Parmesan cheese
1/2 pound ground beef
1/2 cup chopped green pepper
1/2 cup onion, chopped
4-ounce can mushrooms
8-ounce package Mozzarella cheese, grated

Cook macaroni according to package directions; drain. Beat together egg, milk, 1 teaspoon Parmesan cheese and salt. Blend into macaroni and spread in greased 9 x 13-inch baking pan. Pour spaghetti sauce over macaroni. Add small bits of raw ground meat. Sprinkle on green pepper, onion, mushrooms and remaining Parmesan cheese. Top with Mozzarella cheese. Bake at 350 degrees for 20 minutes. Let stand 5-10 minutes before cutting.

Evelyn Evanaski, Homestead, PA

SHRIMP BALL

1 (8-ounce) package cream cheese, softened
1 small can shrimp (rinsed, drained, shredded)
2 tablespoons grated Romano/ Parmesan cheese
1 teaspoon parsley flakes
1/2 teaspoon onion salt
1/2 teaspoon garlic salt
2 tablespoons catsup
Chopped walnuts

Mix all ingredients thoroughly (a food processor is helpful). Form into a ball. Roll ball in chopped walnuts. Chill 24 hours before serving. This appetizer freezes well.

Susan J. Defendorf, Holley, N.Y.

ZUCCHINI APPETIZERS
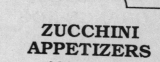
Makes 4 dozen

3 cups thinly sliced zucchini
1 cup Bisquick
1/2 cup chopped onion
1/2 cup grated Parmesan cheese
2 teaspoons snipped parsley
1/2 teaspoon salt
1/2 teaspoon seasoned salt
1/2 teaspoon oregano
Dash of pepper
1 clove garlic, chopped
1/2 cup oil
4 eggs, slightly beaten

Heat oven to 350 degrees. Grease an oblong 9x13x2-inch pan. Mix all ingredients and spread in pan. Bake until golden brown for about 25 minutes. Cut into pieces, about 2x1-inch.
Sue Thomas, Casa Grande, Ariz.

Beverages
TO DRINK

BANANA BREAKFAST DRINK

1 cup (8-ounces) plain yogurt
1 medium-sized ripe banana
1/2 cup milk
2 - 3 tablespoons orange juice concentrate
2 ice cubes, crushed
2 tablespoons honey (optional)

Combine all ingredients in blender; blend until smooth. Serve immediately in chilled glasses. Garnish with banana and orange slices.

Mrs. Bonnie Olson, Hibbing, MN

BREAKFAST ORANGE NOG
Serves 4

2 cups orange juice
1/4 cup honey
2 cups milk
2 eggs
1 teaspoon vanilla
8 ice cubes

In blender, combine all ingredients; blend for 1/2 minute or until ice cubes are crushed and mixture is frothy.

Jean Roczniak, Rochester, MN

CHOCOLATI
Serves 8

3/4 cup nonfat dry milk powder
1/3 cup cocoa
1/4 cup sugar
1 envelope unflavored gelatin
2 cups skim milk
1/4 cup creme de cacao

Early in day or up to a week ahead: In heavy 2-quart saucepan, combine nonfat dry milk powder, cocoa, sugar, and gelatin; stir in skim milk. Cook over medium-low heat, stirring constantly, until gelatin is completely dissolved, about 5 minutes. Remove saucepan from heat; stir in creme de cacao.

Pour mixture into large bowl; freeze until partially firm, about 4 hours. With mixer at high speed, beat mixture until smooth, scraping bowl with rubber spatula. Spoon mixture into eight (6-ounce) freezer-safe dessert glasses. Freeze until firm.

To serve, remove Chocolati from freezer and let stand at room temperature 10 minutes for creamier texture. (105 calories per serving).

Claire-Marie J. Heroux

CHOCOLATE SYRUP DRINK MIX
Makes 4 cups

2 cups sugar
1 quart water
4 squares baking chocolate
1/2 teaspoon salt
2 tablespoons cornstarch dissolved in 2 tablespoons cold water
2 teaspoons vanilla

Boil sugar and water for 5 minutes; add chocolate, salt and dissolved cornstarch. Stir until smooth; cook 3 minutes. Cool. Add vanilla. Store in quart jar or other glass jar in refrigerator.

To use: Stir 2 tablespoons syrup into 8-ounce glass of milk. Optional: Top with whipped cream or ice cream.

Agnes Ward, Erie, PA

COFFEE PUNCH
Makes 3-1/2 quarts

1 pint milk
2 quarts strong coffee, cooled
2 teaspoons vanilla extract
1/2 cup sugar
1 quart vanilla ice cream, softened
1/2 pint whipping cream, whipped
Ground nutmeg

Combine milk, coffee, vanilla and sugar; blend well. Place ice cream in a punch bowl; pour in coffee mixture. Top with whipped cream and nutmeg.

Barbara Beauregard-Smith, Northfield, South Australia

THIRST QUENCHER PUNCH
50 servings

1 package unsweetened cherry Kool-Aid
1 - 6 ounce can frozen orange juice
1 - 6 ounce can frozen lemonade
1 - 18 ounce can pineapple juice
13 cups water
1 cup sugar
1 quart ale

Combine all above ingredients, stir well to blend various fruit juices, Kool-Aid, water and sugar. Keeps will in refrigerator. For party punch, add ginger ale just before serving and serve over ice.

Kit Rollins, Cedarburg, WI

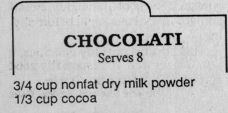

Breads
TO MAKE

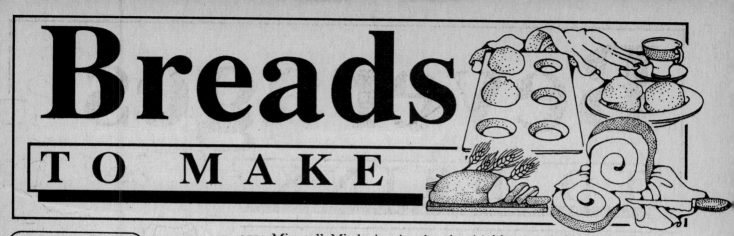

FRENCH BREAD BUTTER

1 pound butter or margarine
1 teaspoon thyme
1/2 teaspoon dry parsley flakes
1 teaspoon celery seeds
4 finely-chopped green onions
1/2 teaspoon garlic powder

Butter should be at room temperature. Mix all together and let stand 2 hours before using. Slice French bread; butter both sides. Freeze about 3 days before needed. Keeps about 6 weeks frozen. Bake frozen at 400 degrees for 45-50 minutes.

Lorraine Schroeder, Fallbrook, CA

BANANA DOUGHNUTS

Makes 22 doughnuts

3 cups solid shortening or peanut oil
4 cups flour
3/4 cup sugar
4 teaspoons baking powder
1 teaspoon salt
1/2 teaspoon cinnamon
1/2 teaspoon nutmeg
1/4 cup butter
1 cup ripe bananas, mashed
2 eggs, well beaten

Topping:
3/4 cup sugar
2 teaspoons cinnamon

In deep-fat fryer, heat oil to 375 degrees. In a large bowl, mix flour, sugar, baking powder, salt, cinnamon and nutmeg. Cut in butter. Make a well in the center and add the bananas and

eggs. Mix well. Mix by hand as dough is heavy. Turn out on a lightly floured board and roll 1/2 inch thick. Cut with 2-1/2 inch doughnut cutter. Deep-fry, until golden brown. Drain on absorbent paper. Combine topping and dip warm doughnuts in the mixture.

Mrs. Agnes Ward, Erie, PA

POPOVERS

2 eggs
1 cup milk
1 tablespoon melted butter
1 cup flour
1/4 teaspoon salt

Put all ingredients in a large bowl and mix thoroughly, without overbeating. Half-fill greased muffin tins or custard cups. Put them in a *cold* oven and set the heat for 450 degrees. Bake for 15 minutes, then reduce heat to 350 degrees, and bake for another 15 - 20 minutes. Test one to be sure it is done by removing it from the pan. It should be crisp on outside and moist and tender on inside.

NOTE: The secret in making good popovers is to start them in a *cold* oven. Try it! You'll like it!

Lucille Roehr, Hammond, IN

WHOLE-GRAIN APPLE MUFFINS

1-1/4 cups whole wheat flour
1/4 teaspoon salt
2 tablespoons brown sugar
1-1/4 cups low-fat milk
3 tablespoons vegetable oil

1 tablespoon baking powder
1/2 teaspoon cinnamon
2 cups Nutra Grain wheat cereal
1 egg
1/2 cup finely chopped apple

Stir flour, baking powder, salt, cinnamon, and sugar together. Measure Nutra Grain cereal and milk into large bowl. Stir. Let stand 5 minutes. Add egg and oil; beat well. Add flour mixture. Stir in apples. Spread evenly into 12 greased muffin pans/cups. Bake at 400 degrees for 20 minutes or until lightly browned. Serve warm.

1966 Queen Carole Cota Gelfuso

FRESH CARROT BREAD

2 cups granulated sugar
3 eggs
1 cup salad oil
3 cups unbleached flour, sifted
1/4 teaspoon baking powder
1 teaspoon baking soda
1 teaspoon salt
1 teaspoon cinnamon
2 cups grated, raw carrots
1 cup chopped pecans

Mix sugar, oil, and eggs in a bowl. Add sifted flour, baking powder, soda, salt, and cinnamon. Stir in carrots and nuts.

Pour into two greased bread pans and bake in a 350-degree oven for 40 minutes. Turn bread out of pans onto wire rack and cool thoroughly. Best if allowed to cool overnight before slicing.

This bread is not only delicious, it also freezes well. It's especially good spread with soft cream cheese.

Arlene Shovald, Salida, Colo.

PARSLEY BREAD

Makes 2 loaves

1 package yeast
1 cup warm water
2 tablespoons oil
1 teaspoon salt
1/2 cup wheat germ
1/4 cup milk
2-1/4 - 3 cups flour
Sugar

Filling:

1 cup chopped parsley
1/4 cup chopped green onions
2 cloves garlic, minced
1/2 teaspoon pepper
2 tablespoons soft butter
2 tablespoons mustard

Dissolve yeast in the water with a pinch of sugar. Gradually add oil and combined salt, wheat germ, milk, and flour. Mix well and knead until a soft dough is formed. Place in a greased bowl. Cover and let rise about 1 hour.

Meanwhile, mix together the filling ingredients until well blended. Cut the dough in half. Roll each into a rectangle 1/4 inch thick, spread with the filling. Roll up tightly, taper the ends. Make 3-4 slits in the top of each loaf. Let rise about 30 minutes until loaves are fluffy. Bake at 375 degrees for 30 minutes. Cool on a wire rack.

Linda Corley, Sperry, OK

GARLIC BREAD

1 loaf French Bread
Soften 1 stick butter in microwave
Add 2 minced garlic cloves
1 cup Parmesan cheese
1/4 cup chopped parsley
Paprika

Cut bread into 1-1/2 inch slices and spread with butter/garlic mix. Sprinkle with Parmesan cheese, parsley, and paprika. Place bread under broiler and cook until golden brown, about 3 minutes, watching closely. Serve hot.

Renee Dennis Wells, Columbia, SC

GARLIC CHEESE BREAD

1/2 pound margarine or butter
1/4 teaspoon garlic powder
1/2 teaspoon sesame seed
1/2 teaspoon poppy seed
1/2 teaspoon caraway seed
1/4 pound grated cheddar cheese

Blend thoroughly. Spread on French bread, cut lengthwise and broil with medium heat until brown and bubbly. May also use wiener buns or hamburger buns. Great on toast for breakfast, as well. Keeps real well in refrigerator.

Ilene Ongman, Klamoth Falls, ON

CHEESE CARAWAY BATTER BREAD

1 package active dry yeast
1-1/4 cups warm water (105-115 degrees)
1 cup shredded sharp Cheddar cheese (about 4 ounces)
2 tablespoons shortening
2 tablespoons sugar
2 teaspoons salt
1 teaspoon caraway seed
2-2/3 cups Gold Medal flour
Melted butter or margarine

In large mixer bowl, dissolve yeast in warm water. Add cheese, shortening, sugar, salt, caraway seed, and 2 cups of the flour. Blend 30 seconds on low speed, scraping bowl occasionally. (By hand, beat 300 vigorous strokes). Stir in remaining flour until smooth. Scrape batter from side of bowl. Cover; let rise in warm place until double, about 30 minutes.

Stir down batter by beating about 25 strokes. Spread evenly in greased loaf pan, 9x5x3 inches. Smooth out top of batter by patting into shape with floured hands. Cover; let rise until double, about 40 minutes. Heat oven to 375 degrees; bake 45 minutes or until loaf sounds hollow when tapped. Brush top with melted butter. Remove loaf from pan; cool on wire rack.

Sharon Jones, Galveston, Texas

FIESTA BREAD

Makes 2 loaves

1/4 cup butter
1/2 cup catsup
1 cup shredded Cheddar cheese
1/2 cup chopped black olives
1/3 cup chopped green pepper
1/3 cup chopped onions
(2 loaves) brown and serve French bread

Mix above ingredients together except for bread. Cut each loaf of bread in half and spread with mixture. Wrap in foil and bake as bread wrapper directs. Bake approximately 15 minutes at 425 degrees.

Agnes Ward, Erie, PA

HAWAIIAN SWEET BREAD

Makes 2 loaves

1/4 cup instant mashed potato flakes
2/3 cup boiling water
1/4 cup dry milk
1/2 cup butter
2 packages yeast
1/3 cup warm water
4-1/2 - 5 cups flour, divided
3 eggs
1 teaspoon salt
1/2 teaspoon vanilla
1/4 teaspoon lemon extract
1 egg beaten

Put potato flakes, boiling water, dry milk, and butter in pan; bring to boil. Let cool to 100 degrees. In large mixing bowl, combine yeast and warm water. Blend in potato mixture. Add 2 cups flour and beat to blend. Stir in eggs, salt, vanilla, and lemon extract until smooth. Add 1-1/2 cups flour; mix. Add more flour, as needed, to make dough stiff. Knead 15-20 times or until satiny. Put into greased bowl, knead lightly and let rise 10 minutes. Make into 2 rounds. Bake in preheated 350 degree oven 25-30 minutes or until toothpick inserted in center comes out clean.

Kit Rollins, Cedarburg, WI

ALOHA TEA BREAD

Makes 2 loaves

1 cup butter
2 cups sugar
4 eggs
1 cup mashed bananas
4 cups flour
2 teaspoons baking powder
1 teaspoon baking soda
3/4 teaspoon salt
8 ounces of crushed pineapple, undrained
1 cup shredded coconut

Cream sugar and butter. Add eggs, mixing well. Add mashed bananas and flour, sifted together with the baking powder, baking soda, and salt. Fold in pineapple and coconut. Bake in 2 greased 9x5-inch loaf pans. Bake at 350 degrees for 70 minutes.

Cynthia Kannenberg, Brown Deer, WI

PEANUT BUTTER BACON BREAD

1 cup sugar
1 tablespoon melted shortening
1 cup milk
1 egg, well beaten
1 cup peanut butter
1/2 teaspoon salt
2 cups flour
3 teaspoons baking powder
1 cup chopped unsalted peanuts
1 cup bacon chips, crisp

Mix sugar, shortening, and milk with well-beaten egg. Add peanut butter. Mix in salt, flour, and baking powder, which have been sifted together. Add nuts and bacon chips. Let stand in a greased and floured loaf pan for 20 minutes. Bake in a 350 degree oven for 1 hour, or until tested done.

Agnes Ward, Erie, Pa.

SWISS CHEESE-BACON BREAD

3-1/2 cups buttermilk baking mix
1/4 cup sugar
1-1/2 cups (6 ounces) shredded Swiss cheese
6 crisply cooked bacon slices, crumbled
1-1/3 cups milk
1 egg, beaten

Preheat oven to 350 degrees. Combine baking mix and sugar; add cheese and bacon. Stir combined milk and egg into dry ingredients, mixing just until blended. Spoon batter into greased 9x5 inch loaf pan. Bake until wooden pick inserted near center comes out clean, about 45 minutes. Cool 5 minutes; remove from pan.

Diantha Susan Hibbard, Rochester, N.Y.

OLIVE PIZZA BREAD

1 egg, slightly beaten
1 cup pitted ripe black olives, drained and chopped
1/2 cup green olives with pimento centers, drained, and sliced
5 slices bacon, crisp fried, well drained, and chopped
1/3 cup margarine, melted
1 small onion, minced
1 teaspoon Worcestershire sauce
Dash hot pepper sauce
2 cups (8 ounces) process American cheese
3 cups packaged biscuit mix
1 cup milk
Pre-heat oven to 425 degrees

Mix together, in a large bowl: Egg, onion, olives, margarine, bacon, Worcestershire sauce, pepper sauce and cheese.

In another bowl combine the biscuit mix and milk; stir well to make a soft dough.

Spread dough in a greased 14 inch pizza pan. Spoon olive mixture evenly over the top of dough. Bake in a hot oven 425 degrees for 20-25 minutes.

Marie Fusaro, Manasquan, NJ

GOLDEN SPIKE BREAD

Serves 12

6 hot dog buns
1/4 cup butter
2 tablespoons chives
1 teaspoon Worcestershire sauce
1 (15 ounce jar) cheese spread

Cream the butter with chives, Worcestershire sauce; then beat in the cheese spread with the electric mixer. Spread the cheese mixture on each half of the hot dog bun. Heat on foil on the barbecue grill.

APPLE-STREUSEL COFFEE BREAD

1 - 16 ounce loaf frozen white bread dough
2 tablespoons butter or margarine, softened
1-1/2 cups finely chopped, peeled apples
1/2 cup packed brown sugar
1 teaspoon cinnamon
1 tablespoon butter or margarine, melted
2 tablespoons all-purpose flour
2 tablespoons sugar
1 tablespoon butter or margarine
1/3 cup slivered almonds (optional)

Thaw dough per package directions; divide in half; let rest 10 minutes. On floured board roll each dough half into an 8-inch square. Spread each with 1 tablespoon softened butter. Arrange half of apples down center of each square. Combine brown sugar and cinnamon; sprinkle over apples. Cutting toward filling, make 2-inch cuts in dough at 1-inch intervals on both sides of apples. Fold alternately over apples; fold under ends. Place loaves in greased 15 x 10 x 1 inch pan and brush with melted butter. Stir together flour and sugar. Cut in the 1 tablespoon butter until mixture is crumbly; sprinkle half over each loaf. Top with almonds. Cover; let rise until doubled. Bake in 350 degree oven - 30 minutes or until brown. Serve warm.

Agnes Ward, Erie, PA

SUPER EASY DELICIOUS WHITE BREAD

Makes 2 loaves

6 cups all-purpose flour
1-1/2 teaspoons salt
1/4 cup sugar
1/2 teaspoon baking soda
1-1/2 teaspoons baking powder
1/2 cup shortening (preferably lard)
1 envelope active dry yeast
1-3/4 cups buttermilk (preferably 7 tablespoons Saco dry buttermilk with dry ingredients and 1-3/4 cups water as liquid)

Sift dry ingredients. Add shortening and cut in with pastry blender as for pie crust. Add yeast mixed with 1/2 cup lukewarm water and thoroughly dissolve. Add buttermilk and beat with spoon until all ingredients are thoroughly mixed. Cover tightly and put in refrigerator overnight.

Next day, if possible, leave at room temperature for an hour or two. Knead dough for 5-7 minutes until smooth and blistery. Divide in half and form into loaves by rolling dough out and rolling up tightly like a jellyroll. Place each loaf in a greased 9" x 5" loaf pan. Brush with melted butter. Let rise until double. Bake in moderate oven (375 degrees) for 40 minutes.

This has replaced all my other bread recipes as it is by far the easiest I have made with delicious flavor and good texture. The dough can be raised in the microwave using microwave-safe bread pans.

Dawn Thompson, Rockford, IL

BOSTON BROWN BREAD

A slow pot recipe

1/2 cup whole wheat flour
1/4 cup white flour
1/4 cup corn meal
1/2 teaspoon baking powder
1/4 teaspoon baking soda
1/4 teaspoon salt

1 beaten egg
1/4 cup molasses
2 tablespoons sugar
2 teaspoons oil
3/4 cup buttermilk or sour milk
1/4 cup raisins

Stir dry ingredients together. Combine egg, molasses, sugar and oil. Add flour mixture alternately with milk. Beat well; add raisins. Turn into two well-greased vegetable cans (divide batter evenly). Cover cans with foil and tie tightly with string. Place in slow pot with about 2 inches of water. Cover pot and cook on high for three hours. Remove cans from cooker; cool 10 minutes before taking breads from cans.

Mary Grills, New London, CT

BANANA ORANGE NUTMEG BREAD

2 extra ripe, medium bananas
1 cup chopped walnuts
1 cup all-purpose flour
1 teaspoon baking powder
1 teaspoon soda
3/4 teaspoon ground nutmeg
1/4 teaspoon salt
1/4 cup butter, softened
3/4 cup sugar
1 egg
1/4 cup orange juice
1 tablespoon grated orange peel
1 cup raisins

Puree bananas in blender (1 cup). Pulverize walnuts in blender; combine with flour, baking powder, soda, nutmeg and salt. Cream butter with sugar until light and fluffy. Beat in egg, orange juice and peel until blended. Beat in flour mixture in thirds alternately with pureed bananas. Stir in raisins. Pour into greased 9 x 5 inch loaf pan. Bake in 325 degree oven 1 hour 20 minutes or until toothpick inserted comes out clean. Cool in pan 10 minutes. Turn onto wire rack to cool.

Mrs. Kit Rollins, Cedarburg, WI

E-Z RAISIN BREAD

3 cups unsifted flour
1 package dry yeast
1 teaspoon sugar
1 teaspoon salt
1/2 cup ice cold skim milk
3/4 cup boiling water
1/2 cup raisins

Put flour in bowl; stir in yeast, sugar, and salt. In another mixing bowl, combine skim milk and boiling water. Sprinkle 1/2 of the flour mixture onto the milk mixture; beat well. Stir in raisins and remaining flour mixture to make a stiff, sticky batter. Place in a sprayed, non-stick bread pan or loaf pan. Cover with a clean towel (do not use a terry cloth towel) and put in a warm place for 45 minutes to rise until double. Bake in a preheated 400 degree oven for 25 minutes. Slice thinly when cool; toast; and serve. Makes about 20 slices, 80 calories each.

Joy Shamway, Freeport, Ill.

APRICOT BREAD

Makes 2 small loaves

1 cup dried apricots
1 cup sugar
2 teaspoons margarine
1 egg
1/4 cup water
1/2 cup orange juice
2 cups flour
2 teaspoons baking powder
1/4 teaspoon soda
1 teaspoon salt
1/2 cup nuts

Soak the apricots in water until soft. Drain; cut into small pieces. Mix the sugar, margarine, and egg together. Stir in water and orange juice. Sift the dry ingredients together and add to the creamed mixture. Fold in apricots and nuts. Bake in a 350 degree oven for 50-60 minutes. One package of dried apricots will make a double recipe. This bread freezes well.

Dorothy Pelster, Hastings, NE

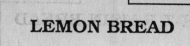

LEMON BREAD

1/2 cup shortening
1 cup sugar
2 eggs, slightly beaten
1-1/4 cups flour
1 teaspoon baking powder
1/4 teaspoon salt
1/2 cup milk
1/2 cup finely chopped walnuts or
    pecans
1 lemon - grated rind and juice
1/4 cup sugar

Cream together the shortening and sugar. Sift together the flour, baking powder, and salt. Stir this mixture into the creamed mixture alternately with the milk. Add the walnuts or pecans and grated rind of lemon. Bake at 350 degrees for about 1 hour in a 9 x 5 inch loaf pan. Remove the bread from the oven and pierce surface with a small skewer or toothpick to make small holes. Combine the sugar and lemon juice. Pour over hot bread very slowly.

When cool store in an air-tight container. Slice in thin slices. Great with cream cheese.

A. Mayer, Richmond, VA

JOSEPHINE HANEL'S RHUBARB BREAD

This makes two, quite solid loaves and slices well.
1-1/2 cups brown sugar
2/3 cup salad oil
1 egg
1 teaspoon vanilla
1/4 teaspoon salt
1 teaspoon baking soda
1 cup sour milk
1-1/2 cups diced rhubarb
2-1/2 cups flour: half white and half
    whole wheat although bread CAN
    be made with only the white.
1/4 cup wheat germ (optional)

Mix sugar, salad oil, and egg; add vanilla and salt.

Mix soda into sour milk; add to egg-sugar-oil mixture.

Then add flour, stirring as you add. Place into two 4 x 8" greased pans.

Bake about an hour, at 350 degrees.

1/4 cup of sugar mixed with a tablespoon of soft margarine is a nice addition. Add to top when you take loaves from oven, while they are warm.

HAWAIIAN ISLE CARROT BREAD

1 (8-1/4 ounce) can crushed pineapple (Dole)
1-1/2 cups sifted flour
3 teaspoons baking powder
1 teaspoon salt
1/2 teaspoon baking soda
1/2 teaspoon cinnamon
1/4 teaspoon nutmeg
1 cup unsifted whole wheat flour
1/4 cup wheat germ
2 large eggs
1/2 cup light brown sugar, packed
1 cup grated raw carrots
2 tablespoons syrup from pineapple
1/2 cup salad oil

Drain pineapple, and save the syrup. Into a bowl resift flour with baking powder, salt, soda, and spices. Stir in whole wheat flour, and wheat germ. In another bowl beat eggs. Stir in sugar, carrots, 2 tablespoons pineapple syrup, drained pineapple, and oil. Add to dry mixture. Mix well. Divide between (2) 7-1/2 x 3-1/2 x 2-1/4-inch greased loaf pans. Spread smooth. Bake below center of oven at 350 degrees for 45 minutes. Let stand in pans 10 minutes. Remove and cool on wire rack.

Cynthia Mae Kannenberg, Brown Deer, WI

ORANGE APPLE BREAD

Makes 2 round loaves

2 cups flour
1/2 cup butter
1 cup sugar
1/3 cup orange juice
1/4 cup nuts
1 tablespoon grated orange rind
1 egg
1 teaspoon salt
1/2 teaspoon baking soda
1 teaspoon baking powder
3/4 cup raisins (golden seedless)
1 cup apples, chopped

Bake in two family-size soup cans, filled 2/3 full, or a 46-ounce juice can. Grease cans. Bake 1 hour at 350 degrees.

Jennie Lien, Stoughton, WI

FRESH APPLE BREAD

1/3 cup margarine, softened
1 cup sugar
1 egg
2 cups sifted flour
1 teaspoon baking powder
1/2 teaspoon baking soda
1/2 teaspoon salt
1/3 cup fruit juice
3/4 cup white or seedless raisins
1/3 cup chopped pecans
1 cup finely-chopped, peeled, tart
    apples

With electric mixer, cream together margarine, sugar, and egg. Add sifted flour, baking powder, baking soda, and salt, alternately, with the fruit juice. When thoroughly combined, add raisins, pecans, and chopped apples; fold in. Pour into 3 small (7-1/2x3-1/2x2-1/4 inches) bread pans, which have been greased with vegetable shortening. Bake for 45 minutes in a 350 degree oven. Serve warm, right from bread pans.

Agnes Ward, Erie, Pa.

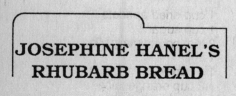

CALUMET PRIZE BAKING POWDER BISCUITS

Makes 1 dozen

2 cups sifted cake flour
2 teaspoons Calumet baking
  powder
1/2 teaspoon salt
4 tablespoons butter or shortening
2/3 cup milk

Sift flour once; measure; add baking powder and salt; sift again. Cut in shortening. Add milk all at once; stir carefully until flour is dampened. Stir vigorously until mixture forms soft dough and follows spoon around bowl. Turn out on lightly floured board and knead 30 seconds. Roll 1/2 inch thick; cut with floured 2-inch biscuit cutter. Bake on ungreased cookie sheet at 450 degrees for 12-15 minutes.

Dianna Shimizu, Spokane, Wash.

BUTTERMILK BISCUITS

Makes 10 biscuits

2 cups flour
1 tablespoon sugar
2-1/2 teaspoons baking powder
1/4 teaspoon salt
1/4 teaspoon baking soda
6 tablespoons butter
3/4 cup buttermilk

Preheat oven to 425 degrees. Sift dry ingredients into mixing bowl. Cut in butter until mixture resembles coarse crumbs. Add buttermilk all at once; stir until dough clings together. Turn out onto floured surface and knead about 10 times. Roll out to 1/2 inch thickness. Cut with 2-1/2 inch biscuit cutter. Bake on an ungreased sheet for 12 minutes.

Agnes Ward, Erie, Pa.

SAUSAGE BISCUITS

Makes 3 dozen

3/4 pound bulk pork sausage
2-2/3 cups all-purpose flour
2 tablespoons sugar
1 teaspoon baking powder
1/2 teaspoon baking soda
1/2 teaspoon salt
1/2 cup shortening
1 package dry yeast
1/4 cup warm water
1 cup buttermilk
Melted margarine

Cook sausage in skillet until browned; stirring to crumble; drain well. Set aside. Combine next 5 ingredients, mixing well; cut in shortening until mixture resembles coarse meal. Dissolve yeast in warm water; let stand 5 minutes. Add yeast mixture to buttermilk, stirring well. Add buttermilk mixture to dry ingredients, stirring just until dry ingredients are moistened. Knead in sausage. Turn dough out onto lightly floured surface; knead lightly. Roll dough to 1/2 inch thickness; cut with a 1-3/4 inch round cutter. Place biscuits on ungreased baking sheet. Brush tops with melted butter. Bake at 425 degrees for 10 minutes or until golden brown.

Note: Biscuits may be frozen. To freeze, place uncooked biscuits on an ungreased baking sheet; cover and freeze until firm. Transfer frozen biscuits to plastic bags. To bake, place frozen biscuits on ungreased baking sheet; bake at 425 degrees for 10 minutes.

Suzanne Dawson, Cypress, Texas

HAMBURGER BUNS

Makes 4 dozen

1-3/4 cups sugar
1 cup lard
1 package yeast
1 tablespoon sugar
12 cups flour
4 cups water
1 tablespoon salt
1/2 cup warm water
3 beaten eggs

Boil the sugar and water together for 5 minutes; add lard and salt. Cool 1 hour. Mix yeast, warm water, and remaining sugar. Add with the remaining ingredients to first mixture. Cover and let rise. Allow to rise; punch down for the second time. Shape into rolls. Put onto greased pans and cover. Let rise for several hours. Bake buns at 350 degrees for 15-20 minutes.

Marcella Swigert, Monroe City, MO

HONEY BUNS

1 can (10 ounce) refrigerated big
  flaky biscuits
1/4 cup chopped pecans
3/4 teaspoon cinnamon
1/3 cup honey
2 tablespoons brown sugar
1/3 cup margarine (melted)
2 tablespoons margarine (melted) for
  topping
Pre-heat oven to 350 degrees.

Combine pecans, honey, and 1/3 cup melted margarine in a small bowl and pour into an ungreased 9 x 4 inch loaf pan. Separate refrigerator biscuit dough into 10 biscuits. In small bowl combine the brown sugar and cinnamon. Take each biscuit and press about 1 teaspoon of sugar-cinnamon mixture into each side of biscuit. Stand biscuits on edge slightly overlapping in 2 rows of 5 biscuits each in pan holding nut-honey mixture. Drizzle 2 tablespoons melted margarine over top and bake 25-30 minutes at 350 degrees until browned. Cool 3 minutes before turning out onto serving plate. Serve warm.

Jodie McCoy, Tulsa, OK

APPLESAUCE MUFFINS

2 cups all-purpose flour
1/2 cup brown sugar
1 tablespoon baking powder
1 teaspoon salt
1/2 teaspoon cinnamon
1/2 teaspoon nutmeg
1/2 stick (1/4 cup) butter
1 cup thick applesauce
1/4 cup milk
1 egg
1/2 cup raisins

Heat oven to 425 degrees. Grease muffin cups. In large bowl, combine dry ingredients and blend. Melt butter in saucepan. Turn off heat; stir in applesauce and milk. Beat in egg. Stir applesauce mixture into dry ingredients and, when well-blended, stir in raisins. Spoon batter into muffin tins. Bake 15-20 minutes. Let cool 5 minutes before removing from muffin tin.

Peggy Fowler Revels, Woodruff, S.C.

PINEAPPLE OATMEAL MUFFINS
Makes 1 dozen

1 (8-ounce) can crushed pineapple, undrained
1 cup rolled oats
1/2 cup sour cream or buttermilk
1/3 cup shortening
1/3 cup brown sugar
1 teaspoon grated orange peel
1 egg, beaten
1-1/4 cups sifted all-purpose flour
1 teaspoon baking powder
1/2 teaspoon baking soda
1 teaspoon salt

Combine undrained pineapple, oats, and sour cream; let stand 15 minutes. Cream shortening, sugar, and peel together thoroughly; stir in egg. Sift flour with baking powder, soda, and salt; add to creamed mixture alternately with oat mixture. Bake in well-greased muffin tins in 400-degree oven for 25 minutes.

Ida Bloedow, Madison, Wis.

WHOLE-GRAIN ENGLISH MUFFINS
Makes 6

1-1/2 cups wheat flour
1/2 cup cornmeal
2-1/2 teaspoons baking powder
1/2 cup dry milk powder
2 tablespoons vegetable oil
2 tablespoons sugar
1-1/2 cups plus 1 tablespoon water

Mix flour, baking powder, cornmeal, and dry milk powder together. Add oil and sugar. Add 1 cup water and stir until all moisture is absorbed. Add more water for a thick, but spreadable, batter. Oil the electric frying pan and set for 325 degrees or medium. Oil the insides of tuna cans with the bottoms removed, or English muffin rings, and place in skillet. Fill the rings with batter about 1/3 full. Cover pan and let cook for 6 to 7 minutes. When the tops of the muffins look dry, flip over the batter and the rings with a spatula. Cook 3 minutes more. Use a knife to loosen muffins from the rings. Muffins freeze well.

Doris Williams, Brainerd, Minn.

SPICE MUFFINS

2 cups pancake mix
1/4 cup sugar
1 teaspoon cinnamon
1 teaspoon allspice
2 teaspoons sugar
1 egg, beaten
2/3 cup milk

Combine pancake mix, sugar, cinnamon, allspice, and sugar in a mixing bowl. Add egg and milk. Beat until smooth. Fill muffin cups 2/3 full. Bake at 400 degrees for 15 minutes.

CRANBERRY MUFFINS
Makes 12 muffins

1-1/4 cups sugar
1/4 cup butter or margarine
2 eggs
1/2 cup milk
2 cups all-purpose flour
2 teaspoons baking powder
1/4 teaspoon salt
2 cups Ocean Spray fresh or frozen cranberries, coarsely chopped

Preheat oven to 350 degrees. In a bowl, cream together sugar and butter. Add eggs, one at a time, beating after each addition. In a bowl, sift together flour, baking powder, and salt; add alternately with milk to the creamed sugar mixture. Stir in chopped cranberries. Spoon into 12 paper-lined 2-1/2-inch muffin cups, filling 3/4 full. Bake 25 to 30 minutes.

ENGLISH MUFFIN BREAD
Makes 2 loaves

2 packages active dry yeast
6 cups flour
1 tablespoon sugar
2 teaspoons salt
2 cups milk
1/4 teaspoon baking soda
1/2 cup water
Cornmeal

Combine 3 cups flour, yeast, sugar, salt, and soda. Heat liquids until very warm. Add to dry mixture; beat well. Stir in rest of flour to make a stiff batter. Spoon into two 8-1/2x4-1/2-inch loaf pans that have been greased and sprinkled with cornmeal. Sprinkle top with cornmeal. Cover. Let rise in warm place for 45 minutes. Bake at 400 degrees for 25 minutes. Remove from pans immediately and cool.

Althea Kaufman, Hollsapple, Pa.

CORNBREAD WITH PARMESAN CHEESE
Serves 4-6

3-3/4 cups milk
1-1/2 cups yellow cornmeal
3 eggs, lightly beaten
1/8 teaspoon cayenne pepper
1/2 teaspoon salt
Pinch black pepper
1 cup grated Parmesan cheese, divided
4 tablespoons butter

Heat oven to 425 degrees. Heat milk in 3-quart saucepan, over moderately high heat, to just below boiling point. Reduce heat to moderate; gradually stir in cornmeal. Cook, stirring constantly to avoid lumping, for 5 minutes or until thick. Remove from heat. Beat eggs into mixture, using wire whisk. Add seasonings and 1/4 cup cheese. Pour mixture into buttered 13x9x2-inch baking dish. Dot with butter; sprinkle on rest of cheese. Bake, uncovered, for 30 to 35 minutes or until firm. Cut into squares and serve with butter and honey or favorite jelly.

Edna Askins, Greenville, Texas

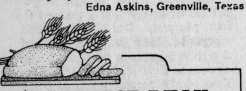

CHEESE DILLY BREAD

3 cups biscuit mix
1-1/2 cups grated sharp Cheddar cheese
1 tablespoon sugar
1-1/4 cups milk
1 egg, lightly beaten
1 tablespoon vegetable oil
1/2 teaspoon dill weed
1/2 teaspoon dry mustard

Preheat oven to 350 degrees. Grease 9x5-inch loaf pan or 6-cup bundt pan. Combine biscuit mix, cheese, and sugar in bowl. Combine remaining ingredients in second bowl and mix well. Stir into dry mixture, blending well. Beat slightly to remove lumps. Turn into pan and bake 45-50 minutes.

Kit Rollins, Cedarburg, Wisc.

BACON CORN BREAD
Serves 4

1 cup stone-ground cornmeal
1 cup unbleached flour
1/4 cup sugar
2-1/2 teaspoons baking powder
1/4 teaspoon salt
1 cup buttermilk
1 cup diced, crisp-cooked bacon
6 tablespoons butter, melted
1 egg, slightly beaten

Preheat oven to 400 degrees. Grease a 9-inch baking pan or skillet and place in oven to heat well. Stir dry ingredients together in a bowl. Stir in buttermilk, bacon, butter, and egg. Mix well. Pour batter into hot pan and bake for 25 minutes or until edges are light brown. May also spoon batter into greased muffin cups and bake 20 minutes.

Mary Linger, Jacksonville, Fla.

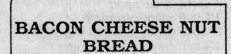

BACON CHEESE NUT BREAD

12 slices bacon, cooked crisp and crumbled
1 egg
3 cups biscuit mix
3/4 cup shredded sharp cheese
1 cup milk
2 tablespoons minced onion
Dash Tabasco sauce
3/4 cup coarsely chopped walnuts

Beat egg lightly. Stir in biscuit mix and shredded cheese. add milk, onion and Tabasco sauce. Mix well. The dough will be stiff. Stir in bacon and walnuts. Turn into greased 9x5x3" pan. Bake in 350—degree oven for 50 minutes or until loaf tests done. Let stand 5 minutes; then turn out onto cake rack to cool. It's great!

Barbara Nowakowski, No. Tonawanda, Ny.

PIMIENTO CHEESE BREAD

3-1/2 cups biscuit mix
1 egg, beaten
1-1/2 cups milk
1 cup grated Cheddar cheese
1 (4-ounce) jar (or can) pimientos, drained and chopped

Preheat oven to 350 degrees. Mix all ingredients together; pour into well greased loaf pan. Bake 60 minutes.

Joy Shamway, Freeport, Ill.

CHEESY DROP BISCUITS
Makes 18 biscuits

2 cups sifted flour
1/2 teaspoon salt
4 tablespoons shortening
2 teaspoons baking powder
1 cup grated American cheese
1 cup milk

Sift flour and measure; add baking powder and salt and sift again. Cut in cheese and shortening. Add milk gradually until soft dough is formed. Drop by teaspoon onto ungreased cookie sheet. Bake at 450 degrees for 12-15 minutes.

These are great and from a 1953 cookbook. Biscuits are great with a salad for lunch.

Jodie McCoy, Tulsa, Okla.

MASHED POTATO BISCUITS

1 teaspoon salt
1-3/4 cups all-purpose flour
1 cup chilled butter
2 tablespoons sour cream
1 cup cold mashed potatoes
4 egg yolks

Stir the salt with the flour; cut in the butter. Add cream, potatoes, and 3 of the egg yolks. Blend and knead together; form into a ball. Chill until firm. Repeat the kneading and chilling process. After chilling, roll out to 1/4-inch thickness. Brush with remaining egg yolk; cut with 2-inch biscuit cutter. Bake at 400 degrees for 15 minutes, or until golden in color.

Gwen Campbell, Sterling, VA

ICE WATER FUDGE LOAF
Serves 8-10

2 cups light brown sugar
1/2 cup butter, softened
2 eggs, separated
1 teaspoon vanilla extract
1/2 cup dairy sour cream
1 teaspoon baking soda
3 squares semi-sweet chocolate, melted
1/2 cup ice cold water
2 cups cake flour, sifted

Thoroughly cream brown sugar and butter. Add egg yolks; beat until mixture is light and fluffy; add vanilla. Mix sour cream and baking soda together; let stand 2 minutes. Add sour cream to the sugar mixture; beat. Add melted chocolate; beat again. Alternately, add the ice water and flour; beating after each addition. Beat egg whites to stiff peaks; gently fold into batter. Pour into a 10x5-inch greased loaf pan. Bake at 375 degrees for 40 minutes or until tested done in middle of loaf.

Gwen Campbell, Sterling, Va.

QUICK YEAST BUNS
Makes 15-18

1-1/2 cups water
1/4 cup Crisco
3 tablespoons sugar
1 teaspoon salt
1 package dry yeast
1 beaten egg
3-1/2 cups flour

Heat water, Crisco, sugar, and salt in saucepan; stir until Crisco melts. Cool to lukewarm, then add yeast and let it dissolve. Add egg and mix well. Stir in flour. Spoon dough into greased muffin pans, filling each 1/2 full. Let rise 1 hour or until doubled in size. Bake at 425 degrees for 12-14 minutes or until golden brown.

Ruth Voges, Riesel, Texas

YUM-YUM BUNS
Makes 8-10

1/2 pound pork sausage links
1 (8-ounce) package refrigerated biscuits
1/2 cup orange marmalade
2 tablespoons raisins
2 tablespoons chopped pecans

Preheat oven to 400 degrees. Cook pork sausage links according to package directions. Separate biscuits and place on ungreased baking sheet. Flatten into ovals measuring 5x3 inches. Top each with a pork sausage link. Combine marmalade with raisins and spoon over sausage. Sprinkle with nuts. Bake 10 to 12 minutes, or until biscuits are done.

CROUTONS FOR FRUIT SOUPS
Makes 14-18 cubes

4 slices stale bread
1/2 cup whipping cream
2 tablespoons butter or margarine
1/4 cup confectioners' sugar

Cut bread into 1-inch cubes. Dip cubes into cream; quickly sauté in butter. Dust with confectioners' sugar.

LOW-CAL GINGERBREAD
Serves 12

1 cup sifted flour
1/2 teaspoon baking soda
1/4 teaspoon salt
1 teaspoon cinnamon
1-1/2 teaspoons ginger
1/4 teaspoon nutmeg
1 egg
2 tablespoons dark brown sugar
1-1/8 teaspoons liquid Sucaryl or equivalent in a dry sugar substitute
1/4 cup molasses
1/2 cup buttermilk or sour skim milk
3 tablespoons melted butter or melted margarine

Preheat oven to 350 degrees. Grease an 8-inch square pan and dust lightly with flour. Sift flour, soda, salt, cinnamon, ginger, and nutmeg together. Beat egg, brown sugar, sugar substitute, and molasses together until light. Add buttermilk and butter (or margarine), then the flour mixture. Beat until smooth. Turn into the prepared pan. Bake 35 minutes or until a cake tester comes out clean. Cool on cake rack. May be topped with whipped cream, whipped topping, or chocolate sauce (means added calories). (35 calories per serving)

Mrs. H.W. Walker, Richmond, Va.

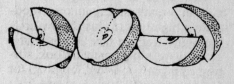

APPLE PASTRY

Sweet Dough recipe
1 tablespoon margarine
2 cups apples, cored/peeled
1/2 cup brown sugar
1 teaspoon cinnamon

Using the Sweet Dough recipe, pat 1/2 of dough into a greased 9-inch pie plate. Brush with melted margarine. Arrange apples on top of dough and sprinkle with sugar and cinnamon. Let rise about 1-1/2 hours. Bake at 375 degrees for 12 minutes

BUTTERSCOTCH TREATS

Sweet Dough recipe
1/4 cup brown sugar
1 teaspoon cinnamon
3/4 cup brown sugar
2 tablespoons margarine (divided)

Using the Sweet Dough recipe, roll dough on a well-floured board. Brush with 1 tablespoon margarine and sprinkle with 1/4 cup brown sugar and cinnamon mixture. Roll; seal edges; cut in slices.

Mix 3/4 cup brown sugar with 1 tablespoon margarine and place in a 15x9-inch pan, placing rolls on top. Let rise about 1-1/2 hours. Bake at 375 degrees for 20 minutes.

FRUIT BREAD

1 (8-ounce) package cream cheese, softened
1 cup margarine (2 sticks), softened
1-1/2 cups sugar
1-1/2 teaspoons vanilla extract
4 eggs
2-1/4 cups all-purpose flour
1-1/2 teaspoons baking powder
1 (16-ounce) can fruit cocktail, drained
1/2 cup chopped nuts

Line two 9x5x3 inch loaf pans with aluminum foil. Grease bottoms and sides of foil. Combine cream cheese, margarine, sugar, and vanilla; add eggs, one at a time, beating well after each addition. Gradually, add flour and baking powder; fold in fruit and nuts. Spoon batter into prepared pans. Bake at 325 degrees for 1 hour or until tests done with a tooth pick. Cool in pans for 5-10 minutes; remove from pans; cool thoroughly. Slice and serve. Delicious with ice cream. Fruit bread freezes well.

Jeannie Looney, Bartlesville, Okla.

BANANA-CHOCOLATE TEA BREAD

Makes 2 loaves

1 cup butter, softened
2 cups sugar
4 eggs
3 cups all-purpose flour
4 tablespoons cocoa
2 teaspoons baking soda
6 bananas, mashed
1 teaspoon cinnamon
2 teaspoons vanilla
1 cup commercial sour cream
1 cup chopped walnuts or pecans
1 cup semi-sweet chocolate morsels

Cream butter, gradually adding sugar; beat until light and fluffy. Add eggs, one at a time, beating well after each addition. Combine flour, cocoa, soda, and cinnamon; sift together.

Sift flour mixture into egg mixture. Blend well. Add vanilla; stir in bananas, sour cream, walnuts, and chocolate morsels. Spoon batter into 2 greased and floured 7-1/2 x 3 x 2-inch loaf pans. Bake at 350 degrees for 55 minutes or until wooden pick comes out clean. Cool in pan for 10 minutes. Remove from pan; cool on wire rack.

P. Mahoney, Bolingbrook, IL.

PINEAPPLE PECAN BREAD

1/4 cup butter or margarine
3/4 cup brown sugar
1 egg
1-3/4 cups flour
1/4 cup wheat germ
1 teaspoon baking powder
1/2 teaspoon salt
1 (6-ounce) can frozen orange juice concentrate
1 (8-3/4 ounce) can crushed pineapple
1/2 cup chopped pecans

Cream butter and sugar together until light and fluffy. Add egg; beat well. Sift together flour, wheat germ, baking powder, and salt. Thaw orange juice concentrate and add alternately with flour to the creamed mixture. Add pineapple and nuts; stir into batter. Place in a greased and floured 9-inch loaf pan; bake in 350-degree preheated oven for 60 minutes or until done.

Agnes Ward, Erie, PA

FRESH STRAWBERRY BREAD

1 cup sliced, fresh strawberries
1 cup sugar, divided
2 eggs
1 stick melted margarine
1-1/2 cups flour
1/2 teaspoon baking soda
1/2 teaspoon cinnamon
1/2 teaspoon nutmeg (freshly grated if possible)

Toss berries with 1/2 cup sugar; set aside. Beat eggs, remaining 1/2 cup sugar and melted butter. In another bowl, mix dry ingredients and add to liquid and berries. Pour into greased 9x5-inch loaf pan. Bake at 350 degrees for 50 minutes. If this is not enough strawberry, mash several berries; add powdered sugar and 1 teaspoon lemon juice to spreading consistency and drizzle over bread—Try it toasted!

HONEY PEAR BREAD

1 (28-ounce) can Bartlett pear halves
2/3 cup brown sugar
3/4 cup honey
1/2 cup cooking oil
2 eggs
2 teaspoons grated orange rind
1 teaspoon grated lemon rind
3/4 cup chopped pecans or walnuts
4 cups sifted flour
3 teaspoons baking powder
1 teaspoon baking soda
1 teaspoon pumpkin pie spice
1-1/4 teaspoons salt

Drain pear halves, reserving two for garnish and saving pear juice. Finely chop remaining pear halves. Combine brown sugar, honey, oil, pear syrup, eggs, orange rind, and lemon rind. Stir in chopped pears and nuts. Sift flour, baking powder, baking soda, spice, and salt. Add to pear mixture, stirring just until blended. Pour into two greased 4-1/2x8-1/2-inch loaf pans. Slice reserved pear halves and arrange on top of batter. Bake at 350 degrees for 50-60 minutes, or until toothpick inserted in center comes out clean. Remove from pans and cool. For best flavor let stand overnight. Store wrapped in foil.

Mrs. Terry A. Cobb, San Jose, Calif.

FRUIT AND BRAN MUFFINS

Makes 18 muffins

1-1/2 cups whole bran cereal (not bran flakes)
1/2 cup boiling water
1 egg or 2 egg whites, lightly beaten
1 cup buttermilk
1/2 cup honey
1/4 cup melted butter, margarine, or salad oil
1-1/2 cups mixed dried fruit (choose from raisins, chopped dates, prunes or figs.)
1/2 cup chopped nuts (walnuts or almonds)
1/2 cup whole wheat flour, unsifted
3/4 cup all-purpose flour, unsifted
1/2 teaspoon salt
1-1/4 teaspoons soda

In a large bowl, combine the bran cereal with water; stir to moisten evenly, then allow to cool until luke-warm. Add the egg, buttermilk, honey, butter, dried fruit, and nuts. Stir until well blended.

In another bowl, mix together the whole wheat and all-purpose flours, salt, and soda. Combine the dry and liquid ingredients and stir just until evenly moistened. Spoon into greased or paper-lined medium-sized muffin pans, filling them 3/4 full.

Bake in a 425 degree oven until a pick inserted in center comes out clean, 20 to 25 minutes.

Mrs. Max Mockler, Center Moriches, NY

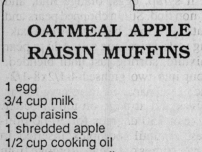

OATMEAL APPLE RAISIN MUFFINS

1 egg
3/4 cup milk
1 cup raisins
1 shredded apple
1/2 cup cooking oil
1 cup all-purpose flour
1 cup quick oats
1/3 cup sugar
3 teaspoons baking powder

1 teaspoon salt
1 teaspoon nutmeg
2 teaspoons cinnamon

Sift flour, salt, nutmeg, cinnamon, baking powder, and sugar together. Beat egg; add milk and cooking oil. Then add raisins, apple, oats, and flour mixture. Mix just to moisten. Pour into 12 greased or paper lined muffin cups until 3/4 full. Bake at 400 degrees for 15-20 minutes. Serve cool or piping hot with butter.

Note: The chunks of apple in the muffins make them very moist. They have a rich, spicy flavor.

Flo Burnett, Gage, Okla.

SPICE MUFFINS

Makes 84 small muffins

1 cup margarine
2 eggs
4 cups flour
3 teaspoons cinnamon
2 teaspoons allspice
2 cups sugar
1 cup chopped nuts
2 cups hot applesauce
1 teaspoon cloves
2 teaspoons soda
1/2 teaspoon salt

Mix all ingredients together. Bake in muffin tins, filling cup half full. Bake at 350 degrees for 15-20 minutes. Take out of oven and roll in powdered sugar. This mixture will keep in refrigerator for a long time and can be baked fresh, as desired. You may also freeze muffins, if batter is baked all at once.

Mrs. Melvin Habiger, Spearville, Kan.

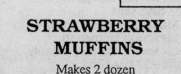

STRAWBERRY MUFFINS

Makes 2 dozen

1 pound fresh strawberries, cleaned, hulled
3-1/2 cups flour
2 cups sugar
1 tablespoon cinnamon
1 teaspoon salt
1 teaspoon baking soda
1-1/4 cups cold corn oil
4 eggs, beaten
1 cup pecans, chopped.

Preheat oven to 375 degrees. Combine flour, sugar, cinnamon, salt, and baking soda. Add oil and eggs; blend lightly. Add nuts and strawberries; blend until dry ingredients are just moistened. Put batter into greased muffin tins, filling the cups two-thirds full. Bake 20-25 minutes or until done.

Kit Rollins, Cedarburg, WI

ZUCCHINI NUT MUFFINS

Makes 18

2 eggs
1/2 cup brown sugar
1/2 cup honey
1/2 cup melted margarine
1 teaspoon vanilla
1-3/4 cups flour
1 teaspoon soda
1 teaspoon salt
1/2 teaspoon baking powder
1/2 teaspoon nutmeg
2 teaspoons cinnamon
1 cup rolled oats
1/2 cup chopped nuts
1/2 cup raisins
2 cups shredded zucchini

In a large bowl, beat eggs, then beat in sugar, honey, margarine and vanilla. In another bowl, mix flour, soda, salt, baking powder, nutmeg and cinnamon. Add to egg mixture and stir until moist. Stir in oats, nuts, raisins and zucchini. Spoon into well-greased muffin tins (or use paper liners), filling 3/4 full. Bake at 350 degrees for 25 minutes, or until toothpick comes our clean. Serve warm.

Freezes very well, but cool completely first. Nice to have on hand in the winter for breakfast.

Vicki Hardekopf, Canyonville, OR

Brunch
FARE

BAKED WESTERN OMELET
Serves 4

4 large eggs
1/4 cup water
4 ounces cooked ham, cut into thin strips
1 cup sliced mushrooms
1/2 cup chopped tomato
1/4 cup sliced scallions
1/4 cup chopped green bell pepper
1/8 teaspoon freshly ground pepper

Preheat oven to 375 degrees. Lightly spray a 10-inch glass pie pan with non-stick cooking spray. In medium bowl, with wire whisk, beat eggs with 1/4 cup water until well-blended. Stir in remaining ingredients. With rubber spatula, scrape into prepared pie pan. Bake 20-30 minutes until omelet is set, slightly puffed, and browned. Cut into four servings and serve at once. (141 calories per serving)

Ann Huff, Boonville, Mich.

BRUNCH PIE
Serves 6

3 tablespoons margarine
2 (15-ounce) cans corned beef hash
3 eggs
1/2 cup chopped onion
1 cup grated cheddar cheese
1 (16-ounce) can mixed vegetables, drained
1/2 cup evaporated milk
1 tablespoon flour
1/2 teaspoon dry mustard
Dash garlic powder

Coat a 9-inch pie pan with margarine. Mix hash and 1 beaten egg; press into plate to form crust. Bake at 375 degrees for 10 minutes. Sauté onion in 3 tablespoons margarine. Layer cheese, sautéed onion, and vegetables all into crust. Beat together remaining eggs, evaporated milk, flour, mustard, and garlic powder. Pour over mixture in crust. Bake at 350 degrees for 30-40 minutes, until filling is set. Let stand 10 minutes before cutting.

Mrs. Albert H. Foley, Lemoyne, Pa.

PEACH AND COTTAGE CHEESE SALAD
Single serving

2/3 cup cottage cheese
1/8 teaspoon cinnamon
Artificial sweetener to equal 2 teaspoons sugar
1/2 cup cooked, enriched rice
1 medium peach, sliced
1/4 cup skim milk

Combine cottage cheese, cinnamon, and sweetener; mix well. Add rice and peach. Toss lightly until well-mixed. Chill. Just before serving, pour skim milk over mixture.

Mrs. Robert E. Dowling, Titusville, Pa.

GRANOLA BARS

3 cups oats
1 cup peanuts
1 cup raisins
1 cup sunflower meats
1-1/2 teaspoons cinnamon
1 can sweetened condensed milk
1/2 cup butter, melted

Preheat oven to 325 degrees. Line 15x10-inch jelly-roll pan with foil; grease. In large bowl, combine all ingredients; mix well. Press evenly into prepared pan. Bake 25-30 minutes or until golden brown. Cool slightly; remove from foil. Cut into 48 bars. Store covered at room temperature.

Dawn Counsil, Williamsport, Pa.

CINNAMON RAISIN BATTER BREAD

1 package active dry yeast
1-1/2 cups warm water (105-115 degrees)
2 tablespoons honey
2 tablespoons butter
1 teaspoon salt
3 cups flour, divided
1 tablespoon cinnamon
1 cup raisins

In a large bowl, dissolve yeast in warm water. Stir in honey. Add butter, salt, and 2 cups of the flour. Beat with electric mixer on low speed until blended. Beat 1 minute on high speed. Stir in remaining flour with a wooden spoon. Cover and let rise in a warm place until doubled in size. Punch down by stirring with a heavy spoon. Add cinnamon and raisins. Spoon batter into a loaf pan. Let rise again until batter reaches the top of the pan (not over!). Bake in preheated 350-degree oven for about 40 minutes or until loaf sounds hollow when lightly tapped. Cool on wire rack.

This batter bread is a wonderful treat for breakfast or in the "munchkin's" lunch sack as a peanut-butter-and-jelly sandwich.

Phyliss Dixon, Fairbanks, Alaska

OMELET SUPREME

Serves 3

3 slices bacon, cut into small pieces
2 small potatoes, peeled and sliced
8 fresh spinach leaves, stems removed, sliced into 1/4 inch slices
6 eggs, lightly beaten with fork
1/2 cup yogurt
Salt and pepper to taste

In skillet, heat bacon; add potatoes; fry until bacon is crisp, and potatoes lightly browned. Add spinach; remove mixture to bowl. In shallow bowl, mix eggs, yogurt, salt, and pepper; pour into skillet. Distribute potato mixture evenly over eggs; cook over low heat without stirring. As eggs set on bottom, lift edges; let uncooked mixture run underneath. When omelet is set, fold with fork. Serve immediately.

June Harding, Ferndale, Mich.

OLD FASHIONED BREAD OMELET

Combine and soak for 10 minutes:
2 cups bread cubes
1 cup milk

Preheat oven to 325 degrees.

Combine in bowl:
5 eggs, beaten
1/2 cup grated cheese
1 cup alfalfa sprouts, chopped
1 small onion, finely chopped
1 tablespoon parsley flakes
1 teaspoon garlic powder
Salt and pepper to taste
Bread and milk mixture

Heat in skillet:
1/4-1/2 cup bacon pieces until done

Pour in egg mixture and cook over medium heat without stirring, about 5 minutes. When browned underneath, place pan in oven for 10 minutes to finish cooking the top. Turn out onto hot platter. Omelet can be folded in half.

Christine Nofziger, Elmworth, Alberta, Canada

BROCCOLI OVEN OMELET

Serves 6

9 eggs
1 (10 ounce) package frozen chopped broccoli, thawed and drained
1/3 cup finely chopped onion
1/4 cup grated Parmesan cheese
2 tablespoons milk
1/2 teaspoon salt
1/2 teaspoon dried basil
1/4 teaspoon garlic powder
1 medium tomato, cut into 6 slices
1/4 cup grated Parmesan cheese

Beat eggs with whisk in bowl until light and fluffy. Stir in broccoli, onion, 1/4 cup Parmesan cheese, milk, salt, basil, and garlic powder. Pour into ungreased 11x7x2 inch baking dish. Arrange tomato slices on top. Sprinkle with 1/4 cup Parmesan cheese. Bake uncovered in 325 degree oven until set, 25-30 minutes.

Great for holiday brunch, also as vegetable side dish.

Cheryl Santefort, Thornton, Ill.

QUICHE LORRAINE

1 (9-inch) pie crust
1 tablespoon soft butter
12 bacon slices
4 eggs
2 cups whipping cream
3/4 teaspoon salt
1/8 teaspoon nutmeg
1/4 pound natural Swiss cheese, shredded (1 cup)

Spread crust with soft butter; beat eggs, cream, salt, and nutmeg with wire whisk; stir in cheese and pour egg mixture into crust. Fry bacon until crisp and brown. Drain on paper towels and crumble; sprinkle in pie crust. Bake 15 minutes at 400 degrees; turn oven to 325 degrees and bake 35 minutes. Quiche is done when knife inserted in center comes out clean. Let stand 10 minutes before serving.

1933 Queen Dorothy Edwards Conlon

GARDEN MEDLEY

Serves 6

1/4 cup butter or margarine
2 cups cauliflower
1/4 cup chopped onion
2 cups sliced zucchini
1/2 cup halved cherry tomatoes
1/4 teaspoon salt
1/4 teaspoon thyme leaves, crushed
2 tablespoons grated Parmesan cheese, if desired

In large skillet, melt butter. Add cauliflower and onion; sauté 2-3 minutes. Add zucchini; cover and cook over medium heat, stirring occasionally, 3-5 minutes, or until vegetables are crisp-tender. Stir in tomatoes, salt, and thyme; cook 1-2 minutes until thoroughly heated. Spoon into serving dish; sprinkle with Parmesan cheese. (100 calories per serving)

Mrs. Sherwin Dick, Inman, Neb.

QUICK AND EASY BUCKWHEAT PANCAKES

1/2 cup bread crumbs
2-1/2 cups scalded milk
2 cups buckwheat flour
1/2 teaspoon salt
1/2 yeast cake
2 tablespoons molasses
1/4 teaspoon baking soda

Add bread crumbs and salt to scalded milk. Cool. When lukewarm add yeast and stir until yeast is dissolved. Add buckwheat flour and stir until smooth. Put in warm place overnight. In the morning add molasses and soda mixed with a little lukewarm water. Beat smooth. Bake on hot griddle.

These pancakes are delicious and more healthful than the regular kind. Your family will love them!

Suzan L. Wiener, Spring Hill, Fla.

LUNCHEON TUNA IN TOAST CUPS

2 ribs celery, thinly sliced
1 medium onion, chopped
1 small green pepper, chopped
1 tablespoon vegetable oil
1 package white sauce mix
1 cup American cheese, cut into small cubes
1 (7-ounce) can tuna, drained and flaked
3 tablespoons pimiento, chopped
Toast cups (recipe follows)

In a skillet, cook celery, onion, and green pepper, in vegetable oil until tender. Prepare white sauce as instructed on package. Into the white sauce, stir the celery, onion, green pepper, cheese, tuna, and pimiento; heat until cheese melts and is hot and bubbly. Serve in warm toast cups.

Toast Cups:

Trim crusts from fresh wheat or white bread; spread lightly with soft butter. Press buttered side down into muffin cups. Bake 10-12 minutes in a 350 degree oven or until lightly toasted.

Gwen Campbell, Sterling, VA

ELEGANT QUICHE LORRAINE

3 eggs, slightly beaten
1 cup light cream
5 slices bacon, crisply cooked and crumbled
3 tablespoons Dijon type mustard
1/4 cup finely minced onion
1 cup grated Swiss cheese
1/4 teaspoon salt
1/8 teaspoon pepper
1 unbaked 9-inch pie shell

Combine all ingredients, except pie shell. Pour into pie shell and bake in a pre-heated 375 degree oven for 35-40 minutes, or until knife inserted in filling comes out clean.

Agnes Ward, Erie, Pa.

BACON ROLL-UPS
Makes 6 dozen

1/2 cup margarine
3 cups herb-seasoned stuffing mix
2 eggs, beaten
1/4 pound ground beef
1/4 pound hot sausage, crumbled
1 pound sliced bacon, cut slice into thirds

Melt margarine in 1 cup water in saucepan. Remove from heat. Combine with stuffing. Mix in large bowl, mixing well; chill. Add remaining ingredients except bacon, mixing well.

Shape into pecan-shaped balls. Wrap with bacon; secure with toothpicks. In baking dish, bake at 375 degrees for 35 minutes or until bacon is crisp.

Marcella Swigert, Monroe City, MO

CHEESE, HAM 'N OLIVE SWIRLS
Makes 45

1-one pound loaf frozen ready-dough
6 thin slices cooked ham (4 x 7 inches)
4 ounces softened cream cheese
6 tablespoons chopped olives (black or green)

Let frozen dough thaw until pliable. (To thaw dough in the microwave, wrap in plastic wrap and cook on lowest setting for six minutes, rotating occasionally.) On a lightly floured board, roll thawed dough out to a 14-inch square. Cut in half. Cover each half with three slices of meat. Spread each half with two ounces softened cream cheese and sprinkle with 3 tablespoons chopped olives.

Beginning with 14-inch sides, roll each half in jelly-roll fashion. Pinch long edge to seal. Cut rolls into 1/2 inch slices. Place slices on greased baking sheets. Let rise for 30 minutes. Bake in 350 degree oven for 15 minutes or until golden brown. Remove from pan immediately.

Peggy Fowler Revels, Woodruff, SC

ZUCCHINI QUICHE
Serves 8

2 cups zucchini, sliced thin
1 cup onion, sliced
3 tablespoons oil
1 clove garlic, minced
1-1/2 teaspoons salt
4 eggs, beaten
1 cup milk
1 cup heavy cream
1/2 cup mozzarella cheese, grated
10-inch pie crust

Saute zucchini, onion, and garlic in oil. Season with salt. Cover pie crust with this mixture. Combine remaining ingredients and pour into pie shell. Bake in preheated 375 degree oven 30-35 minutes until custard is set. Serve hot.

Fay Duman, Eugene, OR

COCONUT CRUNCH CEREAL
Yields 8 cups

3 cups rolled oats
1-1/2 cups shredded coconut
1/3 cup wheat germ
1 cup toasted, unsalted sunflower kernels
1/3 cup sesame seeds
1/4 cup soy flour
2 teaspoons cinnamon
1/4 cup honey
1/4 cup vegetable oil
1/2 cup water
1 cup almonds, chopped

Mix first seven ingredients. Heat honey and water; pour slowly over cereal. Pour oil over cereal and mix until crumbly. Pour mixture into a heavy, shallow baking pan that has been oiled. Bake in a 325 degree oven for 1-1/2 hours; stirring every 15 minutes. Add chopped almonds and bake for 30 additional minutes. Cereal should be crisp. Turn off the oven; cool. Store cereal mixture in a tightly covered container. Serve plain with fresh fruit or milk.

Agnes Ward, Erie, PA

BREAKFAST EGG DISH

Serves 6

8 slices bread
1/2 cup melted butter
1 cup grated Cheddar cheese
Bacon or ham bits
Chopped green pepper
Sliced mushrooms, optional
2 cups milk
1/4 teaspoon salt
1/8 teaspoon pepper

Cut crust off the slices of bread and cube bread. Put in a 9x13 inch buttered pan. Pour the melted butter over the bread cubes; sprinkle on bacon bits, green pepper, and mushrooms.

Separate the eggs. Beat the yolks with the milk, salt, and pepper; pour over ingredients in the pan. Beat egg whites until stiff. Seal above mixture with egg whites. Cover and keep in the refrigerator overnight.

Bake at 325 degrees for 40-45 minutes.

EGG 'N' CHIPS

Serves 6

6 hard-boiled eggs, chopped
2 tablespoons chopped green pepper
1/2 teaspoon salt
2/3 cup mayonnaise or salad dressing
1-1/2 cups diced celery
3/4 cup coarsely chopped walnuts
1 teaspoon minced onion
1/4 teaspoon pepper
1 cup grated Cheddar cheese
1 cup crushed potato chips

Combine eggs, celery, walnuts, green pepper, onion, salt, pepper and salad dressing or mayonnaise. Toss lightly, but thoroughly, so ingredients are evenly moistened. Use additional salad dressing if needed. Place in a greased 1-1/2 - quart baking dish. Sprinkle with cheese and top with crushed chips. Bake at 375 degrees for about 25 minutes or until thoroughly heated and cheese has melted.

Shirley Anne Crist, Marion, IN

FOOLPROOF SCRAMBLED EGGS

Serves 3-4

6 eggs
1/3 cup light cream
3/4 teaspoon salt
1/8 teaspoon pepper
1/2 teaspoon Worcestershire sauce

Beat eggs; beat in cream and seasonings. Cook in upper part of double boiler, over hot water, until just set, stirring often. Serve at once with toast.

Agnes Ward, Erie, PA

SCRAMBLED BAGEL ROYALE

Serves 2

2 bagels
1-1/2 tablespoons butter
  or margarine
4 eggs
2 tablespoons milk
3 tablespoons chopped onion
1/4 cup lox pieces or smoked salmon
2 ounces cream cheese
2 slices tomato garnish

Slice bagels in half horizontally. Lightly spread with one tablespoon of butter or margarine; toast lightly. Over medium high heat, saute chopped onion in remaining half tablespoon of butter or margarine until translucent. Beat eggs with milk; add to onions. Stir eggs. When eggs are almost set, add lox pieces and cream cheese that has been cut into small chunks; scramble in pan until cheese begins to melt.

Spoon mixture over bagels. Garnish with tomato slices.

TOLEDO HAM AND EGGS

Serves 6

1 cup chopped, cooked ham
1 tablespoon olive oil
2 cups cooked peas
2 canned pimentos, chopped
1/4 cup chopped green olives
Salt and pepper, if desired
6 eggs
2 tablespoons olive oil

Saute ham in olive oil for 2-3 minutes. Combine with peas, pimento, and olives. Heat well; add salt and pepper if desired. Put in the middle of a hot platter and surround with the eggs, which have been slowly cooked in the 2 tablespoons of olive oil.

Agnes Ward, Erie, PA

TUNA STUFFED EGGS

Makes 24 halves

12 eggs
6 slices bacon
1 - 3-1/4 to 3-1/2 - ounce can tuna, drained and finely flaked
3/4 cup mayonnaise
1 tablespoon lemon juice
1/2 teaspoon hot pepper sauce
1/2 teaspoon salt

In 4-quart saucepan, place eggs and enough water to come one inch above tops of eggs over high heat; heat to boiling. Remove saucepan from heat; cover tightly and let eggs stand in hot water 15 minutes; drain.

Meanwhile, in 10-inch skillet, cook bacon until browned, remove to paper towel to drain. Crumble bacon, set aside.

Peel and slice eggs lengthwise in half. Remove yolks and place in medium bowl. With fork, finely mash yolks. Stir in tuna, mayonnaise, lemon juice, hot pepper sauce and salt until smooth. Pile egg yolk mixture into egg whites center. Sprinkle with bacon. Cover and refrigerate.

Dorothy K. Garms, Anaheim, CA

BACON PUFFED PANCAKES

Makes about 15

2 eggs
3/4 cup sweet milk
2-1/3 cups baking mix (I use Bisquick)
2 tablespoons sugar
1/4 cup oil
8 slices bacon, fried and crumbled

Beat eggs with mixer on high speed for about 5 minutes or until thick and lemon colored. Add remaining ingredients. Pour about 1/4 cup batter onto hot, ungreased griddle or use skillet. Cook as usual, turning once.

Kids love these because they are so light and have the bacon right inside. Awfully good on a cold day or any day!

Jodie McCoy, Tulsa, OK

OATMEAL PANCAKES

2 cups milk
1-1/2 cups quick rolled oats (uncooked)
1 cup sifted flour
2-1/2 teaspoons baking powder
1 teaspoon salt
2 tablespoons sugar
2 eggs, beaten
1/3 cup melted butter or margarine

Pour milk over oats and let stand 5 minutes. Sift together flour, baking powder, salt, and sugar. Add beaten eggs to rolled oats mixture. Add butter. Add sifted dry ingredients; mix quickly and lightly. If not used right away, store in refrigerator and mix again just before using. Keeps for several days in refrigerator.

POTATO PANCAKES

Serves 6

4 large potatoes
1 small onion
1/2 cup milk
1 teaspoon salt

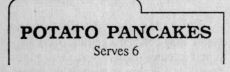

1 egg, beaten
2 tablespoons flour
Fat for frying

Peel and grate potatoes; mix with onion and milk. Mix with salt, egg, and flour. Drop by tablespoonsful into hot fat in skillet. Brown on both sides and serve immediately.

Susan L. Wiener, Spring Hill, Fla.

POTATO PANCAKES WITH CHEDDAR

Serves 4

1 egg
1/3 cup milk
1/2 teaspoon salt
3 tablespoons flour
1 small onion, grated or chopped fine
1/2 cup grated Cheddar cheese
4 medium potatoes
Shortening or salad oil for frying
Applesauce

In bowl, beat egg; beat in milk, salt and flour. Add grated or chopped onion and grated cheese. Wash and peel potatoes. Grate directly into egg mixture, working rapidly as grated potatoes tend to darken.

In heavy skillet, heat shortening or salad oil, using enough to coat surface generously. Add potato mixture by tablespoons; cook until brown and crisp on both sides. Serve hot with applesauce.

Velma Carbonara, Woodridge, IL

SOUFFLE PANCAKES

Serves 6

6 egg yolks
1/3 cup pancake mix
1/3 cup sour cream
1/2 teaspoon salt
6 egg whites

Beat egg yolks until thick and lemon colored; fold in pancake mix, sour cream and salt, until well blended. Beat egg whites until stiff but not dry. Carefully fold into yolk mixture. Drop by tablespoonsful onto

hot, well greased griddle. Cook until golden brown on both sides.

Serve hot with butter, maple syrup, honey or favorite fruit sauce.

Lucille Roehr, Hammond, IN

MAPLE PANCAKE SYRUP

Makes 2-1/2 cups

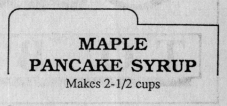

2 cups sugar
2 cups water
1 teaspoon maple flavoring

Combine sugar, water, and maple flavoring in small saucepan. Bring to boil; cook for 5 minutes. Bottle and refrigerate.

Marcella Swigert, Monroe City, Mo.

CORN FRITTERS

1 to 2 cups corn
1 egg, well beaten
1 teaspoon sugar
1/2 teaspoon salt
1 tablespoon butter, melted
2 teaspoons baking powder
1 cup flour
2/3 cup milk

Mix thoroughly. Drop spoonfuls of batter into fat in hot frying pan. Brown both sides.

Mrs. Elizabeth Dunn, Harrisonville, NJ

BUFFET RYE SLICES

1 cup Swiss cheese, grated
1/4 cup bacon, cooked and crumbled
1/4 cup mayonnaise
1 teaspoon Worcestershire sauce
1/4 cup green onions, chopped
1/2 cup chopped ripe olives

Mix all ingredients and spread on party rye slices. Bake in 375 degree oven for 8-10 minutes; serve warm.

Camille Mucha, Santa Monica, Calif.

Cakes
TO BAKE

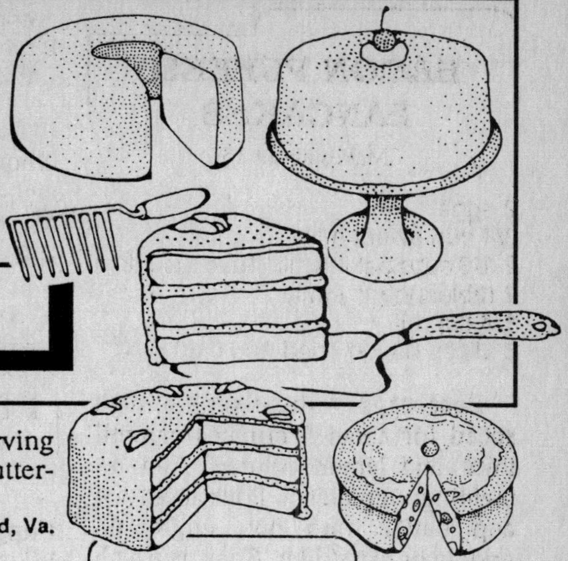

minutes, then unmold onto serving plate. Decorate with white buttercream icing and chopped nuts.

Nora Leigh, Richmond, Va.

APPLESAUCE LOAF CAKE

1/2 cup shortening
1 cup sugar
1 egg
1 cup unsweetened applesauce
1-3/4 cups sifted flour
1 teaspoon baking soda
1-1/2 teaspoons cinnamon
1 teaspoon allspice
1 teaspoon nutmeg
1/4 teaspoon cloves
1/2 teaspoon salt

Cream shortening and sugar until fluffy; add egg; beat well. Add applesauce. Sift remaining ingredients and mix. Bake in greased and floured 8x5x3 or 11x4-1/2x2-1/2 inch pan. Bake at 350 degrees for 1 hour. Frost with butter frosting. Decorate with whole walnuts. Delicious!!

Sarah Burkett, Centralia, Ill.

BANANA-GINGERBREAD DELIGHT

4-5 medium bananas, peeled (2 cups mashed)
3 tablespoons lemon juice
1 (14-ounce) package gingerbread mix
1 cup golden raisins

Sprinkle bananas with lemon juice and mash with potato masher. Add to gingerbread mix and beat until well mixed. Fold in raisins and pour batter into well-greased gingerbread mold. Bake at 350 degrees for 35-40 minutes. Allow to stand in mold for 10

REJOICE CAKE

2 cups flour
2-1/2 teaspoons baking soda
2 teaspoons cinnamon
1 teaspoon salt
1 cup cooking oil
2 cups sugar
3 eggs
1 (8-ounce) can crushed pineapple in juice
2 cups grated carrots
1-1/3 cups flaked coconut
1/2 cup chopped walnuts
1 (3-ounce) package cream cheese
1/4 cup margarine
3 cups sifted powdered sugar
1 tablespoon milk
1/2 teaspoon vanilla

Mix flour, soda, cinnamon, salt. Beat oil, sugar, and eggs thoroughly. Add flour mixture. Beat until smooth. Add pineapple, carrots, 1/3 cup coconut, and walnuts. Pour into greased 9 x 13-inch pan. Bake at 350 degrees for 50-60 minutes. Cool 10 minutes, then remove from pan and cool on rack.

Frosting:

Toast 1 cup coconut, cool. Cream together cream cheese and margarine. Add powdered sugar, milk, and vanilla. Beat until smooth. Add 1/2 of the coconut. Frost cake and top with remaining coconut.

Cheryl Santefort, Thornton, IL

14-KARAT CAKE

Mix:
2 cups flour
2 teaspoons baking powder
1 teaspoon baking soda

Blend:
1-1/2 cups cooking oil
1-2/3 cups sugar
4 eggs
4 teaspoons cinnamon
1 teaspoon salt

Add:
2 cups grated raw carrots
1 small flat can crushed pineapple (reserve 3 tablespoons for frosting)
1 cup chopped walnuts or pecans

Mix all ingredients together and blend well. Pour into 3 layer cake pans. Bake 25 minutes at 350 degrees. Cool on wire racks.

Frosting:

1 pound confectioners' sugar, sifted
1/2 pound (2 sticks) butter
8 ounces cream cheese
3 tablespoons crushed pineapple
1 teaspoon lemon extract

Blend together confectioners' sugar and softened butter. Add softened cream cheese, crushed pineapple, and lemon extract. Blend thoroughly and spread between layers, on top and sides of cooled cake.

Mrs. E. O'Brien, Richmond, VA

NO-COOK FROSTING

1/4 teaspoon salt
2 egg whites
1/4 cup sugar
3/4 cup Karo syrup, red or blue label
1-1/4 teaspoons vanilla

Beat salt and egg whites until mixture peaks. Add sugar, 1 tablespoon at a time, beating until smooth and glossy. Continue beating and add Karo syrup gradually, until frosting peaks. Fold in vanilla. Add vegetable coloring, if desired; frost top and sides of two 9 inch layers.

Mrs. Olen Begly, West Salem, Ohio

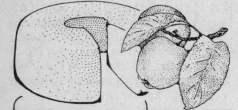

APPLE BUTTER CAKE

1/2 cup shortening
1 cup sugar
3 eggs
1 cup apple butter
2-1/2 cups sifted cake flour
3 teaspoons baking powder
1/2 teaspoon baking soda
1/2 teaspoon salt
1/2 teaspoon cinnamon
1/4 teaspoon nutmeg
1/2 cup apple butter
1 cup sour milk

Cream together shortening and sugar. Beat in eggs, one at a time; beat until light and fluffy. Stir in 1 cup apple butter. Sift together flour, baking powder, soda, salt, cinnamon, and nutmeg. Add dry ingredients to creamed mixture, alternately with sour milk. Turn into 2 greased and floured 9 inch cake pans. Bake at 350 degrees for 30-35 minutes. Cool thoroughly. Spread bottom layer of cake with 1/4 cup of remaining apple butter. Top with frosting. Cover with top cake layer. Frost top and sides with any marshmallow frosting. Swirl remaining apple butter on top for marbled effect.

Leah Daub, Milwaukee, Wis.

DUTCH APPLE CAKE
Makes 1 13 x 9-inch cake

1 (18-1/2 ounce) package spice cake mix
1/2 cup butter or margarine, melted
2 eggs
1 (21 ounce) can apple pie filling
3/4 cup brown sugar, firmly packed
1 teaspoon cinnamon
1/4 cup butter or margarine, softened
1/2 cup chopped nuts

In large bowl, combine dry cake mix, melted butter, and eggs. Blend well. Spread on bottom of 13 x 9 inch baking pan. Spoon pie filling evenly over batter. In small bowl combine brown sugar and cinnamon; cut in softened butter; stir in nuts. Sprinkle over pie filling. Bake at 350 degrees for 50 minutes or until cake springs back when lightly touched.

Agnes Ward, Erie, Pa.

APPLESAUCE CAKE

1 stick (1/2 cup) butter or margarine, softened
1 cup sugar
1 large egg
1-1/2 cups applesauce
2 cups all-purpose flour
2 teaspoons baking soda
1 teaspoon cinnamon
1 teaspoon nutmeg
1/4 teaspoon ground cloves
1 cup chopped, pitted dates
1/2 cup chopped walnuts

In a large bowl cream the butter, add the sugar, a little at a time. Beat the mixture until light and fluffy. Beat in the egg and add the applesauce. Into a bowl sift together the flour, soda, and spices, gently stir the mixture into the applesauce mixture with the dates and walnuts. Transfer the batter into a well greased baking pan, 12 x 8 x 2 inches, and bake in a preheated oven 350 degrees for approximately 45 minutes. Let the cake cool in pan on a rack. Frost if desired.

Very moist cake. Raisins may be used instead of dates.

Paula L. Walton, Fort Pierce, FL

APPLESAUCE LAYER CAKE

2 eggs
1-1/2 cups sugar
1-1/2 cups applesauce
1/2 cup butter or shortening
1 teaspoon soda
1 teaspoon salt
1 teaspoon cinnamon
1 teaspoon nutmeg
1/2 cup nut meats
2 cups flour
1 cup raisins (if desired)

Cream together the shortening and sugar. Add eggs, applesauce; and then sift the flour, soda, salt, and spices together. Add to creamed mixture; stir in raisins.

Grease (2) 8-inch round cake pans or use typing paper cut to fit inside pans. Pour batter into pans and bake at 325 degrees for 40 minutes or until cake tests done.

This cake is especially tasty with a mocha or caramel frosting.

Betty Slavin, Omaha, NE

SAUCY APPLE SWIRL CAKE
Serves 16

1/4 cup sugar
1 teaspoon cinnamon
1 package yellow cake mix
 (Pillsbury Plus best)
1 (15 ounce) jar (1-1/2 cups) applesauce
3 eggs

Heat oven to 350 degrees. Grease and flour 12-cup fluted pan or 10-inch tube pan. In small bowl, combine sugar and cinnamon; set aside. In large bowl, blend cake mix, applesauce, and eggs until moistened. Beat 2 minutes at high speed. Pour 1/2 of batter into prepared pan. Sprinkle with sugar mix. Cover with remaining batter. Bake 35-45 minutes until toothpick comes out of center clean. Cool upright in pan 25 minutes; turn onto serving plate. Cool completely. Dust with powdered sugar.

Judie Betz, Lomita, Calif.

"500" CAKE

1/2 cup butter
1 cup sugar
2 eggs
1/2 cup sour cream
1 cup mashed bananas
2 cups flour
1/2 teaspoon salt
1 teaspoon baking soda
1 teaspoon baking powder
1/2 cup chopped dates
1/2 cup chopped nuts
1 teaspoon vanilla

Cream butter and sugar. Add eggs. Add sour cream and mashed bananas alternately with sifted dry ingredients. Fold in nuts and dates which have been dusted with a little of the flour. Add vanilla. Pour into greased cake pans or cupcake tins. Bake at 350 degrees for 30 minutes.
Note: Buttermilk may be used instead of sour cream.

Leah Maria Daub, Milwaukee, Wis.

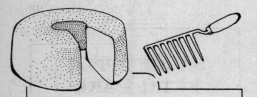

SOUR CREAM CAKE

1/2 cup chopped pecans
1/2 cup sugar
1 teaspoon cinnamon
4 eggs
1 package yellow cake mix
1 package instant vanilla pudding mix
1/2 cup oil
1 cup sour cream

Combine pecans, sugar, and cinnamon; set aside. Combine remaining ingredients; beat for 4 minutes. Spoon half the batter into well-greased and floured bundt or spring pan. Sprinkle half of the pecan mixture over batter, then add remaining batter and remaining pecan mixture over top. Bake in a preheated 350-degree oven for 1 hour. Cake may be glazed with thin icing or dusted with confectioners' sugar.

Leota M. Baxter, Ingalls, Kan.

APPLE CAKE WITH TOPPING

3 cups flour
2 cups sugar
1-1/2 teaspoons soda
1 teaspoon salt
3/4 cup cooking oil
2 eggs, beaten
1 teaspoon vanilla
1 cup chopped walnuts
3 cups chopped apples (unpeeled)

Mix oil, sugar, and eggs. Add dry ingredients and vanilla by hand. Add nuts and apples. Bake at 350 degrees for 1 hour in a well-greased tube or bundt pan. Remove from oven and pour topping over cake. Return cake to oven and bake 15 minutes more. Slide knife around cake to loosen.

Topping:
1 cup light brown sugar
1 stick butter or margarine
1/4 cup orange juice

Cook over low heat for 3 minutes after the mixture starts boiling. Pour over cake as directed above.

Trenda Leigh, Richmond, Va.

POPPY SEED CAKE
Serves 10-12

1 (18-1/2–ounce) package yellow cake mix
1 (3-3/4-ounce) package instant vanilla pudding mix
4 eggs
1 cup sour cream
1/2 cup (1 stick) melted butter
1/2 cup cream sherry
1/3 cup poppy seeds

Preheat oven to 350 degrees. Grease bundt cake pan and flour lightly, shaking out excess. Combine all ingredients in large bowl and beat 5 minutes with electric mixer. Pour batter into pan. Bake until tester in center comes out clean, about 1 hour. Let cool completely in pan. Invert onto platter and serve. Garnish each serving with sliced fruit.

Frances Falk, W. Palm Beach, Fla.

ORANGE PEANUT– BUTTER CAKE
Serves 12

2 oranges
1 (18-ounce) package yellow cake mix with pudding
1-1/4 cups water
3 eggs
1/2 cup peanut butter
1 teaspoon ground cinnamon
1/3 cup packed brown sugar

Grate peeling from oranges; reserve. Peel oranges and cut into bite–size pieces; drain well. In large bowl, combine cake mix, water, eggs, peanut butter, and cinnamon; mix according to package directions. Stir in orange peel and pieces. Pour batter into greased and floured 13x9x2-inch cake pan. Sprinkle brown sugar over top of batter. Bake at 350 degrees for 35-40 minutes or until done. Serve warm or cool.

Kit Rollins, Cedarburg, Wis.

PRALINE CHEESECAKE
Serves 12

Crust:
1-1/2 cups graham cracker crumbs
6 tablespoons butter, melted
1/4 cup sugar
2 tablespoons pecans, finely chopped

Filling:
1-1/2 pounds cream cheese
1 cup dark brown sugar
2 tablespoons flour
3 eggs
1/2 teaspoon vanilla
1/4 cup pecans, finely chopped

Combine all crust ingredients. Press on bottom and up sides of 9-inch springform pan.
For filling beat together cheese and sugar until creamy. Add flour, then eggs. Blend in vanilla and pecans. Pour into crust. Bake at 350 degrees for 50 minutes. Allow to cool. Chill in refrigerator before serving.

Lisa Varner, Baton Rouge, La.

OATMEAL CAKE

1 cup quick oatmeal
1 1/4 cups boiling water
1 stick butter or margarine
2 eggs, beater
1 cup white sugar
1 cup brown sugar
1 1/2 cups flour
1 teaspoon soda
1 teaspoon cinnamon
1/2 teaspoon salt
1 teaspoon vanilla

Stir together the oatmeal, boiling water and butter until butter melts. Let cool. Add the eggs and beat, then add sugar and beat mixture again. Sift together the flour, soda, cinnamon and salt and add to cake mixture with the vanilla. Beat all well.

Pour into greased and floured 9x 13" pan. Bake at 350-degrees for about 32 minutes.

When done and still hot, spread with the following topping. Mix together in heavy pan 3/4 cup brown sugar, 3/4 cup pecan pieces (or other chopped nuts), 6 tablespoons butter and 1/2 cup condensed milk (1/2 cup coconut, optional). Cream and cook until thick (but not too long).Evenly place mixture on cake. Place cake under broiler until topping becomes bubbly.

Karen Shea Fedders, Dameron, Md.

$100 CHOCOLATE CAKE

1/2 cup butter
2 cups sugar
4 ounces semi-sweet chocolate, melted
2 eggs, beaten
2 cups sifted cake flour
1/4 teaspoon salt
2 teaspoons baking powder
1-1/2 cups sweet milk
1 teaspoon vanilla
1 cup chopped nuts

Cream butter and sugar. Add melted chocolate. Add beaten eggs. Add flour, salt, baking powder mixture, and vanilla, alternately with milk. Beat with hand beater, not mixer, after addition. Put in 2 (9-inch) cake pans. Bake in 350 degree oven for 45 minutes. Batter is thin.

Frosting:
1/2 cup butter
2 ounces semi-sweet chocolate, melted
1 egg, beaten
1/4 teaspoon salt
1 teaspoon lemon juice
1 teaspoon vanilla
1-1/2 cups confectioners' sugar
1 cup chopped nuts

Mix first 6 ingredients, then stir in confectioners' sugar. Beat until thick enough to spread. (Beat by hand.) Sprinkle chopped nuts on top.

Sandra Russell, Gainesville, Fla.

ORANGE KISS ME CAKE

1 (6-ounce) can frozen orange juice, (3/4 cup thawed)
2 cups flour
1 cup sugar
1 teaspoon soda
1 teaspoon salt
1/2 cup shortening
1/2 cup milk
2 eggs
1 cup raisins
1/3 cup chopped walnuts

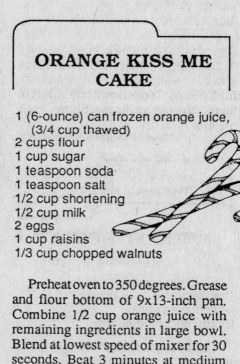

Preheat oven to 350 degrees. Grease and flour bottom of 9x13-inch pan. Combine 1/2 cup orange juice with remaining ingredients in large bowl. Blend at lowest speed of mixer for 30 seconds. Beat 3 minutes at medium speed. Bake 40-45 minutes. Drizzle remaining orange juice over warm cake and sprinkle with topping (recipe follows).

Topping:
1/3 cup sugar
1/4 cup chopped walnuts
1 teaspoon cinnamon
Combine in a bowl.

Susan Kirch, Dexter, N.Y.

SUNSHINE CAKE

7 egg yolks
1 teaspoon lemon extract
1-1/2 cups powdered sugar
10 egg whites
1 teaspoon cream of tartar
1 cup cake flour
1/4 teaspoon salt

Preheat oven to 325 degrees. Line bottom of a 10-inch tube pan with wax paper; cut to fit. Beat egg yolks; add lemon extract and 1 cup of the powdered sugar. Beat until thick and pale; set aside. Beat egg whites until foamy; add the cream of tartar, and beat until whites form soft peaks. Gradually, add remaining 1/2 cup powdered sugar and beat until stiff. Stir a fourth of the whites into the yolk mixture. Spoon remaining whites on top of the yolk mixture and sift flour and salt over them. Carefully fold until blended. Spoon into pan and bake for 50-60 minutes, until a toothpick comes out clean. Invert pan on a rack and let cake cool completely before removing from the pan. Frost with your favorite icing.

Lucille Roehr, Hammond, Ind.

NO-BAKE PEPPERMINT ICE CREAM CAKE

10-inch angel food cake
6 chocolate peppermint patties
1/2 cup nuts
1/8 teaspoon peppermint extract
1 quart vanilla ice cream

Cut cake in 4 layers. Chop patties and nuts. Soften ice cream slightly. Stir in candy, nuts, and extract. Spread thick layer of ice cream mixture between cake layers and rebuild the cake. Cover top with ice cream mixture. Keep in freezer; no thawing necessary.

Sally Jonas, Lafayette, Ind.

ZUCCHINI PINEAPPLE CAKE

3 eggs
2 cups sugar
2 teaspoons vanilla
1 cup cooking oil
2 cups zucchini, peeled and grated
3 cups flour
1 teaspoon baking powder
1/2 cup raisins
1 teaspoon salt
1 teaspoon nuts
1 cup crushed pineapple, drained

Beat eggs until fluffy; add sugar, vanilla, oil, and zucchini. Blend well. Add dry ingredients and mix well. Stir in pineapple, raisins, and nuts.

Bake in one large greased and floured loaf pan or two small loaf pans. Bake in 325-degree oven for 1 hour. Cool in pan on wire rack. When cool wrap in foil to store.

Mrs. L. Mayer, Richmond, VA.

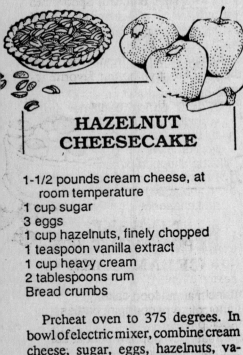

HAZELNUT CHEESECAKE

1-1/2 pounds cream cheese, at room temperature
1 cup sugar
3 eggs
1 cup hazelnuts, finely chopped
1 teaspoon vanilla extract
1 cup heavy cream
2 tablespoons rum
Bread crumbs

Preheat oven to 375 degrees. In bowl of electric mixer, combine cream cheese, sugar, eggs, hazelnuts, vanilla extract, heavy cream, and rum. Butter a 10x3-inch deep layer-cake or springform pan and coat with bread crumbs. Pour batter into pan. Put pan with the cheesecake batter into a deep pan. Fill outside pan with water until water reaches halfway up sides of cheesecake pan. Bake for 45 minutes. Cool and serve.

Irene Donner, Jamestown, N.Y.

ELEGANT APPLE CHEESECAKE

2 (8-ounce) packages cream cheese, softened
1 (16-ounce) carton cream-style cottage cheese
1-1/2 cups sugar
4 eggs
3 tablespoons cornstarch
1-1/2 tablespoons lemon juice
1 tablespoon vanilla
1/4 pound butter, melted and cooled
2 cups dairy sour cream
1 (21-ounce) can apple pie filling

Lightly butter a 9-inch springform pan. In a large mixing bowl, combine cheeses; beat until light and fluffy. Add sugar; blend well. Add eggs, one at a time, beating well after each addition. Add cornstarch, lemon juice, vanilla, and butter; blend until smooth. Blend in sour cream. Pour batter into prepared pan. Bake at 325 degrees for 1 hour and 10 minutes, or until center is set. Turn oven off. Let cheesecake stand in oven, with the door closed, for 2 hours. Cool completely. Chill 6 hours. Spoon apple pie filling over the top.

Gwen Campbell, Sterling, Va.

APRICOT NECTAR CAKE

1 (46-ounce) can apricot nectar
7 tablespoons cornstarch
1-1/2 cups sugar
1 large angel food cake

Combine the first three ingredients and cook over medium heat until mixture becomes clear and bubbly. Watch closely, stirring constantly. Take off heat and pour over a large angel food cake, which has been torn into small pieces and placed in a greased 9x13 glass baking dish. Cover and allow it to chill 24 hours in refrigerator. Serve with a scoop of whipped topping. This is a quick and easy cake that is absolutely delicious!!

Denise Winchell, Pleasant Hill, Ill.

CRANBERRY CAKE

3 cups sifted flour
1-1/2 cups sugar
1 teaspoon soda
1 teaspoon salt
1 cup mayonnaise
1 cup chopped nuts
3/4 cup whole cranberry sauce
2 tablespoons orange peel
1/3 cup orange juice

Sift dry ingredients. Add remaining ingredients. Pour into greased 9x13-inch pan. Bake at 350 degrees for 45 minutes.

Icing:
2 tablespoons butter
2 cups sifted confectioners' sugar
1/4 cup whole cranberry sauce

Combine ingredients and spread on hot cake.

Sharon McClatchey, Muskogee, Okla.

ORANGE HONEY CAKE

2 cups sifted cake flour
3-1/2 teaspoons baking powder
3/4 teaspoon salt
1/2 cup butter or shortening
1/2 cup sugar
2/3 cup honey
2 egg yolks
1/2 cup orange juice
2 egg whites, stiffly beaten

Sift flour; measure; add baking powder and salt; sift 3 times. Cream butter thoroughly; add sugar gradually; cream until light and fluffy. Add honey; blend. Add egg yolks and beat thoroughly. Add flour alternately with orange juice, a small amount at a time, beating well after each addition until smooth. Fold in egg whites. Bake in 2 greased 9-inch layer pans in 350-degree oven for 30-35 minutes.

Agnes Ward, Erie, Pa.

CARROT CAKE

1/2 cup oil
1 cup sugar
2 eggs, well beaten
1/2 cup grated carrots, packed
1/2 cup crushed pineapple
1-1/2 cups sifted flour
1/2 teaspoon salt
1/2 teaspoon baking soda
1/2 teaspoon baking powder
1/2 teaspoon cinnamon
1 teaspoon vanilla
1/2 cup chopped walnuts

Combine oil and sugar; add well-beaten eggs, carrots, and crushed pineapple. Mix just to combine. Sift flour, salt, baking soda, baking powder, and cinnamon. Stir into oil mixture. Add vanilla and nuts. Mix to combine. Pour batter into a greased and floured 9x13-inch pan. Bake at 350 degrees for 30 minutes or until done. Cool.

Icing:

1 (3 ounce) cream cheese
3 ounces margarine
1-1/2 cups powdered sugar
1 teaspoon walnuts, chopped fine
1 teaspoon crushed pineapple

Mix together cream cheese, margarine, and powdered sugar. Beat until light and fluffy. Add nuts and pineapple. Ice cooled cake.

Leona Teodori, Warren, Mich.

NO-FUSS FRUITCAKE

3/4 cup brown sugar
1/2 cup margarine or butter
1 egg
2-1/2 cups all-purpose flour
1 teaspoon baking soda
1/4 teaspoon *each* nutmeg and cloves
1/2 teaspoon cinnamon
1/4 cup orange or pineapple juice
1 cup applesauce, unsweetened or diced
2 cups chopped candied fruit
1 cup *each* raisins and chopped walnuts

In large bowl cream sugar and margarine or butter; add egg; beat well. Mix flour with spices and soda; stir into creamed mixture alternately with applesauce and juice. Fold in fruits, raisins, and nuts. Pour into two greased, floured 7-1/2 x 3-1/2 x 2 inch loaf pans. Bake for 1 hour at 325 degrees or until tests done with toothpick. Remove from pans; cool. Lightly glaze tops with mixture of confectioners' sugar and enough fruit juice or water to spread thinly. When glaze is set, press halved candied cherries over the top. Wrap in foil; store in cool place or freeze until needed.

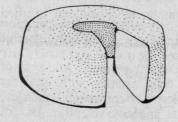

GRAPEFRUIT CHIFFON CAKE

2 cups all-purpose flour
1-1/2 cups sugar
3 teaspoons baking powder
1/2 teaspoon salt
1/2 cup oil
6 egg yolks
3 teaspoons grated grapefruit peel
2/3 cup grapefruit juice
6-7 egg whites
1/4 teaspoon cream of tartar

In a small mixer bowl stir together flour, sugar, baking powder, and salt. Make a well in center; in order add oil, egg yolks, peel, and juice. Beat smooth with an electric mixer. Wash beaters and in large bowl beat egg whites with the cream of tartar until stiff.

Gradually pour flour mixture (it will be thick) in a thin stream over surface and fold in gently. Bake in a 10-inch ungreased tube pan for 55 minutes at 350 degrees or until it tests done when lightly touched with the finger the cake springs back. Invert. Cool completely on cake cooling rack, loosen edges, and remove to cake plate. Glaze with the following:

2 cups sifted powdered sugar
3 teaspoons grapefruit peel, grated
1 teaspoon vanilla
2-3 tablespoons grapefruit juice

Mix all ingredients together using enough grapefruit juice to make it spread easily and drizzle down the sides when spread on top of cake.

Judy Smith, Indianapolis, IN

HAWAIIAN CAKE

1 package yellow cake mix
1-6 ounce package instant vanilla pudding mix
1-1/4 cups cold milk
1-8 ounce package cream cheese
1-8 or 9 ounce container frozen whipped topping
1-20 ounce can crushed pineapple, well drained
1/2 cup chopped pecans
1/2 cup flaked coconut
1/2 cup Maraschino cherries, drained and chopped

Prepare cake according to directions on package. Pour into greased 10 x 15 jelly roll pan. Bake in preheated oven 350 degrees 15-20 minutes, or until done. Cool in pan.

Blend pudding mix with milk, beat in cream cheese (room temperature); then fold in frozen whipped topping. Spread on cooled cake. Sprinkle drained pineapple over pudding, then cherries, nuts, and coconut. Refrigerate until ready to cut. Can be made a day ahead. This not only makes a big beautiful cake but is very delicious. I've taken this to a lot of potlucks and someone always wants the recipe.

Roselyn Finan, Fort Wayne, IN

LEMON CRACKLE CAKE

20 soda crackers (2" squares)
3/4 cup brown sugar
1 cup flour
1 teaspoon baking soda
1/2 cup butter or oleo
1 cup coconut

Crush crackers in bowl; add brown sugar, flour and soda. Work in butter; add coconut. Pat 3/4 of mixture into greased and floured 8 or 9-inch baking pan. Carefully spread on filling; cover with rest of crumb mixture. Bake at 350 degrees for 30 to 35 minutes or until slightly brown.

Lemon Filling:

1 cup sugar
2 tablespoons cornstarch
1 cup cold water
2 eggs, beaten
Juice of 2 lemons or 1/2 cup lemon juice
1/4 cup butter
1 teaspoons vanilla

In sauce pan, combine sugar and cornstarch. Gradually stir in water. Add remaining ingredients. Cook over medium heat until thickened. Cool before adding to cake.

Mrs. Stanley M. Lewis, Sussex, WI

ORANGE - KISS ME CAKE

Serves 12

1-6 ounce can (3/4 cup) frozen orange juice concentrate, (thawed)
2 cups flour
1 cup sugar
1 teaspoon baking soda
1 teaspoon salt
1/2 cup shortening
1/2 cup milk
2 eggs
1 cup raisins
1/3 cup chopped walnuts

Grease and flour bottom of 13 x 9 inch pan. Combine 1/2 cup orange juice concentrate with remaining ingredients in large mixer bowl. Blend at lowest speed of mixer for 30 seconds. Beat 3 minutes at medium speed. Pour into pan. Bake at 350 degrees for 40-45 minutes. Drizzle remaining orange juice concentrate over warm cake; sprinkle with sugar-nut topping (recipe follows).

Sugar-Nut Topping:

1/3 cup sugar
1/4 cup chopped walnuts
1 teaspoon cinnamon

Combine all ingredients in small bowl.

Barbara Nowakowski, N. Tonawanda, NY

CREAM CHEESE TOPPED PINEAPPLE CAKE

2 eggs
2 cups sugar
2 cups all-purpose flour
1 (20-ounce) can crushed pineapple packed in own juice, undrained
1/2 cup chopped pecans
2 teaspoons baking soda
1 teaspoon vanilla

Preheat oven to 350 degrees. Lightly grease 9 x 13-inch baking pan. Beat eggs in large bowl until light and fluffy. Add sugar and beat until thick. Stir in flour, pineapple, pecans, baking soda, and vanilla; mix thoroughly. Pour into pan and bake until tester inserted in center comes out clean. Bake 40-45 minutes. Let cake cool in pan on rack.

Cream Cheese Frosting:

2 cups powdered sugar
1 (8-ounce) cream cheese (room temperature)
1/4 cup (1/2 stick) butter (room temperature)
1 teaspoon vanilla
Additional chopped pecans for garnish

Combine powdered sugar, cream cheese, butter, and vanilla; mix until fluffy. Spread over cooled cake and sprinkle with chopped nuts. Cut into squares to serve.

This is a quick and easy cake to make and is delicious!

Lois Conway, Coloma, WI

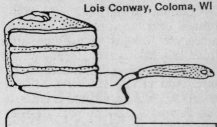

PINEAPPLE UPSIDE DOWN CAKE

1/2 cup packed brown sugar
1/4 cup butter
1 - can sliced pineapple (drained - reserve 1 tablespoon juice)
Maraschino cherries, halved
1 - 16 ounce container frozen pancake batter, thawed
1/4 cup granulated sugar

Heat oven to 350 degrees. Melt butter and put in glass pie plate. Add brown sugar and stir till smooth. Cut pineapple slices in half and arrange pineapple and cherries on sugar mixture in a decorative manner. Open top of pancake batter container completely. Add granulated sugar and reserve pineapple juice. Stir well. Pour over pineapple. Bake 30-35 minutes until golden brown and toothpick inserted in center comes out clean. Cool 5 minutes. Loosen edges of cake with small knife. Invert cake on serving platter.

This is a delicious and unusual way to make an upside-down cake. If pineapple is arranged pinwheel fashion, with a half-cherry in each curve, you get a lot more fruit on your cake.

Helen Weissinger, Levittown, PA

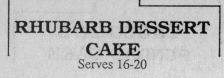

RHUBARB DESSERT CAKE
Serves 16-20

2 cups half and half
2 cups sugar
3 cups diced rhubarb
1 box yellow cake mix

Mix cake as directed on box. Pour into greased 9x13 inch pan. Mix cream, sugar, and rhubarb together. Pour over cake. Bake at 350 degrees for 1 hour. May be served with whipped cream.

Ida Bloedow, Madison, WI

FOURTH OF JULY WATERMELON CAKE

3 cups sifted flour
3 teaspoons baking powder
1/4 teaspoon salt
1/2 cup shortening
1-1/2 cups sugar
3 egg whites, stiffly beaten
1 cup milk
1 teaspoon vanilla
1/2 teaspoon red food coloring
1/2 cup raisins

Sift together flour, baking powder, and salt. Cream shortening. Add sugar gradually and cream together. Add flour alternately with milk, beating until smooth. Add vanilla and fold in egg whites. Divide batter into 2 parts. To one part, add food coloring and floured raisins. Put layer of white batter in bottom of greased melon mold. Place layer of red batter in center and a layer of white on top. Bake in a 350 degree oven for about 30 minutes. Frost with green-tinted icing.

Pour into greased 13x9x2 inch pan. Sprinkle with 1/2 cup chopped nuts. Bake in preheated oven at 350 degrees for 40 to 45 minutes or until pick comes out clean. Cool in pan on rack. Cut in bars.

**Optional if desired: sprinkle with powdered sugar or drizzle with powdered sugar frosting.

Gertrude Krisch, Milwaukee, WI

EASY PUMPKIN CHEESECAKE
Serves 8

10-1/2 or 12-1/8 package no-bake cheese cake mix
1 teaspoon ground cinnamon
1/2 teaspoon ground nutmeg
1/4 teaspoon cloves
3/4 cup milk
3/4 cup canned pumpkin
1/2 teaspoon vanilla
Whipped cream
Ground cinnamon

Prepare graham cracker crust in the cheesecake mix according to package direction; press into 9-inch pie plate. Chill in freezer while preparing pie filling. In small mixer bowl, combine cheesecake filling mix, teaspoon cinnamon, nutmeg and cloves. Add milk, pumpkin and vanilla. Beat at low speed of electric mixer until blended; beat 3 minutes at medium speed. Pour mixture into crust. Chill at least 1 hour. Garnish with whipped cream and additional cinnamon, if desired.

For easy serving, let stand at room temperature for five minutes before slicing.

Theresa Guillaume, Mosinee, WI

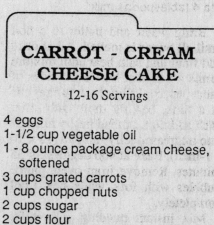

CARROT - CREAM CHEESE CAKE
12-16 Servings

4 eggs
1-1/2 cup vegetable oil
1 - 8 ounce package cream cheese, softened
3 cups grated carrots
1 cup chopped nuts
2 cups sugar
2 cups flour
2 teaspoons soda
1 teaspoon salt
1-1/2 teaspoon cinnamon
1 teaspoon vanilla

Beat cheese and sugar together at medium speed of mixer until smooth and creamy. Add eggs and oil; blend well. Gradually add remaining ingredients and blend well. Pour batter into

a greased and floured 13 x 9 x 2 inch pan and bake at 350 degrees, 45-55 minutes. Cool. Dust with powdered sugar. Cut into squares and serve with dollops of whipped cream.

Lisa Varner, Baton Rouge, LA

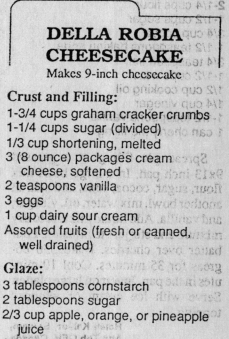

DELLA ROBIA CHEESECAKE
Makes 9-inch cheesecake

Crust and Filling:
1-3/4 cups graham cracker crumbs
1-1/4 cups sugar (divided)
1/3 cup shortening, melted
3 (8 ounce) packages cream cheese, softened
2 teaspoons vanilla
3 eggs
1 cup dairy sour cream
Assorted fruits (fresh or canned, well drained)

Glaze:
3 tablespoons cornstarch
2 tablespoons sugar
2/3 cup apple, orange, or pineapple juice
1/2 cup apple or currant jelly

Preheat oven to 350 degrees. For crust, combine crumbs, 1/4 cup sugar, and melted shortening. Press firmly in bottom and up side of ungreased 9 inch springform pan. Set aside. For filling, beat cream cheese in large bowl at low speed of electric mixer, just until smooth. Gradually add remaining 1 cup sugar and vanilla. Beat in eggs, one at a time. Blend in sour cream. Pour into prepared pan. Bake 1 hour, or 1 hour and 10 minutes, or until set. Turn off oven. Open door slightly. Leave cheesecake in oven 1 hour. Chill 4 hours or overnight. Top with fruit and glaze 1-2 hours before serving.

For glaze, combine cornstarch and sugar in small saucepan. Stir in juice; add jelly. Cook and stir until mixture is smooth and thickened. Cook about 2 minutes; cool slightly. Spoon 1/3 cup over top of cheesecake. Arrange fruit in circles on top of glaze. Gently spoon and spread remaining glaze in thin layer over top of fruit. Chill until serving time.

CHOCOLATE CHERRY UPSIDE-DOWN CAKE

2-1/4 cups flour
1-1/2 cups sugar
3/4 cup cocoa
1-1/2 teaspoons baking soda
3/4 teaspoon salt
1-1/2 cups water
1/2 cup cooking oil
1/4 cup vinegar
1-1/2 teaspoons vanilla
1 can cherry pie filling

Spread pie filling in a greased 9x13-inch pan. In a large bowl mix flour, sugar, cocoa, soda, and salt. In another bowl, mix water, oil, vinegar, and vanilla. Add liquid mixture to dry mixture and stir just to moisten. Pour batter over cherries. Bake 350 degrees for 35 minutes. Cool 10 minutes in the pan. Invert on large platter. Serve with ice cream or whipped topping.

Helen Keillor, Berwyn, Alta Toh OEH, Canada

CHOCOLATE CHIP CAKE

2 cups all purpose flour
1 cup packed brown sugar
1/2 cup granulated sugar
3 teaspoons baking powder
1 teaspoon salt
1/2 teaspoon baking soda
1/2 cup shortening
1-1/4 cups milk
3 eggs
1/2 cup semi-sweet chocolate chips finely chopped or
1/2 cup miniature semi-sweet chocolate chips
1-1/2 teaspoons vanilla

Heat oven to 350 degrees. Grease and flour oblong pan, 13 x 9 x 2 inches or 2 round layer pans, 8 or 9 inch x 1-1/2 inches. Beat all ingredients in large mixer bowl on low speed, scraping bowl constantly, 30 seconds. Beat on high speed, scraping bowl occasionally, 3 minutes.

Pour into pans. Bake in a 350 degree oven for 40-50 minutes. Bake until wooden pick inserted in center comes out clean. While cake is cooling, prepare Chocolate Butter Frosting.

CHOCOLATE ECLAIR CAKE

Serves 15

1 cup flour
1 stick (1/2 cup) butter or margarine
1/4 teaspoon salt
1 cup water
4 eggs (best at room temperature)
2 packages instant French vanilla pudding
2-1/2 cups cold milk
8 ounces cream cheese, softened
12 ounces (large container) Cool Whip or other whipped topping
3 ounces chocolate chips (1/2 of 6-ounce bag)
2 tablespoons butter or margarine
1 cup confectioners' sugar
3 to 4 tablespoons milk

Bring water and butter to a boil until all butter is melted. All at once add flour and salt; beat until mixture forms a ball that leaves the sides of saucepan; cool slightly. Add eggs one at a time, beating thoroughly after each addition. Spread pastry mixture into ungreased jelly roll pan (15 x 10 x 1-inch). Bake at 400 degrees for 35 minutes. Remove from oven; pierce bubbles with fork while hot. Cool completely.

Mix instant pudding with milk; add softened cream cheese, beat together thoroughly. Spread whipped topping over pudding mixture. Melt chocolate chips and butter over low heat, mix to add confectioners' sugar and milk, alternately until thin glaze forms. Pour or drizzle chocolate glaze over whipped topping. Refrigerate at least 1 hour or longer. Cut into squares to serve.

CHOCOLATE SUNDAE CAKE

1 package devil's food cake mix
1 cup brown sugar
1/3 cup cocoa
2 cups water
2 cups miniature marshmallows
1 cup pecans, chopped

Combine brown sugar, cocoa, and water. Mix well. Pour into a 13x9-inch pan. Place marshmallows evenly on top.

Make cake batter following package directions. Pour into pan. Top with nuts. Bake at 350 degrees for 30 minutes. Cool in pan on wire rack. Cut into bars or squares to serve.

Mrs. P. B. Brothers, Richmond, Va.

COOKIES 'N CREAM CAKE

1 package white cake mix
1-1/4 cups water
1/3 cup oil
3 egg whites
1 cup crushed, creme-filled chocolate sandwich cookies
10 whole cookies

Frosting:

3 cups powdered sugar
3/4 cup shortening
1 teaspoon vanilla
2 egg whites

Heat oven to 350 degrees. Grease and flour 2 round cake pans. In large bowl, combine all cake ingredients, except cookies. Mix at low speed until moistened. Beat 2 minutes at high speed. Stir in crushed creme-filled chocolate cookies. Bake at 350 degrees for 25-35 minutes or until it tests done. Cool layers.

In small bowl combine 1/2 cup of the powdered sugar, shortening, vanilla, and egg whites. Blend well. Beat in remaining sugar until frosting is smooth. Fill and frost cake. Arrange whole cookies on end and on top of frosted cake.

Suzanne Dawson, Cypress, TX

CHOCOLATE YOGURT CAKE

2 cups unsifted all-purpose flour
1-1/2 cups sugar
1/2 cup unsweetened cocoa
2 teaspoons baking soda
1 teaspoon salt
1 cup plain yogurt
3 eggs
2/3 cup oil
1-1/2 teaspoons vanilla

Preheat oven to 350 degrees. Grease and flour two 9-inch round layer pans. Set aside. Mix flour, sugar, cocoa, baking soda and salt in large mixing bowl. Add yogurt, eggs, oil, and vanilla. Beat with electric mixer at low speed until ingredients are moistened; scraping bowl constantly. Beat at medium speed 2 minutes; scraping bowl occasionally. Pour into prepared pans. Bake at 350 degrees, 30-35 minutes, or until wooden pick inserted in center comes out clean. Cool 10 minutes. Remove from pans. Cool completely on wire rack.

Frosting:

1 package (6 ounces) semi-sweet chocolate chips
1/4 cup butter or margarine
2/3 cup plain yogurt
1/2 teaspoon vanilla
1/8 teaspoon salt
2-1/2 - 3 cups confectioners sugar

Combine chocolate chips and butter in small saucepan. Cook over low heat; stirring constantly, until melted. Transfer mixture to medium mixing bowl. Cool slightly. Blend in yogurt, vanilla and salt. Stir in enough confectioners sugar until frosting is thick enough to spread. Frost the layers of the cooled cake.

Ida Bloedow, Madison, WI

FUDGE SURPRISE CAKE

1 cup butter or margarine

1/4 cup cocoa
1 cup water
1/2 cup buttermilk
2 eggs, beaten
2 cups sugar
2 cups flour
1 teaspoon baking soda
1 teaspoon vanilla

In saucepan, combine the butter, cocoa, water, buttermilk, and eggs. Stir constantly over low heat until mixture bubbles. In large bowl, mix together the sugar, flour, and baking soda. Stir in the hot cocoa mixture, beat until smooth. Stir in vanilla, spread evenly in a greased and floured 9 x 13 pan. Bake 25-30 minutes at 350 degrees, until firm to the touch in center. Cool.

Filling:

In bowl, mix 1 cup creamy peanut butter with 1 tablespoon oil, until smooth. Spread over the cooled cake.

Frosting:

1/2 cup butter or margarine
1/4 cup cocoa
6 tablespoons buttermilk
1 pound powdered sugar
1 teaspoon vanilla

In saucepan, heat butter, cocoa, and buttermilk until bubbly. Place sugar in bowl, beat in hot mixture until smooth. Stir in vanilla. Spread mixture over the peanut butter layer. . . .Enjoy!

Mary Young, Spencer, IA

GERMAN CHOCOLATE CAKE

2 cups sugar
1/2 cup shortening
1/2 cup pure butter (1 stick)
4 eggs
1 teaspoon vanilla
4 tablespoons cold black coffee
1/4 teaspoon salt
1 teaspoon baking soda
4 tablespoons cocoa
2 1/2 cups flour
1 cup buttermilk

Cream shortening, butter and sugar together; add eggs one at a time. Sift dry ingredients together. Add to creamed mixture, alternately with buttermilk one half at a time. Add coffee and vanilla. Bake in three 9-inch round cake pans at 350 degrees for 35 minutes.

Filling and Icing:

1 cup cream (half & half)
3 egg yolks
1/4 pound butter (1 stick)
1 cup chopped pecans
1 cup sugar
1 teaspoon vanilla
1 cup coconut

Place cream, sugar, egg yolks, vanilla and butter in saucepan. Cook together for 10 minutes, stirring constantly. Add coconut and nuts. Cool. Spread and cool cake.

Pauline M. Terrell, Grafton, DE

INSIDE-OUT CHOCOLATE BUNDT CAKE

4-1/2-ounce package instant chocolate flavor pudding
2-layer size chocolate or Devil's Food cake mix
.12 ounces chocolate chips
1-3/4 cups milk
2 eggs

Combine pudding mix, cake mix, chips, milk and eggs in bowl. Mix by hand until well blended, about 2 minutes. Pour into greased and floured 12-cup tube or Bundt pan. Bake at 350 degrees for 50 to 55 minutes, or until cake springs back when lightly pressed with fingers. Do not overbake. Cool 15 minutes in pan, remove and continue cooling on rack.

If you love chocolate, this is for you. It's moist and easy to make, and doesn't need frosting. However, if you like, you can sift confectioners' sugar on top.

Marian E. Reichenbach, Trenton, MI

CHOCOLATE ANGEL FOOD CAKE

1/4 cup cocoa
1 cup cake flour
1-3/4 cups sugar
1-1/2 cups egg whites
3/4 teaspoon salt
1-1/2 teaspoons cream of tartar
1 teaspoon vanilla
1/4 teaspoon almond extract

Sift cocoa, cake flour, and 3/4 cup sugar together four times. Beat egg whites and salt until foamy. Sprinkle cream of tartar over egg whites; continue beating until stiff, but not dry. *Fold* in remaining sugar, one tablespoon at a time. Add vanilla and almond extract. *Fold* in dry ingredients, a little at a time. Pour into ungreased 10 inch tube pan. Bake 60-70 minutes at 325 degrees. Frost, if desired, although it is delicious plain.

Mrs. Melvin Habiger, Spearville, Kan.

OLD-FASHIONED TRIPLE FUDGE CAKE

1 package devil's food cake mix
1/2 cup chopped nuts
1/2 cup semi-sweet chocolate pieces
1 (12 ounce) jar thick fudge ice cream topping
Ice cream, whipped topping, or whipped cream

Mix cake as directed on package. Stir in nuts; spread batter in a greased and floured 13 x 9 x 2 inch pan. Sprinkle chocolate pieces evenly over batter; bake as directed on package. Immediately after baking, poke deep holes through top of hot cake (still in pan), space holes about 1 inch apart. Spoon fudge topping evenly over cake. Topping will melt into holes. Serve when completely cool. Top with ice cream or whipped cream.

Pauline Dean, Uxbridge, Mass.

OREO COOKIE CAKE

1 pound oreo cookies
1 cup melted margarine
8 ounce soft cream cheese
2 - 8 ounce containers whipped topping
1 cup powdered sugar
1 large package instant chocolate pudding

Crush cookies and (set aside 1/2 cup). Mix crumbs with butter, and press into 9 ix 13 pan. Refrigerate 1 hour. Mix cream cheese, sugar, 1 carton whipped topping. Spread over cookie crust. Refrigerate 1 hour. Prepare pudding mix by directions on package. Spread over cheese mixture. Refrigerate 1 hour. Top with whipped topping, sprinkle with rest of cookie crumbs. Garnish with maraschino cherries.

Lowela C. McDaniel, Roanoke, VA

TURTLE CAKE

1 package German chocolate cake mix
1 (14-ounce) package caramels
1/2 cup evaporated milk
6 tablespoons margarine
1 cup chopped pecans
1 cup chocolate chips

Prepare cake mix according to directions. Pour 1/2 batter into greased and floured 9 x 13 inch pan. Set other batter aside. Bake at 350 degrees for 18 minutes. Melt caramels and milk together, then stir in pecans. Sprinkle baked part of cake with chocolate chips, and pour caramel mix over that. Pour remaining batter over top. Return pan to oven and bake 20 minutes. Cut into squares to serve.

Cheryl Santefort, Thornton, IL

BUTTERMILK COFFEE CAKE

9 Servings

2 cups sifted flour

1 cup sugar
1/2 teaspoon ground cinnamon
1/4 teaspoon baking powder
1/4 teaspoon salt
1/2 cup butter or margarine
1 teaspoon ground cinnamon
1/2 teaspoon baking soda
3/4 cup buttermilk
1 teaspoon vanilla

Sift together flour, sugar, 1/2 teaspoon cinnamon, baking powder and salt into bowl. Cut in butter with pastry blender or two knives until mixture is crumbly. Reserve 1/2 cup crumb mixture. Combine reserved crumbs with 1 teaspoon cinnamon; set aside. Dissolve baking soda in buttermilk. Add buttermilk mixture and vanilla to remaining crumb mixture, stirring just enough to moisten. Spread batter in greased 8 inch square pan. Sprinkle with reserved crumbs. Bake in 375 degree oven 35 minutes or until done. Cut into squares and serve warm. If you love cinnamon you will love this coffee cake.

Barbara Beauregard-Smith, Northfield, Australia

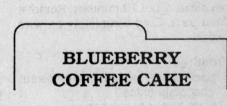

BLUEBERRY COFFEE CAKE

2 cups flour
1 cup sugar
3 teaspoons baking powder
1/4 teaspoon salt
1/2 cup butter or margarine
2 eggs, beaten
1 cup milk
1-1/2 cups blueberries
1/2 cup coconut
1/2 cup chopped nuts

Mix flour, sugar, baking powder, and salt; cut in butter until mixture resembles cornmeal. Combine beaten eggs and milk; stir in dry ingredients. Stir only until dry mixture is well moistened. Do not overmix! Fold in blueberries. Grease a 9 x 12-inch pan and pour cake batter into pan. Sprinkle with coconut and chopped nuts. Bake in a 350 degree oven for 25-30 minutes. "Great for breakfast."

Agnes Ward, Erie, PA

CINNAMON PULL-APART COFFEE CAKE
Serves 8-10

1 cup Frosted Rice Crispies, crushed to 1/2 cup
1-1/3 cups all-purpose flour
1 tablespoon baking powder
1/2 teaspoon salt
1/4 cup shortening
1/2 cup milk
1/4 cup butter, melted
1/2 cup sugar
1 teaspoon cinnamon

Stir together Rice Crispies cereal, flour, baking powder, and salt. Cut in shortening until mixture resembles coarse crumbs. Add milk; stir with a fork until dough leaves sides of bowl. Shape dough into balls, about 1 inch in size. Roll dough balls in melted butter, then in sugar-cinnamon mixture. Arrange in single layer on ungreased 8-inch round cake pan. Bake at 425 degrees for 18-20 minutes. Serve warm.

Agnes Ward, Erie, Pa.

CHERRY CRUMB COFFEE CAKE

1/4 cup margarine
1 cup sugar
2 eggs
1 cup low fat plain yogurt
1/4 cup milk
2 cups flour
1/2 teaspoon baking soda
1/4 teaspoon vanilla
1/4 teaspoon almond extract
1 (21 ounce) can cherry pie filling

Topping:
1/2 cup flour
1/4 cup brown sugar
1 teaspoon cinnamon
3 tablespoons margarine
1/2 cup chopped pecans

In mixing bowl, cream together margarine and sugar. Add eggs, one at a time. Mix well. Add remaining cake ingredients, except cherry pie filling. Beat well. Spread 1/2 of the batter in a greased 9x13-inch baking pan. Spread cherry filling over batter and cover with remaining batter.

For topping, combine all ingredients, except butter and nuts, into a small mixing bowl. Cut in butter and stir in nuts. Sprinkle topping over batter. Bake at 350 degrees for 45 minutes until cake springs back when lightly touched with fingers.

Mrs. Don Shamway, Freeport, Ill.

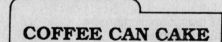

COFFEE CAN CAKE

3-1/2 cups flour
2 teaspoons baking soda
1 teaspoon salt
1 teaspoon cinnamon
1 teaspoon nutmeg
3 cups sugar
4 eggs
2 cups pumpkin (fresh is preferred, but if not available, use canned)
2/3 cup water
1 cup vegetable oil
1 cup raisins
1 cup nuts
1 cup candied cherries

Sift flour, baking soda, salt, cinnamon and nutmeg together in a bowl. In separate bowl, mix eggs, pumpkin, water and oil. Slowly stir in dry ingredients. When all ingredients are mixed, add raisins, nuts and cherries. Pour mixture into large, well-greased coffee cans. Fill only halfway to allow room to rise. Bake at 350 degrees for about 1 hour. Cool in cans on wire rack before removing from cans. This cake resembles fruit cake and is delicious served with hard sauce or a wine-flavored sauce.

Trenda Leigh, Richmond, VA

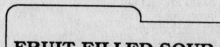

FRUIT FILLED SOUR CREAM COFFEE CAKE

1/2 cup butter or margarine
1 cup sugar
2 eggs
1 cup sour cream
2 cups flour
1-1/2 teaspoons baking powder
1/2 teaspoon baking soda
1/2 teaspoon salt
1 teaspoon vanilla
1 can fruit pie filling (any kind)

Grease and flour 9 x 13 inch pan. Mix dry ingredients together. Cream butter and sugar. Add eggs and vanilla. Add sour cream alternately with dry ingredients. Pour 1/2 batter into pan. Smooth pie filling gently over this. Add remaining batter, spread over filling. Bake in 350 degree oven for 45 - 50 minutes or until tested done.

Topping:
2 tablespoons butter or margarine
1/2 cup sugar
2 tablespoons flour
1/2 cup chopped nuts
1 teaspoon cinnamon

Melt butter. Mix together remaining ingredients, add melted butter and mix. Add to the top of the cake about half way through the baking time. **Lillian Harris, Edwards, IL**

HEATH COFFEE CAKE

1/4 pound butter (1 stick)
1/2 cup white sugar
1 cup brown sugar
1 egg
1 teaspoon soda
2 cups flour
1 teaspoon vanilla
1 cup buttermilk

Blend flour, sugars, and butter. Take out 1/2 cup of crumb mixture. To rest of mixture, add buttermilk, soda, egg, and vanilla. Blend well; pour into greased and floured 10 x 14 x 2-inch pan.

Sprinkle on topping of:
3/4 cup chopped Heath bars
1/4 cup nuts
1/2 cup mixture (reserved earlier)

Bake 350 degrees for 30 minutes. This is a great coffee cake, so tasty and very moist!!

Mrs. Merle Mishler, Hollsopple, Pa.

QUICK COFFEE-CHOCOLATE CAKE

1 package yellow cake mix
1/2 cup brewed coffee
1 teaspoon flavoring

Prepare cake mix according to package directions, using coffee as part of the liquid and add vanilla. Bake according to package directions.

Topping:
3 tablespoons butter or margarine, room temperature
1/2 box confectioners' sugar
1 square unsweetened chocolate, room temperature
Brewed coffee
1 teaspoon vanilla flavoring
1 teaspoon chocolate flavoring (optional)

In a saucepan, brown the butter or margarine. Add chocolate and stir until melted. Pour over confectioners' sugar in bowl and mix, adding enough coffee until spreading consistency. Add flavoring and spread on cake.

Alice McNamara, Eucha, OK

SNICKERDOODLE COFFEE CAKE

1 cup flour
1 cup sugar
1 teaspoon baking powder
1/2 teaspoon salt
1 tablespoon ground cinnamon
1/2 cup milk
1/4 cup melted margarine
1 egg

Mix together the flour, sugar, baking powder, salt, cinnamon, milk, margarine and egg. Pour into a greased and floured 8 or 9 inch square pan. Sprinkle top heavily with sugar (this gives a crusty top). Bake at 400 degrees for 25 minutes. Best when served warm.

Karen Krugman, Tampa, FL

ORANGE BUTTERSCOTCH COFFEE CAKE

Batter:
1/2 cup butter or margarine
1 cup granulated sugar
1 egg
1 teaspoon vanilla
1-1/2 cups sifted all-purpose flour
1-1/2 teaspoons baking powder
1/2 teaspoon cinnamon
1/2 teaspoon salt
1 cup milk
3/4 cup uncooked oats

Topping:
1/4 cup firmly packed brown sugar
1 tablespoon all-purpose flour
1 tablespoon butter or margarine, melted
2 teaspoons grated orange peel

Beat together butter and sugar until light and fluffy; add egg and vanilla; blend well. Sift together flour, baking powder, cinnamon and salt; add to creamed mixture alternately with milk; stir in oats. Pour batter into greased and floured 8 inch square baking pan. Combine all topping ingredients and sprinkle evenly over batter. Bake in preheated 350 degree oven for 40 to 45 minutes. Cool in pan 15 minutes before serving.

ALMOND POUND CAKE

3 cups sugar
2 sticks (1/2 pound) butter or margarine
1/2 cup shortening
5 large eggs
1/4 teaspoon salt
3 cups flour
1 small can evaporated milk (3/4 cup) plus water to make 1 cup liquid
2 teaspoons almond extract

Cream sugar and shortening. Add eggs and salt, cream well. Add remaining ingredients. Pour into a very lightly greased 12 cup bundt pan. Put into cold oven; set temperature at 320 degrees. Bake 1 hour and 30 minutes. Cool 15 minutes and remove from pan.

Leah M. Daub, Milwaukee, WIS

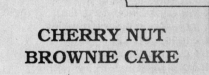

CHERRY NUT BROWNIE CAKE

1/2 cup maraschino cherries
3/4 cup flour, spooned lightly into cup
1/2 teaspoon baking powder
1/4 teaspoon salt
1/2 cup butter or margarine, softened
1 cup sugar
2 large eggs
2 envelopes Choc-bake (or 2 squares unsweetened chocolate, melted)
1 teaspoon vanilla
1/2 cup chopped walnuts or pecans

Quarter cherries with scissors; place on paper towel to drain; set aside. Measure flour, baking powder and salt into small bowl; whisk to blend; set aside.

In large bowl, beat butter or margarine briefly; beat in sugar. Beat in eggs one at a time; beat in chocolate and vanilla. By hand or on lowest mixer speed, beat in dry ingredients. Stir in cherries and nuts. Spread in greased and floured or foil-lined 8-inch squares pan. Bake at 350 degrees until firm in center, about 35 minutes. Cool on rack. Ice as directed below. Freeze leftovers in serving size units.

Chocolate Icing:
Looks and tastes like fudge icing.
2 tablespoons cocoa
2 tablespoons water
2 tablespoons butter or margarine
1 teaspoon maraschino cherry juice
1-1/8 cups unsifted confectioners' sugar (1/8 cup is 2 tablespoons)

Measure cocoa, water, butter and cherry juice into medium saucepan. Heat, stirring, just until smooth. Remove from heat; whisk in sugar. Icing should be just thin enough to pour. Add a little more sugar if necessary. Pour over cool cake; spread to edges. Allow icing to set before cutting cake.

PECAN CAKE WITH PRALINE GLAZE

Makes 1 (10-inch) cake

1 cup raisins
1/2 cup bourbon
1 cup butter or margarine, softened
2-1/4 cups sugar
5 eggs
3-1/4 cups all-purpose flour
1 teaspoon baking powder
1/2 teaspoon baking soda
1-1/2 teaspoons ground nutmeg
1 cup buttermilk
2 cups coarsely-chopped pecans
Praline Glaze (recipe follows)

Combine raisins and bourbon, stirring well. Cover and refrigerate at least 1 hour. Cream butter; gradually add sugar, beating well. Add eggs, one at a time, beating well after each addition. Combine flour, baking powder, soda, and nutmeg; add to creamed mixture alternately with buttermilk, beginning and ending with flour mixture. Mix well after each addition. Fold in pecans and reserved raisin mixture. Mix well to thoroughly blend.

Pour batter into greased and floured 10-inch tube pan. Bake at 325 degrees for 1 hour and 30 minutes or until wooden pick inserted in center comes out clean. Cool in pan 10 minutes; remove to wire rack, and drizzle Praline Glaze over cake. Cool completely.

Praline Glaze:

1/2 cup firmly-packed brown sugar
1/4 cup sugar
1/4 cup butter or margarine
1/4 cup whipping cream
1/2 cup pecan halves

Combine first 4 ingredients in a heavy saucepan. Cook over low heat, stirring constantly, until mixture reaches soft ball stage (240 degrees). Remove from heat and stir in pecans. Makes about 1 cup glaze.

Mrs. C. B. Williams, Richmond, Va.

NUTTY PRETZEL BUNDT CAKE

1 cup vegetable shortening
2 cups sugar
6 eggs
1/2 cup milk
1-1/2 cups very finely crushed pretzels (a blender can be used)
1-1/2 cups sifted all-purpose flour
3 tablespoons baking powder
2 teaspoons cinnamon
1 cup raisins
1 cup chopped nuts

Cream shortening and sugar in large bowl. Beat with electric mixer until fluffy. Add eggs, one at a time, beating until smooth after each addition. Beat in milk. Fold in pretzels, along with flour, baking powder, and cinnamon. Blend thoroughly. Add raisins and chopped nuts gradually, mixing well after each addition.

Pour batter into a well-oiled and lightly floured Bundt pan. Bake in pre-heated oven of 350 degrees 45-50 minutes, or until cake tests done. Cool in pan on wire rack 10 minutes. Turn out and complete cooling.

Glaze:

1-1/2 cups confectioners' sugar
2-3 tablespoons fresh lemon juice

Combine confectioners' sugar with lemon juice until well blended and drizzle over the cooled cake.

Mrs. E. O'Brien, Richmond, VA

BUTTERSCOTCH SPICE CAKE

1 cup brown sugar
1/2 cup sugar
1/2 cup corn oil
1-1/2 cups flour
1-1/2 teaspoons baking soda
1 teaspoon cinnamon
1/2 teaspoon nutmeg
2 eggs
2 tablespoons molasses
1 cup quick cooking oatmeal
1 cup water
3/4 teaspoon salt
1 teaspoon vanilla

Cream sugars and oil. Add eggs and beat. Add molasses, oatmeal, and water. Beat together. Add the rest of the ingredients; beat. Pour into a 13 x 9 inch pan, which has been greased and floured. Bake in a 350 degree oven for approximately 25-28 minutes. Cool and frost.

Creamy Frosting:

1/4 cup butter, softened
1 cup powdered sugar
2 tablespoons cream
1 teaspoon vanilla

Whip for 4 minutes with electric mixer.

Anna Pritchard, Marysville, Wash.

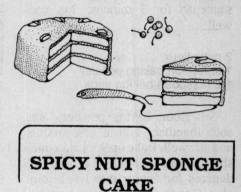

SPICY NUT SPONGE CAKE

5 eggs, separated
3 tablespoons Sucaryl
1 tablespoon lemon juice
1/2 cup water
2-1/2 cups sifted cake flour
1/4 teaspoon salt
1/2 teaspoon baking powder
1 teaspoon cinnamon
1/2 teaspoon nutmeg
1/2 teaspoon cloves
1/2 teaspoon allspice
3/4 teaspoon cream of tartar
1/2 cup finely chopped nuts

Beat egg yolks until thick and lemon colored. Add Sucaryl, lemon juice and water. Beat on high speed of mixer until thick, about 10 minutes. Sift together flour, salt, baking powder and spices. Sift a little at a time over egg yolk mixture, folding in gently but thoroughly. Beat egg whites until foamy. Add cream of tartar and beat until stiff peaks are formed. Fold egg yolk mixture gently into whites. Add chopped nuts. Pour into 9-inch ungreased tube pan. Bake 45 to 50 minutes at 350 degrees. Invert and let hang until cold.

Mrs. Peggy Fowler Revels, Woodruff, SC

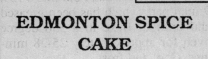

EDMONTON SPICE CAKE

1 cup water
1 cup sugar
1 teaspoon nutmeg
1 teaspoon cinnamon
1 cup raisins
1/3 cup cooking oil
1/2 teaspoon cloves
1/2 teaspoon salt

Boil all above ingredients in saucepan for 3 minutes. Let cool well.

2 cups flour
1 teaspoon baking powder
1/2 teaspoon baking soda

Sift flour, baking powder, and soda together; add to first mixture and stir well. Bake on 9 x 15 x 2-inch shallow pan or jelly roll pan, at 375 degrees for approximately 15 minutes. Good with whipped topping.

Deborah Hooker, San Bernardino, CA

FAVORITE SPICE CAKE

No milk, butter or eggs

2 cups brown or white sugar
2 cups water
1 cup raisins
2/3 cup lard
1/4 teaspoon salt
2 teaspoons cinnamon
1/2 teaspoon nutmeg
1 teaspoon ground cloves
2 teaspoons baking soda mixed with
    1/3 cup water or cold coffee
4 cups flour sifted with 1 teaspoon
    baking powder
1 cup nuts chopped (optional)
Whole or half nuts (optional)

Preheat oven to 350 degrees. Boil sugar, water, lard, raisins, salt and spices for 5 minutes. Let cool; add baking soda and flour mixture. Mix thoroughly (batter should be quite stiff); add chopped nuts. Pour into greased and floured rectangular or square pan. Decorate with nut halves. Bake 350 degrees for 30 to 35 minutes or until knife inserted comes out clean.

Ruth Miles, Cairo, NY

1917 WAR CAKE

Very popular in 1917 when sugar and butter were scarce and eggs too costly for luxuries such as cake. My mother used it for years.

1 cup corn syrup
1 cut cold water
1 teaspoon salt
1/2 teaspoon cloves
1 teaspoon cinnamon
1/2 teaspoon nutmeg
1 tablespoon Crisco
1 teaspoon soda
2 cups flour
1/2 teaspoon baking power

Put first 6 ingredients in saucepan; cook 3 minutes after reaching boiling point. Add Crisco. When cool, add soda dissolved in a little hot water; add flour and baking powder. Stir; pour into greased tube pan. Bake for one hour at 325 degrees.

Rebecca Preston, Weare, NH

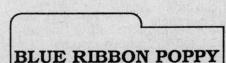

BLUE RIBBON POPPY SEED BUNDT CAKE

1/4 cup poppy seeds
1 cup buttermilk
1 cup butter
1-1/2 cups sugar
4 eggs
1 teaspoon vanilla
2-1/2 cups flour
1/2 teaspoon salt
1 teaspoon soda

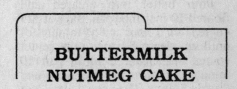

2 teaspoons cinnamon
1/3 cup sugar

Soak poppy seeds for 2 hours in buttermilk. Cream together butter and sugar. Add eggs one at a time, beating well after each; add vanilla. Sift together flour, salt and soda. Add buttermilk-poppy seed mixture and flour mixture, alternately to butter-sugar mixture. Grease well 12-cup bundt pan; spoon in 1/3 of batter; top with half cinnamon-sugar mix; spoon in 1/3 more batter, cinnamon-sugar mix, and end with batter. Bake at 350 degrees for 50 minutes. Let cool in pan 5 minutes before turning onto rack to finish cooling.

Cinnamon-sugar mixture:
2 tablespoons cinnamon
1/3 cup sugar

Mix cinnamon and sugar together. Super to have on hand in the freezer. Just pop into the oven and warm a bit, serve with apricot butter and coffee or tea!

Mary I. Young, Spencer, IA

BUTTERMILK NUTMEG CAKE

1/2 cup butter
1-1/2 cups sugar
3 eggs, beaten
2 cups sifted all-purpose flour
1/4 teaspoon salt
1 teaspoon baking powder
1/4 teaspoon baking soda
2 teaspoons nutmeg
1 cup buttermilk

Preheat oven to 350 degrees. Cream butter; add sugar gradually; cream well. Add eggs; stir. Sift together flour, salt, baking powder, soda, and nutmeg. Add to sugar-butter mixture, alternately, with buttermilk; mix well. Pour batter into two 9-inch layer pans. Sprinkle top of cake batter with sugar and nutmeg before baking. Bake at 350 degrees for 35 minutes or until done. No frosting is necessary; the sugar and nutmeg make a sweet topping.

Jennie Lien, Stoughton, Wis.

DUTCH HUSTLE CAKE

1-1/2 cups flour
1/4 cup sugar
1/2 teaspoon salt
1 package active dry yeast
2 tablespoons soft butter
1/2 cup very hot tap water
1-1/2 cups drained cooked apple slices
2 tablespoons brown sugar
1/4 teaspoon ground cinnamon
1/4 teaspoon ground nutmeg
2 tablespoons butter
Confectioners' sugar glaze (use own recipe)

In large bowl, mix 1/2 cup flour, sugar, salt, yeast and butter. Gradually add water. Beat at high speed in mixer 2 minutes, scraping often. Add 1/2 cup more flour and beat again. Add another 1/2 cup flour (1-1/2 cups in all) and beat until very thick batter is formed. Spread batter evenly in buttered 9-inch square pan. Toss apples with cinnamon, nutmeg and sugar. Arrange on top of batter. Dot with butter. Cover; let rise in warm place, free from drafts, until doubled in bulk, about 1 hour. Bake in 400 degree oven about 25 minutes or until done. Drizzle with confectioners' sugar glaze. Let stand on wire rack about 10 minutes before removing from pan.

Diantha Hibbard, Rochester, NY

GOOEY BUTTER CAKE

1/4 cup sugar
1/4 cup Crisco
1/4 teaspoon salt
1 egg
1 6-ounce cake of yeast
1/2 cup warm milk
2-1/2 cups all purpose flour
1 tablespoon vanilla

Prepare a sweet dough by mixing sugar with Crisco and salt. Add egg and beat with electric mixer one minute until well blended. Dissolve yeast in warm milk. Add flour, then milk and yeast mixture and vanilla to sweet dough batter. Mix 3 minutes with dough hooks or with hands. Turn dough onto floured board and knead for one minute. Place in a lightly greased bowl; cover with a towel and set in a warm place to rise for one hour.

M. Lanff, Philadelphia, Pa.

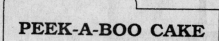

PEEK-A-BOO CAKE

1/2 pound margarine
2 cups sugar
4 eggs, add and beat one at a time
1 teaspoon vanilla extract
Dash of salt
1 cup pie filling (your favorite)
3 cups flour

In a large bowl, mix together margarine, sugar, eggs, vanilla, salt, and flour. Grease a 13 x 9 x 2-inch pan. Spread half of batter in pan, then spoon pie filling over the batter. Drop remaining batter over pie filling. Bake at 350 degrees for 40 minutes.

Melanie Burnell, Pittsfield, Mass.

POUND CAKE

2/3 cup shortening
1-1/4 cups sugar
2/3 cup milk
1 teaspoon lemon extract
2 cups sifted flour
1 teaspoon salt
1/2 teaspoon baking powder
3 eggs

Preheat oven to 325 degrees. Grease and flour 9 x 5 x 3-inch loaf pan. Cream shortening and sugar until light and fluffy. Add milk and lemon extract; blend. Sift dry ingredients; add to creamed mixture. Beat until smooth. Add eggs, one at a time and beat well after each addition. Beat entire mixture well before pouring into loaf pan. Bake for 75 - 80 minutes.

Mrs. E. Bartels, Howard Beach, NY

"PRETTY POSY EASTER CAKE"

1 - 18-1/4 ounce box yellow cake mix
2 egg whites, unbeaten
1-1/4 cups granulated sugar
Dash of salt
1/3 cup water
2 teaspoons light corn syrup
1 teaspoon vanilla extract
2 cups shredded coconut
18 colored jelly beans

Bake in two 8" cake pans according to directions; cool on rack. Combine next 6 ingredients beating well until thick. Spread between layers and on top and sides of cooled cake. Sprinkle coconut generously on top and sides. Place 3 jelly beans together 6 times around top of cake to form posies (flowers).

Gwen Campbell, Sterling, VA

TREASURE TOFFEE CAKE

Serves 16

1/4 cup sugar
1 teaspoon cinnamon
2 cups flour
1 cup sugar
1-1/2 teaspoons baking powder
1 teaspoon baking soda
1/4 teaspoon salt
1 teaspoon vanilla
1 cup sour cream
1/2 cup butter, softened
2 eggs
1/4 cup chopped nuts
3 - 1 1/8 ounce chocolate Toffee bars, coarsely crushed
1/4 cup melted butter
Confectioners' sugar

Combine cinnamon and 1/4 cup sugar. Combine remaining ingredients except nuts, candy, and melted butter.

Blend at low speed with electric mixer until moistened. Beat at medium speed for 3 minutes. Spoon half of the batter into greased and floured 10-inch bundt pan. Sprinkle with 2 tablespoons cinnamon-sugar mixture. Spoon remaining batter into pan. Top with remaining cinnamon-sugar mixture, nuts, and candy. Pour melted butter over top. Bake in a 325 degree oven for 45 minutes. Cool 15 minutes. Remove from pan; dust with confectioners' sugar.

Marcella Swigert, Monroe City, MO

Casseroles

CEATIVE

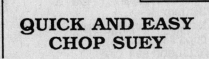

CHEESE SPAGHETTI SOUFFLE
Makes 6 servings

1 cup spaghetti in 1-inch pieces
1 cup milk, scalded
1 cup grated sharp cheese
1/4 cup butter
2/3 cup coarse bread crumbs
1 (10-ounce) package frozen peas, thawed
1 tablespoon minced green pepper
1 tablespoon minced onion
1 tablespoon minced parsley
1 teaspoon salt
3 eggs, separated

Cook spaghetti according to package directions; drain. Combine milk, cheese, and butter; stir until cheese is melted. Add spaghetti; half of bread crumbs, vegetables, parsley and salt. Blend in egg yolks. Fold in stiffly beaten egg whites. Turn into a buttered 1-1/2-quart casserole. Sprinkle remaining crumbs on top. Set casserole in a shallow pan of water. Bake at 350 degrees for about 40 minutes, or until a knife inserted in center comes out clean.

Trenda Leigh, Richmond, Va.

BAKED EGG AND CHEESE CASSEROLE

6 slices white bread
3 tablespoons soft butter
1/2 cup Romano cheese, grated
1/2 cup sliced, stuffed olives
5 eggs

2 cups milk
Salt & pepper to taste
1 tablespoon parsley, finely minced

Trim bread. Toast very lightly. Spread soft butter on toast. Arrange slices in a square, buttered casserole. Sprinkle with half of the grated cheese. Add a layer of sliced olives. Beat eggs with milk, salt, pepper, and parsley. Pour over the bread; sprinkle with remaining cheese and bake in a 350 degree oven for 30-40 minutes or until the casserole's contents are puffed and golden brown.

Agnes Ward, Erie, PA

QUICK AND EASY CHOP SUEY

1/2 pound ground beef round
2-1/2 cups tomatoes
1 cup celery cut into thin strips, about 1-inch long
1 cup onions, finely sliced
2 tablespoons soy sauce
1 cup elbow macaroni
2 tablespoons oil
2-1/2 teaspoons salt

Cook macaroni in 2 quarts boiling, salted water for 10 minutes. Stir occasionally. Drain and rinse. Heat oil in skillet and add onions; cook over medium heat for 5 minutes or until onions are slightly yellow. Add beef and continue cooking for 10 to 15 minutes or until well browned. Stir frequently. Add tomatoes and 1-1/2 teaspoons salt; cover and cook for 10 minutes. Add celery; cook 5 minutes longer. Combine meat sauce and macaroni; season with soy sauce and cook slowly 5 more minutes.

This is very easy and your family will love the taste!

Suzan Wiener, Spring Hill, Fla.

RICE AND MUSHROOM CASSEROLE
Serves 4

1/2 cup rice
2 tablespoons butter or margarine
1/4 pound fresh mushrooms, sliced
1/2 cup chopped onion
1/2 cup chopped celery
1-1/4 cups water
1 beef bouillon cube
1/2 teaspoon salt
1 bay leaf
Some basil (1/4 teaspoon dried - 1/2 teaspoon fresh)
Pepper to taste

Preheat oven to 350 degrees. In a skillet, over medium heat, cook rice, stirring constantly, until rice is golden (about 5 minutes). Use 1/2 tablespoon butter to brown rice. Pour rice into a 1-quart casserole. In same skillet, in 1/2 tablespoon butter, sauté mushrooms, celery, and onions until tender (5 minutes). Add rest of ingredients; heat to boiling. Pour mixture over rice; cover and bake 35 minutes or until liquid is absorbed. Toss in 1 tablespoon butter to make fluffy.

Vivian Nikanow, Chicago, Ill.

LAZY BEEF CASSEROLE
Serves 4

1 pound lean beef chuck, cut into 1-1/2-inch cubes
1/2 cup red wine
1 (10-1/2-ounce) can consomme, undiluted
1/4 cup all-purpose flour
Freshly ground black pepper, to taste
1 medium onion, chopped
1/4 cup fine dry bread crumbs
1/4 teaspoon rosemary

Put meat in a casserole with the wine, consomme, pepper, rosemary, and onion. Mix flour and bread crumbs and stir into the liquid. Cover and bake at 300 degrees, about 3 hours. Serve with rice or noodles. (206 calories per serving)

Ronnie J. Heroux, Uxbridge, Mass.

EASY BEEF GOULASH
Serves 4

1 to 2 tablespoons vegetable oil
1 pound ground beef (chuck)
3 cups uncooked medium egg noodles
2 cups water
1 (8-ounce) can tomato sauce
1 envelope dry onion soup mix

Heat oil in a medium-size skillet over medium heat. Add ground beef and cook until lightly browned, stirring occasionally with a fork to break up meat. Drain off any excess fat. Sprinkle uncooked noodles over meat. Combine water, tomato sauce, and onion soup mix. Pour over noodles in skillet. Do not stir. Cover and bring to a boil. Reduce heat to moderately low and simmer about 30 minutes, or until noodles are tender. Stir and serve.
Note: You may have to add a small amount of water if the noodles seem to be sticking. This is very easy and quick for those hectic days.

Doris L. Rayman, Somerset, Pa.

GERMAN POTATO CASSEROLE

6 medium-size potatoes, peeled and sliced
1 pound hot pork sausage, cooked and drained
8 ounces sour cream
2 teaspoons dry onion soup mix
2 teaspoons lemon juice
1 can cream of mushroom soup
2 teaspoons Dijon mustard
1 can sauerkraut, washed and drained
1 cup buttered bread crumbs
Salt and pepper to taste

Peel, wash, and slice potatoes. Boil in salted water until tender. Mix sour cream, dry onion soup mix, mushroom soup, lemon juice, and mustard. Heat sauerkraut in 2 tablespoons sausage drippings. Alternate layers of potatoes, cream mixture, and sauerkraut. Put bread crumbs on top and bake in 350-degree oven until hot and bubbly, about 20-25 minutes.

Ruby Walsh, West Chicago, Ill.

INDIAN CASSEROLE

1 can hominy, drained
1 pound ground beef
1/2 cup chopped onion
1/2 cup chopped green pepper
1-3/4 cups canned tomatoes
1/2 teaspoon salt
1/4 teaspoon pepper
1 cup grated cheese

Brown beef, salt, onions, and green pepper. Add tomatoes and hominy. Pour into buttered casserole and bake at 350 degrees for 40 minutes. Remove from oven and sprinkle cheese on top. Return to oven and bake 15 minutes.
Note: I tried this recipe and cooked it in an electric skillet. I cooked it on low until thick, then placed slices of cheese over the top and put lid of skillet on until cheese melted. I served it with French bread and a cottage cheese and peach salad.

Corena J. Bennington, Whitestown, Ind.

MOCK OYSTER CASSEROLE
Serves 6

1 large eggplant
1 cup cracker crumbs (approx. 25 soda crackers, crushed)
2 eggs
1/2 cup milk
3 tablespoons butter
1/4 cup chopped celery
1/4 cup chopped green pepper
1/4 cup chopped onion
1 (11 ounce) can mushroom soup
Tabasco sauce to taste

Peel eggplant and cut into cubes. Boil eggplant for 3 minutes in salt water; set aside. Place 1/3 of the crushed crumbs in a buttered 2 quart casserole dish; add 1/2 the eggplant. Repeat layering the cracker crumbs and eggplant. Beat eggs slightly, add 1/2 cup milk, mushroom soup, peppers, onions, celery and Tabasco sauce, mixing well. Pour slowly over eggplant mixture. Dot with butter. Cover and bake at 375 degrees for 30 minutes. Uncover and add more milk if needed. Bake 15 minutes more uncovered, until golden brown.

Rose McBride, Kent, OH

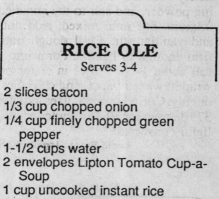

RICE OLE
Serves 3-4

2 slices bacon
1/3 cup chopped onion
1/4 cup finely chopped green pepper
1-1/2 cups water
2 envelopes Lipton Tomato Cup-a-Soup
1 cup uncooked instant rice
1/2 teaspoon garlic salt

In skillet cook bacon until crisp; drain, reserving 2 tablespoons drippings. Crumble bacon; set aside. Add onion and green pepper to skillet; cook until tender. Add water and bring to boil. Stir in Cup-a-Soup, uncooked rice, garlic salt, and crumbled bacon; cover and remove from heat. Let stand for 5 minutes.
Agnes Ward, Erie, Pa.

Cookies &

BARS

BANANA OATMEAL HONEY NUT COOKIES
Makes 3 dozen

1/2 cup shortening
1/2 cup sugar
1 egg, beaten
1/2 cup honey
2 cups all-purpose flour
2 teaspoons baking powder
1 teaspoon salt
1 cup finely chopped nuts
1 teaspoon vanilla

Combine sugar and shortening. Mix egg and honey and add alternately with the combined flour, baking powder, and salt to the creamed mixture. Stir until mixed. Add nuts and vanilla; stir. Chill dough until firm enough to handle. Form into a roll about 1-1/2 inches in diameter; wrap in waxed paper, and chill thoroughly. Cut in 1/8-inch slices. Bake at 375 degrees for 10-15 minutes or until lightly browned.

Leota Baxter, Ingalls, Kan.

COOKIES (DIABETIC)
Makes 2 dozen

3 medium bananas, mashed
1/3 cup oil
1 teaspoon vanilla extract
2 cups old-fashioned rolled oats
1-1/4 cups chopped walnuts
1/4 cup raisins

Combine bananas, oil, and vanilla. Stir in oats, walnuts, and raisins. Drop by tablespoonfuls onto greased cookie sheets. Press down lightly with fork. Preheat oven to 350 degrees. Bake 10-12 minutes until golden brown.

Kit Rollins, Cedarburg, Wis.

CHERRY TWINKS
Makes 2-1/2 dozen

1 cup confectioners' sugar
1 cup butter, softened
1 teaspoon vanilla
1 egg
2 cups flour
2 tablespoons poppy seeds
1/2 teaspoon salt
1/3-1/2 cup cherry preserves

Heat oven to 300 degrees. Beat confectioners' sugar and butter until fluffy. Add vanilla and egg; blend well. Stir in flour, poppy seeds, salt; mix well. Drop by rounded teaspoonfuls onto ungreased cookie sheets. With finger make imprint in center of each cookie. Fill with 1/2 teaspoon preserves. Bake at 300 degrees for 20-25 minutes or until edges are light golden brown. Remove from cookie sheet immediately.

This is a very light and buttery cookie.

Vickie Vogt, Kewaskum, Wis.

DATE BARS

1 pound dates
1 cup walnut meats
1/2 cup flour
1/4 teaspoon baking powder
1/4 teaspoon salt
1 cup sugar
2 eggs
1/4 cup melted butter

Pit dates and cut into quarters. Mix together flour, baking powder, salt, and sugar. Add dates and nuts to flour mixture. Beat eggs. Add melted butter and combine mixtures. Bake in 8x12-inch pan for 30 minutes in moderate oven of 350 degrees. When slightly cool, cut into bars. Roll each bar in powdered sugar.

Suzan L. Wiener, Spring Hill, Fla.

CREAM CHEESE LEMON BARS
Makes 24

1 (18-1/2-ounce) package lemon cake mix
1/2 cup butter or margarine
3 eggs, divided
2 cups canned lemon frosting
1 (8-ounce) package cream cheese, softened

Grease 9x13-inch pan. Combine cake mix, butter, and 1 egg. Stir until moist. Press into pan. Blend frosting into cream cheese. Reserve 1/2 cup mixture to frost bars. Preheat oven to 350 degrees.

Add remaining eggs to remaining frosting mixture. Beat 3-5 minutes at high speed. Spread over base. Bake about 30 minutes. Cool slightly and frost with reserved frosting. Cut into bars.

Kit Rollins, Cedarburg, Wis.

LEMON SUGAR COOKIES

Makes 4 dozen

2-3/4 cups flour
2 teaspoons baking powder
1/4 teaspoon salt
1 cup butter
2 cups sugar
2 eggs
2 teaspoons grated lemon rind
3 tablespoons lemon juice
1 cup quick oats

Sift together flour, baking powder, and salt. In large bowl, cream butter and sugar. Add eggs; beating well. Beat in lemon rind and juice. Gradually add flour mixture, then stir in oats. Chill dough thoroughly (at least 2 hours). Roll level tablespoons dough into balls and place on greased cookie sheets, allowing room for cookies to spread. Using a flat-bottomed glass or custard cup that has been greased and dipped in sugar, flatten each ball to 1/4 inch thickness (dip glass in sugar each time). Bake at 375 degrees until lightly browned around edges, about 8-10 minutes. Cool for one minute, then carefully remove from cookie sheets; cool on racks. These cookies are delicate and delicious.

Barbara Beauregard-Smith, Northfield, South Australia

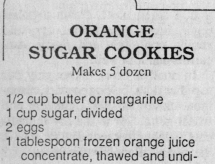

ORANGE SUGAR COOKIES

Makes 5 dozen

1/2 cup butter or margarine
1 cup sugar, divided
2 eggs
1 tablespoon frozen orange juice concentrate, thawed and undiluted
3 tablespoons grated orange rind, divided
2 cups flour
2 teaspoons baking powder

Cream butter and 1/2 cup sugar until light and fluffy. Add eggs, one at a time, beating well after each addition. Blend in orange juice and 1 tablespoon grated orange rind. Combine flour and baking powder; blend into creamed mixture. Wrap dough in waxed paper and refrigerate for 3 hours. Roll out on lightly floured surface to 1/4-inch thickness. Cut with a 2-inch cookie cutter. Place on greased cookie sheet. Combine 1/2 cup sugar and 2 tablespoons grated orange rind; sprinkle mixture over cookies. Bake at 375 degrees for 8-10 minutes.

Barbara Beauregard-Smith, Northfield, South Australia

BUTTERSCOTCH COCONUT COOKIES

Makes 5 dozen

2 cups flour
1/2 teaspoon soda
1/2 teaaspoon salt
1/2 cup margarine, softened
1/2 cup granulated sugar
1/2 cup packed brown sugar
2 eggs
1 teaspoon vanilla
1 cup butterscotch chips
1/2 cup chopped pecans
2-1/2 cups coconut
Pecan halves (if desired)
Candied cherry halves (if desired)

Pre-heat oven to 375 degrees. Combine in a small bowl the flour, soda, and salt; set aside. Using larger bowl, combine softened margarine and both sugars; beat until very light and fluffy. Beat in eggs (one at a time) and vanilla. Add flour mixture; mix well. Stir in butterscotch chips and nuts. Drop dough into coconut. With lightly floured or greased hand; roll to coat with coconut. Form into balls. Bake at 375 degrees on ungreased cookie sheet for 10-12 minutes. Garnish each cookie with pecan half before baking if desired or place half candied cherry on each cookieas you remove from oven. Remove to cooling rack and allow to cool.

Jodie McCoy, Tulsa, OK

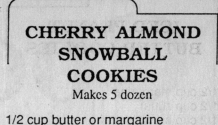

CHERRY ALMOND SNOWBALL COOKIES

Makes 5 dozen

1/2 cup butter or margarine
1/4 cup evaporated milk
1/2 teaspoon grated lemon rind
1-3/4 cups sifted flour
3/4 cup sugar
1/2 teaspoon salt
1 cup finely chopped almonds
6 tablespoons confectioners' sugar
1/2 pound candied cherries

Cream butter; beat in milk, a little at a time, until all is blended with butter. Add lemon rind. Sift flour with sugar and salt; gradually add to butter mixture. Add nuts; mix well. Pinch off pieces of dough, about a teaspoon. Flatten dough in palm of hand. Place a cherry on dough; pinch dough up around cherry completely. Roll between palms. Place on lightly greased, floured cookie sheet. Bake at 375 degrees for 12 minutes. Roll in confectioners' sugar while still warm.

Mrs. Don Shamway, Freeport, Ill.

POPPY SEED COOKIES

Makes 2 dozen

1/2 cup butter or margarine
1/3 cup sugar
2 egg yolks
1 cup flour
1/3 teaspoon salt
1/4 teaspoon grated lemon rind
1/2 teaspoon vanilla extract
2 teaspoons poppy seed

Cream butter and sugar. Beat in egg yolks and other ingredients. Mix well; cover bowl and chill at least 2 hours. Shape dough into 1-inch balls; place on greased cookie sheets. Flatten balls with a fork and bake at 375 degrees for 10 minutes.

Barbara Beauregard-Smith, Northfield, South Australia

ICED PEANUT BUTTER COOKIES

1/2 cup margarine
1/2 cup sugar
1/2 cup brown sugar
2 eggs
1/3 cup peanut butter
1/2 teaspoon baking soda
1/4 teaspoon salt
1/2 teaspoon vanilla
1 cup flour
1 cup rolled oats
1 cup chocolate chips

Mix together margarine, sugar and brown sugar. Blend in eggs, peanut butter, baking soda, vanilla flour and rolled oats. Spread in a greased pan 13 x 9 x 2 inches and bake at 350 degrees for about 20 minutes. As soon as the pan is removed from the oven, sprinkle chocolate bits on the top. Return to oven for a few minutes to melt the chocolate, remove again, spreading chocolate evenly; allow to cool.

Icing:
1/4 cup peanut butter
1/2 cup powdered sugar
2 to 4 teaspoons of milk

Combine peanut butter and powdered sugar. Moisten with milk until consistency to spread. Ice cooled cookies.

Amelia M. Brown, Pittsburgh, PA

PEANUT BUTTER COOKIES
Makes 100 cookies

3-1/3 cups peanut butter
2-2/3 cups shortening
6 eggs
3/4 teaspoon salt
3/4 teaspoon baking soda
2-1/2 cups brown sugar
3 cups white sugar
4-1/2 cups flour
1 tablespoon vanilla

Cream the sugars, peanut butter, and shortening all together. Add well beaten eggs and vanilla. Add dry ingredients sifted together. Roll mixture in balls and place on greased sheets. Flatten with fork dipped in granulated sugar. Bake in preheated oven at 375 degrees for 8 or 9 minutes.

This is a large recipe, but it can be adjusted to needs. I usually make the full amount - some to use right away, some to freeze, and some to give away. I am a head cook at our Chichester School and everyone who has eaten these cookies loves them.

Natalie Henshaw, Pittsfield, NH

MOIST OATMEAL COOKIES

Boil gently for 10 minutes:
1 cup water
1 cup sugar
1 cup shortening
1 cup golden raisins
1/2 teaspoon cinnamon
1/2 teaspoon nutmeg
1/2 teaspoon salt

Set aside to cool. Then add:
2 eggs
1 teaspoon vanilla
2 cups flour
1/2 cup nut meats
2 cups oatmeal

Drop by spoonfuls on greased cookie sheet. Bake 10-12 minutes at 350 degrees. Check bottom of cookie—if evenly browned, it's done and not too crispy.

O. Elizabeth Todd, Minneapolis, Minn.

HAWAIIAN OATMEAL COOKIES
Makes 3 dozen

1 cup flour
1 teaspoon baking powder
1 teaspoon baking soda
3/4 teaspoon salt

1/2 cup shortening
1/2 cup granulated sugar
1/2 cup packed brown sugar
1 egg
1/2 teaspoon vanilla
1 cup rolled oats
1 cup shredded coconut

Sift together flour, baking powder, baking soda and salt; set aside. Cream shortening and sugars until light and fluffy; add egg; mix well. Add vanilla, then flour mixture. Add oats and coconut; mix until well blended. Shape into small walnut size balls, place on ungreased cookie sheets. Bake at 350 degrees about 12 to 15 minutes or until golden.

Margaret Russo, Winsted, CT

OATMEAL-CARROT COOKIES
Makes 24 bars

1/2 cup brown sugar
1 tablespoon honey
1/3 cup margarine, melted
1 egg
1-1/2 teaspoon vanilla
3/4 cup shredded carrots
1 cup whole wheat flour
1 teaspoon baking powder
1 teaspoon cinnamon
1/2 teaspoon ground cloves. (optional)
1/2 cup oatmeal
1/4 cup wheat germ
1/2 cup raisins

In a small bowl, cream together sugar, honey, margarine, egg and vanilla until light and fluffy. Add carrots and mix well.

In another bowl, thoroughly stir together flour, baking powder, cinnamon, cloves (if used), oatmeal and wheat germ. Stir in the dry ingredients into the creamed mixture; fold in the raisins. Pour mixture into a 9 x 2 x 2 inch pan sprayed with vegetable oil. Bake at 350 degrees for 30 minutes. Let cool in pan on wire rack. Cut into bars or squares.

Let cookies set overnight so flavors can blend.

Trenda Leigh, Richmond, VA

ANGEL COOKIES

1-1/2 cups bread crumbs
1/2 cup chopped nuts
1/2 teaspoon vanilla or almond
    extract
2/3 cup sweetened condensed milk
3 drops red food coloring
30 nut halves (walnut or pecan)

Soak bread crumbs in condensed milk to which the extract and coloring have been added. Add chopped nuts. Drop by spoonfuls onto greased cookie sheets. Top each with a nut half; bake at 350 degrees for 12 minutes.

Fun for children to make!

Mrs. Don Shamway, Freeport, Ill.

AMERICAN FLAG COOKIES

1 cup butter or margarine
1-1/2 cups granulated sugar
1 egg, beaten
2-1/2 cups flour
1-1/2 teaspoons baking powder
1 teaspoon flavoring of your choice
Few drops of coloring (red and blue)
(Untinted dough represents white)

Cream butter. Add sugar and beaten egg. Beat until well-blended. Add flour, baking powder, and flavoring; mix until dough is smooth and easy to handle. Divide dough into 3 different bowls and color each portion as desired. Mix thoroughly to get a uniform color. Add more color, a drop at a time, as needed. Form each portion into long bars or flattened cylinders. Wrap each in waxed paper or plastic wrap and refrigerate until well-chilled. Remove wrappings and stack cylinders on top of each other in the desired color arrangement. Wrap entire log in waxed paper or plastic wrap and chill until very firm. Preheat oven to 350 degrees. Slice flag bars 1/4-inch thick. Place on cookie sheet and bake 10 to 12 minutes. Cool on wire rack.

SWEETHEART COOKIES
Makes 6 dozen

1 cup butter or margarine, softened
1-1/3 cups granulated sugar
1-1/3 cups firmly-packed light brown
    sugar
2 eggs
1 teaspoon vanilla extract
3 cups quick-cooking oats
1-1/2 cups chopped nuts (any desired
    kind)
1 cup semisweet chocolate bits

In a large mixing bowl, beat butter or margarine with sugars until thoroughly creamed. Add eggs and vanilla. Beat until fluffy. Sift flour and soda into another large bowl. Add oats and toss until well coated with flour. A cup at a time, stir dry ingredients into batter. When well-mixed, stir in nuts and chocolate bits. (Dough will be stiff.) Drop by teaspoonfuls onto cookie sheet and bake in preheated oven of 375 degrees for 10 to 12 minutes.

Mrs. L. Mayer, Richmond, VA

YULE LOGS OR WREATHS
Makes 4 dozen

2-2/3 cups all-purpose flour
1 teaspoon nutmeg
1 cup softened margarine
3/4 cup sugar
1 egg
1 teaspoon vanilla

Cream margarine, sugar, and nutmeg until fluffy. Add egg and vanilla; beat well. Add flour to creamed mixture, small amounts at a time; beat well. Chill dough for 1 hour. Shape dough by hand into ropes, 3 inches long, 1/2 inch thick, on floured surface; or form circles with the rope-lengths to make wreaths. Place on ungreased cookie sheet, 1 inch apart. Bake at 350 degrees for 12 to 15 minutes until golden on the bottom. Remove from oven and cool; spread with plain white glaze. Sprinkle with chopped nuts, or with colored sugar.

For glaze, add enough water to 1 cup confectioners' sugar to make a thin icing.

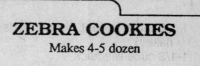

ZEBRA COOKIES
Makes 4-5 dozen

1-1/2 cups sugar
1/2 cup vegetable oil
1-1/4 teaspoons vanilla extract
3 eggs
1-2/3 cups all-purpose flour
1/2 cup cocoa
1/2 tablespoon cinnamon
1-1/2 teaspoons baking powder
1/4 teaspoon salt
1 cup confectioners' sugar

In a mixing bowl combine sugar, oil, and vanilla. Add eggs, one at a time; mix well. Stir in flour, cocoa, cinnamon, baking powder, and salt. Cover; refrigerate 2 hours. Lightly grease baking sheet; set aside. Place confectioners' sugar in a shallow dish. Shape dough into 1-inch balls; roll in confectioners' sugar. Place 2-inches apart on baking sheet. Bake 350 degrees for 11 minutes; cool on rack. (These cookies crack on top as they bake; thus the striped Zebra look).

Gwen Campbell, Sterling, VA

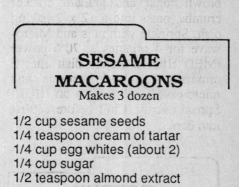

SESAME MACAROONS
Makes 3 dozen

1/2 cup sesame seeds
1/4 teaspoon cream of tartar
1/4 cup egg whites (about 2)
1/4 cup sugar
1/2 teaspoon almond extract

Toast sesame seeds in 350 degree oven for 15 minutes or until golden brown. Pulverize seeds in blender. Add cream of tartar to egg whites; beat until stiff. Gradually add sugar; beating well after each addition. Fold in sesame seeds and almond extract. Drop by teaspoonfuls onto lightly greased baking sheet. Bake in 250 degree oven for 30 minutes. Remove at once from baking sheet.

Agnes Ward, Erie, PA

MACAROONS

1-1/2 cups Instant Potato Buds (not flakes)
1-1/2 cups Bisquick
1 cup sugar
1/4 cup flour
1/2 cup plus 2 tablespoons margarine
1 teaspoon coconut extract
1 egg

Mix all in order given. Chill at least 5 minutes. Roll in balls, flatten with a fork on cookie sheet. Bake in 350 degree oven for 8-10 minutes. These are a crunch cookie.

Kathleen Dwyer, Saginaw, MN

TOFFEE SPLINTERS

11 graham cracker squares, crushed
1/2 cup margarine
3/4 cup packed dark brown sugar
1/4 cup chopped peanuts or pecans
1 - 6 ounce package semi sweet chocolate morsels

Combine melted margarine, brown sugar and graham cracker crumbs, press into a 12 x 7 baking dish. Sprinkle with nuts and Microwave for 4 minutes at 70% power (MED HIGH). Rotate dish after 2 minutes. Top with morsels and microwave for 1 minute on HIGH. Spread evenly. Chill before cutting into bars.

TOFFEE COOKIES

Makes 3 dozen

1-1/2 cups flour
1 teaspoon baking powder
1/2 teaspoon salt
1/2 cup margarine
3/4 cup packed brown sugar
1 egg
1 teaspoon vanilla
1 cup finely chopped Heath bars
1/3 cup coarsely chopped pecans

Mix egg, sugar, and vanilla until smooth and creamy. Stir in dry ingredients. Blend in chopped candy bars and nuts. Drop by spoonfuls, 2 inches apart on greased cookie sheet. Bake at 350 degrees for 12-15 minutes. Remove from cookie sheet. A great crunchy cookie!!

Jodie McCoy, Tulsa, Okla.

CREAM CHEESE SNOWBALLS

Makes 36

1 cup flour
1-1/2 teaspoons baking powder
1/2 cup butter, softened
1 (3-ounce) package cream cheese, softened
1/2 cup sugar
1/4 teaspoon lemon extract
1 cup powdered sugar

Combine flour and baking powder. In small bowl, beat butter and cream cheese until softened. Add sugar and extract; beat until fluffy. Add flour mixture; beat until well blended. Cover and chill for 1 hour or until easy to handle. Shape into 1-inch balls. Place on ungreased cookie sheets and bake at 350 degrees for 12-15 minutes or until done. Cool slightly and roll in powdered sugar. Cool thoroughly; then roll in sugar again.

Shirley Viscosi, Worcester, Mass.

CHOCOLATE BRANDY BALLS

Makes 4 dozen

6-ounce package chocolate chips
3 tablespoons dark Karo syrup
1/2 cup brandy (rum or bourbon)
10-ounce box vanilla wafers, crushed
1/2 cup sifted confectioners' sugar
1 cup finely chopped nuts (your choice)
Granulated sugar

Melt chocolate chips in top of doubler boiler; remove from heat; add syrup and brandy. Set aside. In large bowl, combine vanilla wafer crumbs, confectioners' sugar and nuts. Add chocolate mixture. Mix thoroughly. Let stand 1/2 hour in refrigerator. Form into 1-inch balls and roll in granulated sugar. Let season in covered container for several days.

Esther Haehnel, Ft. Lauderdale, FL

CHOCO DATE BALLS

Makes 3-1/2 dozen

1/2 cup chunky peanut butter
1/4 cup cocoa or carob powder
2 teaspoons vanilla
2 cups uncooked oat cereal
1/4 cup butter or margarine
2/3 cup mild-flavored honey
1 cup finely-snipped dates

In a small mixing bowl, blend the peanut butter, cocoa or carob, and vanilla, using two forks. Mix in oats. In a small saucepan bring butter and honey to a boil; stir 1 minute. Remove from heat and add dates. Blend into oat mixture. Shape into bite-size balls. Chill until firm. When firm, store in refrigerator in plastic bags. Best when served chilled.

Peggy Fowler Revels, Woodruff, SC

PECAN BALLS

Makes 5 dozen

1 cup soft butter
1/2 cup granulated sugar *or* 1/2 cup powdered sugar
1/4 teaspoon salt
1 teaspoon vanilla
2-1/4 cups flour
1 cup chopped pecans

Mix butter, sugar, salt, and vanilla. Work in flour. The last bit of flour may be worked in with hands. Add nuts. Chill dough. Roll into 1-inch balls. Place on ungreased baking sheet and bake at 350 degrees for 10-12 minutes, until set, but not browned. Roll in sifted confectioners' sugar while warm. Cool; roll again.

Betty Slavin, Omaha, Neb.

DATE AND ALMOND BROWNIES

Makes 16-20 bars

2/3 cup flour
1/2 teaspoon baking powder
1/4 teaspoon salt
1/4 cup butter or margarine
2 squares baking chocolate
1 cup sugar
2 eggs, beaten
1/2 cup chopped almonds
1/2 cup chopped dates*
1 teaspoon vanilla extract

Preheat oven to 350 degrees. Grease 8-inch square pan. Sift flour, baking powder, and salt together. Melt butter and chocolate in top of double boiler. Add sugar to eggs; beat well. Add butter and chocolate; stir in flour and add almonds, dates, and vanilla. Turn into pan. Bake 25 minutes. Cool in pan; cut into squares or bars. Decorate with dates or almonds, if desired.
*Chopped, uncooked prunes may be substituted for dates, if desired.

Mrs. A. Mayer, Richmond, Va.

GOLD RUSH BROWNIES

2 cups graham cracker crumbs
1 can condensed milk
1 (6-ounce) package chocolate chips
1/2 cup chopped pecans

Mix together and put into a 8 x 8-inch pan (well greased). Bake at 350 degrees for 30 minutes. Let brownies cool 10 minutes. Cut into squares and remove from pan.

Norma L. Farrar, Sullivan, MO

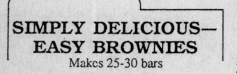

SIMPLY DELICIOUS— EASY BROWNIES

Makes 25-30 bars

Grease 9 x 13 inch baking pan. In large bowl, combine in order given:

1 cup butter or margarine
2 cups sugar

4 eggs (beating after each addition)
2 teaspoons vanilla
1-1/2 cups all-purpose flour
1/2 cup plus 1 tablespoon cocoa
1 teaspoon salt

Mix well and add 1 cup chopped nuts, if desired. Put in pan; bake at 350 degrees for 30 minutes. Check at 25 minutes, if you like brownies chewy. Frost, if desired.

Audrey Reynolds, Lumberport, W.V.

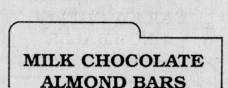

MILK CHOCOLATE ALMOND BARS

1/2 cup softened butter or margarine
1/2 cup dark brown sugar, firmly packed
1-1/4 cup flour
1/4 teaspoon salt
1 - 6 ounce package milk chocolate morsels
1/2 cup chopped almonds

Combine butter and sugar until creamy. Sift flour and salt together and blend into butter and sugar mixture. Press evenly into 13 x 9 x 2 baking dish. Microwave on HIGH for 4 to 5 minutes. Rotate the dish after 2 minutes. Sprinkle milk chocolate morsels over top and return to microwave for 1 minute on HIGH. Spread evenly over top and sprinkle with chopped almonds. Cool before cutting.

ELEGANT KRISPIE BARS

6 ounces white chocolate coating
1 cup peanut butter
4 cups rice cereal
1 cup salted peanuts

Combine coating and peanut butter in a 2 quart bowl and microwave for 2-1/2 to 3 minutes until coating is melted, on HIGH, stir twice. Add cereal and peanuts. Press into 12 x 8 or 13 x 9 baking dish. Refrigerate until set, about 1 hour. Cut into squares.

SUGARLESS BAR

Makes 20 bars
50 calories per bar

1/2 cup raisins
1/2 cup prunes, chopped
1/2 cup dates, chopped
1/2 cup margarine
1 cup water
3 eggs
1 cup flour
1 teaspoon vanilla
1 teaspoon soda
1/4 teaspoon cinnamon
1/4 teaspoon nutmeg
1/2 cup chopped walnuts or pecans

Boil fruit in one cup of water; add margarine. Let cool.

Combine all other ingredients; mix well with fruit mixture. Pour into greased 7 x 11-inch pan. Bake at 350 degrees for 25 to 30 minutes.

Flo Burtnett, Shattuck, OK

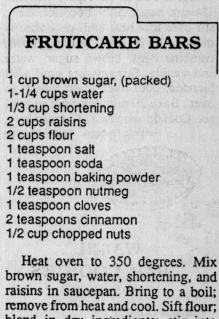

FRUITCAKE BARS

1 cup brown sugar, (packed)
1-1/4 cups water
1/3 cup shortening
2 cups raisins
2 cups flour
1 teaspoon salt
1 teaspoon soda
1 teaspoon baking powder
1/2 teaspoon nutmeg
1 teaspoon cloves
2 teaspoons cinnamon
1/2 cup chopped nuts

Heat oven to 350 degrees. Mix brown sugar, water, shortening, and raisins in saucepan. Bring to a boil; remove from heat and cool. Sift flour; blend in dry ingredients; stir into cooled mixture. Mix in nuts. Spread dough evenly in greased pan, 13x9x2 inches. Bake at 350 degrees for 35-40 minutes or until no imprint remains when touched. Cool and cut into 2x2-1/2 inch bars. Many people like "fruitless" fruitcake; they should love these bars.

Barbara Beauregard-Smith, Northfield, South Australia

CHOCOLATE PECAN PIE BARS

Makes 36 bars

1-1/4 cups all-purpose flour
1/4 cup sugar
1/2 teaspoon baking powder
1/2 teaspoon cinnamon
1/2 cup margarine
1 cup finely chopped pecans
1/4 cup butter
1 square (1-ounce) semisweet chocolate
3 eggs, beaten
1-1/4 cups packed brown sugar
2 tablespoons water
1 teaspoon vanilla

In mixing bowl, stir together flour, sugar, baking powder and cinnamon. Cut in 1/2 cup margarine until mixture resembles coarse crumbs; stir in pecans. Press into bottom of ungreased 13 x 9-inch pan. Bake in 350 degree oven for 10 minutes. Meanwhile, in a small saucepan, combine 1/4 cup butter and chocolate; heat; stir over low heat until chocolate is melted. In a small mixing bowl, combine eggs, brown sugar, water and vanilla. Stir mixture until well blended; pour over crust. Return to oven. Bake 20 minutes more or until set. Cool on wire rack. Cut into bars.

Patricia Habiger, Spearville, KS

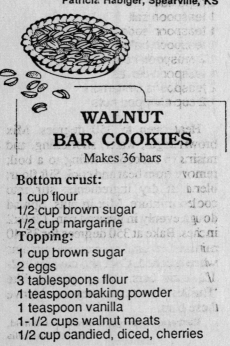

WALNUT BAR COOKIES

Makes 36 bars

Bottom crust:
1 cup flour
1/2 cup brown sugar
1/2 cup margarine
Topping:
1 cup brown sugar
2 eggs
3 tablespoons flour
1 teaspoon baking powder
1 teaspoon vanilla
1-1/2 cups walnut meats
1/2 cup candied, diced, cherries

Crust: Mix flour and sugar in bowl. Cut in margarine with pastry-blender or knives until mixture resembles coarse crumbs. Spread in 13x9x2 inch pan; press down evenly. Bake at 375 degrees for 8 to 10 minutes until firm.

Topping: Beat sugar and eggs together; stir in flour, baking powder, and vanilla. Mix well. Stir in nuts and cherries. Pour over baked crust. Bake at 375 degrees for 18 to 20 minutes or until golden and edges are firm with center slightly soft, but crusted.

CARAMEL O'S BAR

14-16 ounces caramel candies
1/4 cup water
1/2 cup peanut butter
4 cups Cheerios
1 cup salted peanuts

Topping:
1 cup chocolate chips
1/4 cup peanut butter
2 tablespoons margarine

Combine caramels, water, and peanut butter in large mixing bowl. Microwave for 3 to 5 minutes or until melted, stir every minute. Stir in cereal and peanuts, press into buttered 13 x 9 pan. Melt topping ingredients in a 2 cup glass measure by microwaving them for 2 minutes on 50% power (MED). Stir, then microwave 2 more minutes on 50% power, blend well. Spread over bars. Cool before cutting.

COCONUT MARSHMALLOW BARS

Makes 3 dozen

1 cup unsalted butter
1 cup creamy peanut butter
2 (6 ounce) packages butterscotch chips
1 (10-1/2 ounce) bag colored miniature marshmallows
1-3/4 cups flaked coconut

Melt butter, peanut butter, and butterscotch chips together over low heat in large saucepan. Cool slightly. Add marshmallows and 3/4 cup of the coconut. Mix well. Put mixture into a buttered 13 x 9-inch pan. Sprinkle with remaining coconut. Cool in refrigerator until firm, about 3 hours. Cut into bars.

Shirley Viscosi, Worcester, Mass.

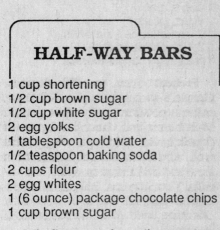

HALF-WAY BARS

1 cup shortening
1/2 cup brown sugar
1/2 cup white sugar
2 egg yolks
1 tablespoon cold water
1/2 teaspoon baking soda
2 cups flour
2 egg whites
1 (6 ounce) package chocolate chips
1 cup brown sugar

Mix first seven ingredients and pat into 13x9 inch pan. Sprinkle with chocolate chips; push chips into mixture. Beat egg whites until stiff and add 1 cup brown sugar. Spread over top of mixture. Do not touch sides of pan. Bake at 325 degrees until golden brown - about 35 minutes.

Mrs. George Brown, Lee, FL

BUTTERSCOTCH BARS
(No Bake)

1 cup sugar
2 eggs
1/2 cup butter
2-1/2 cups graham cracker crumbs
1-1/2 cups marshmallows (cut up)
1 cup butterscotch chips
3 tablespoons peanut butter

In saucepan, bring sugar, eggs, and butter to a boil, stirring constantly. Remove from heat and cool. Stir in cracker crumbs and marshmallows; press into 9x13 inch pan. Melt 1 cup butterscotch chips with peanut butter over hot water. Spread on top of crumbs. Cool. Cut into bars.

Mrs. E. J. Kuchenbecker, Prairie du Chien, WI

QUICK AND EASY BROWNIES

1/2 cup shortening
2 eggs
2 squares bitter chocolate
1/2 teaspoon baking powder
1 cup sugar
1/2 teaspoon salt
1 cup nut meats, chopped
1/4 cup flour
1 teaspoon vanilla

Melt chocolate and shortening together over hot water. Add sugar and eggs; beat thoroughly. Add vanilla and nut meats. Mix baking powder and salt with the flour. Add to first mixture. Mix thoroughly. Pour into a greased 8x12-inch baking pan and bake 25 minutes in a moderate 350-degree oven.

Suzan L. Wiener, Spring Hill, Fla.

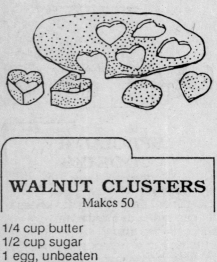

WALNUT CLUSTERS
Makes 50

1/4 cup butter
1/2 cup sugar
1 egg, unbeaten
1-1/4 teaspoons vanilla
1-1/2 squares unsweetened chocolate, melted
1/2 cup flour
1/4 teaspoon baking powder
1/2 teaspoon salt
2 cups unbroken walnuts

Cream butter and sugar until fluffy. Add egg and vanilla; blend well. Stir in chocolate, then flour sifted with baking powder and salt. Add walnuts. Drop by teaspoonsful onto greased baking sheet. Bake at 350 degrees for 10 minutes. Cookies should be soft, almost like candy.

Elizabeth S. Lawson, Delbarton, W.V.

CLOUD 9 COOKIES
Makes 3 dozen

2 stiffly-beaten egg whites
2/3 cup sugar
1/8 teaspoon salt
1 cup chopped almonds
1 cup mini chocolate chips

Preheat oven to 350 degrees for 15 minutes; turn off when putting the cookies in oven. Fold sugar, salt, nuts, and chips into stiffly-beaten egg whites. Drop by teaspoonfuls onto a well-greased cookie sheet. Leave in oven 2-1/2 hours or overnight, but *do not open oven door* until time to remove the cookies. A good lunch box or after-school snack.

Joy Shamway, Freeport, Ill.

ORANGE SUGAR COOKIES
Makes 6 dozen

3/4 cup shortening
1 cup sugar
2 beaten eggs
2 teaspoons grated fresh orange peel
3-1/2 cups flour
3 teaspoons baking powder
1/4 teaspoon salt
1/2 teaspoon vanilla
1/3 cup milk

Cream shortening and sugar; add eggs. Combine sifted flour, baking powder, and salt; sift together. Mix into the creamed mixture; add vanilla and milk. Chill dough until easy to roll out. Cut out cookies into your desired shapes and bake at 375 degrees for 8-10 minutes.

Jodie McCoy, Tulsa, Okla.

DATE BALLS

1 cup margarine
1-1/2 cups sugar
2 cups cut-up dates*
2 eggs, beaten

1 small package or 5 cups Rice Krispies
1 cup flaked coconut

Melt margarine; add sugar. Bring to boil, stirring constantly. Add dates and cook for 5 minutes or until dates are tender and mashed. Remove from heat and cool for a few minutes. Add hot mixture, a spoonful at a time, to beaten eggs, stirring rapidly. Boil for 2 minutes longer; remove from heat. Pour over Rice Krispies. Cool and shape into balls. Roll in coconut and chill.

*Uncooked prunes may be substituted for dates.

Trenda Leigh, Richmond, Va.

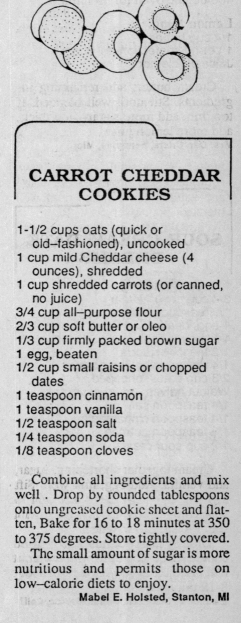

CARROT CHEDDAR COOKIES

1-1/2 cups oats (quick or old-fashioned), uncooked
1 cup mild Cheddar cheese (4 ounces), shredded
1 cup shredded carrots (or canned, no juice)
3/4 cup all-purpose flour
2/3 cup soft butter or oleo
1/3 cup firmly packed brown sugar
1 egg, beaten
1/2 cup small raisins or chopped dates
1 teaspoon cinnamon
1 teaspoon vanilla
1/2 teaspoon salt
1/4 teaspoon soda
1/8 teaspoon cloves

Combine all ingredients and mix well. Drop by rounded tablespoons onto ungreased cookie sheet and flatten. Bake for 16 to 18 minutes at 350 to 375 degrees. Store tightly covered.

The small amount of sugar is more nutritious and permits those on low-calorie diets to enjoy.

Mabel E. Holsted, Stanton, MI

ITALIAN BOW KNOT COOKIES

Makes 6 dozen medium cookies

4 cups flour
4 teaspoons baking powder
2 teaspoons salt
6 beaten eggs
1 cup sugar
1/2 cup oil
1-1/2 teaspoons lemon extract

Blend beaten eggs into dry ingredients, following with all other ingredients. Knead until smooth. Roll into pencil lengths and tie in bow knots. Bake on greased cookie sheets in a 400 degree oven for 15 minutes.

Lemon Icing:
1/4 cup butter
1 pound confectioners' sugar
Juice of 2 lemons

Cream butter; add remaining ingredients. Stir until well blended. If too thin, add more sugar—too thick, add more lemon juice.
Mrs. Dan Crisia, Fennville, Mich.

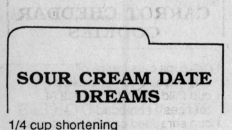

SOUR CREAM DATE DREAMS

1/4 cup shortening
3/4 cup brown sugar
1/2 teaspoon vanilla
1 egg, beaten
1-1/4 cups flour
1/2 teaspoon soda
1/4 teaspoon baking powder
2/3 cup dates, chopped
Walnut halves
1/4 teaspoon salt
1/4 teaspoon cinnamon
1/8 teaspoon nutmeg
1/2 cup sour cream

Cream together shortening, sugar, and vanilla. Add egg; mix well. Sift together dry ingredients and add to shortening mixture, alternately with sour cream. Stir in dates.

Drop by teaspoonfuls onto greased cookie sheet. Top each with a walnut half and bake at 400 degrees for about 8-10 minutes.
Eleanor V. Craycraft, Santa Monica, Calif.

PISTACHIO PUDDING COOKIES

Makes 7 dozen

2-1/4 cups unsifted all-purpose flour
1 teaspoon baking soda
1 cup margarine, well softened
1/4 cup granulated white sugar
3/4 cup brownulated light brown sugar
1/2 teaspoon vanilla
1/2 teaspoon almond extract
1 (4-ounce) package pistachio instant pudding (used dry)
2 eggs
1 (12-ounce) package butterscotch morsels
1 cup chopped walnuts
Few drops green food coloring, if desired

Mix flour and baking soda in medium bowl. Combine margarine, both sugars, both extracts, and instant pudding powder in large mixing bowl. Beat until smooth. Beat in eggs, one at a time. Gradually, stir in flour mixture. Stir in morsels and nuts. Batter will be very stiff; mix well with floured hands. Cover bowl; chill several hours or overnight for easier shaping. Form into smooth balls by *teaspoonfuls*. Place 2 inches apart on ungreased cookie sheets. Bake at 375 degrees for 8-10 minutes. Do not overbake. If desired, drizzle with confectioners' sugar icing mixed with a few drops of green food coloring.

These are absolutely delicious. Don't wait for St. Patrick's Day to enjoy them. Have them anytime during the year when you feel like a special cookie treat!!
Hyacinth Rizzo, Snyder, N.Y.

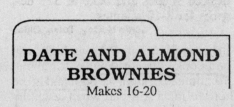

DATE AND ALMOND BROWNIES

Makes 16-20

2/3 cup flour
1/2 teaspoon baking powder
1/4 teaspoon salt
1/3 cup butter or margarine
2 (1-ounce) squares baking chocolate

1 cup sugar
2 eggs, beaten
1/2 cup chopped almonds
1/2 cup chopped dates*
1 teaspoon vanilla

Preheat oven to 350 degrees. Grease 8-inch square pan. Sift flour, baking powder, and salt together. Melt butter or margarine and chocolate in top of double boiler. Add sugar to eggs; beat well. Add butter or margarine and chocolate mixture. Stir in flour mixture, dates, and vanilla. Turn into prepared pan. Bake 25 minutes. Cool in pan on wire rack; cut into squares or bars when cool. Decorate with almonds, if desired.
*Chopped prunes may be substituted for dates, if desired.

This is, indeed, the most delicious brownie I've ever tasted and one of the easiest to prepare. It is a year-round favorite at our home.
Mrs. L. Mayer, Richmond, Va.

SPECIAL K COOKIES

Makes 3 dozen

1 (3-ounce) package cream cheese
1/4 cup butter or margarine
1/2 cup white sugar
2 tablespoons grated lemon rind
1/2 teaspoon lemon flavoring
1 cup unbleached all-purpose flour
2 teaspoons baking powder
1/4 teaspoon salt
1-1/2 cups Special K cereal

Mash cream cheese. Cream together with butter or margarine, sugar, lemon rind, and flavoring. Sift together flour, baking powder, and salt. Add gradually to creamed mixture, beating until smooth. Chill dough about 1 hour. Then shape dough into small balls. Roll each ball in Special K cereal. Place 1-1/2 inches apart on ungreased baking sheet. Bake at 350 degrees for 12-15 minutes.
Eileen Waye

BUTTERSCOTCH COCONUT COOKIES

Makes 5 dozen

2 cups flour
1/2 teaspoon soda
1/2 teaspoon salt
1/2 cup margarine, softened
1/2 cup granulated sugar
1/2 cup packed brown sugar
2 eggs
1 teaspoon vanilla
1 cup butterscotch chips
1/2 cup chopped pecans
2-1/2 cups coconut
Pecan halves (if desired)
Candied cherry halves (if desired)

Pre-heat oven to 375 degrees. Combine in a small bowl the flour, soda, and salt; set aside. Using larger bowl, combine softened margarine and both sugars; beat until very light and fluffy. Beat in eggs (one at a time) and vanilla. Add flour mixture; mix well. Stir in butterscotch chips and nuts. Drop dough into coconut. With lightly floured or greased hand; roll to coat with coconut. Form into balls. Bake at 375 degrees on ungreased cookie sheet for 10-12 minutes. Garnish each cookie with pecan half before baking if desired or place half candied cherry on each cookie as you remove from oven. Remove to cooling rack and allow to cool.

Jodie McCoy, Tulsa, OK

CREAM CHEESE CHOCOLATE CHIP COOKIES

Makes 4 dozen

1 cup margarine
1 cup sugar
1 (3-ounce) package cream cheese
2 eggs
1 teaspoon vanilla
1/2 teaspoon lemon extract
2-1/2 cups flour
1 teaspoon baking powder
1/2 teaspoon baking soda
1 cup coarsely chopped pecans or walnuts
1 cup semi-sweet chocolate pieces

Cream margarine, then add sugar, beating until smooth and fluffy. Add cream cheese; blend in eggs, vanilla, and lemon extract. Mix flour, baking powder, and baking soda together; stir into cream cheese mixture. Add nuts and chocolate pieces. Drop by teaspoon on lightly greased cookie sheet. Bake at 350 degrees for 12-15 minutes.

D. Villines, Clinton, MO

ICED MOLASSES BARS

1 cup butter
1/2 cup sugar
1 cup light molasses
1 egg
3-1/2 cups cake flour, sifted
1 teaspoon soda
1 teaspoon ginger
1 teaspoon cinnamon
1 teaspoon salt
1/2 cup sour cream

Cream butter and sugar until light. Stir in molasses and egg. Add sifted flour, soda, seasonings, and sour cream. Beat until smooth. Spread in greased jelly-roll pan. Bake in moderate oven of 350 degrees for 30 minutes. Cool in pan.

Sour Cream Frosting:
1 cup sour cream
2 cups sugar
Dash of salt
1 teaspoon vanilla

Blend sour cream, sugar, and salt in heavy saucepan. Put over high heat and cook, stirring rapidly, for about 10 minutes or until smooth and mixture forms a soft ball when tested in cold water. Add vanilla. Spread on top of baked layer and cut into bars. (If preferred, the molasses bars may be iced with your favorite chocolate frosting.)

Trenda Leigh, Richmond, Va.

BUTTER PECAN TURTLE BARS

Makes 2 dozen

Crust:
2 cups flour
2 cups firmly packed brown sugar
1/2 cup soft butter

Combine all ingredients. Mix at medium speed with mixer, 2-3 minutes or until particles are fine. Pat into ungreased 9 x 12 inch pan.

Filling:
1 cup pecan halves or hickory nuts
2/3 cup butter
1/2 cup firmly packed brown sugar
1 cup milk chocolate chips

Spread nuts over crust. Cook, stirring constantly, the butter and brown sugar over medium heat until entire surface of mixture begins to boil, about 1 minute. Pour over pecans. Bake for 20 minutes at 350 degrees. Remove from oven; sprinkle with chocolate chips. Marble chips after they have melted.

Ida Bloedow, Madison, WI

STARLIGHT MINT SURPRISE COOKIES

Makes 4-1/2 dozen

3 cups flour
1 teaspoon soda
1/2 teaspoon salt
1 cup butter
1 cup sugar
1/2 cup brown sugar
2 eggs
1 teaspoon vanilla
1 package chocolate mint wafers

Mix first three ingredients, set aside. Cream butter, sugars, eggs, and vanilla. Add flour mixture. Cover and chill 2 hours. Enclose each chocolate mint wafer in 1 tablespoon dough. Place on greased cookie sheet 2 inches apart. Top with pecan half. Bake for 10 minutes in a 375-degree oven.

Ann Sterzer, Lincoln, NE

CANDIED ORANGE PEEL COOKIES

Makes 3 dozen

2 eggs
2/3 cup shortening
1 cup sugar
2/3 cup sour cream
1/2 cup candied orange peel
2-1/3 cups all-purpose flour
2 teaspoons baking powder
1/4 teaspoon salt
1/2 teaspoon baking soda

Beat together first five ingredients. Sift together dry ingredients; add to liquid ingredients. Drop by teaspoonfuls onto greased cookie sheet; press small piece of candied peel into top of each cookie. Bake at 375 degrees for 12 minutes or until lightly browned.

Gwen Campbell, Sterling, Va.

JUMBO PEANUT BUTTER APPLE COOKIES

Makes 1-1/2 dozen

1 cup sifted flour
1 cup sifted whole-wheat flour
2 teaspoons baking soda
1 teaspoon cinnamon
3/4 teaspoon salt
1/3 cup butter, softened
2/3 cup chunk-style peanut butter
1/4 cup sugar
1-3/4 cups brown sugar
2 eggs
1 teaspoon vanilla
1 cup rolled oats
1 cup peeled, diced apples
1/2 cup raisins

Mix and sift first 5 ingredients. Cream butter, peanut butter, and sugars. Add eggs and vanilla; mix. Add sifted dry ingredients to creamed mixture and mix well. Stir in oats, apples, and raisins. Using about 1/4 cup of dough for each, shape into balls. Place on ungreased cookie sheet and flatten slightly. Bake in a 350-degree oven for about 12-15 minutes. Let stand on cookie sheet 1 minute before removing to wire cooling rack.

Melba Bellefeuille, Libertyville, Ill.

chopped nuts. Put on cookie sheet about 2 inches apart. Bake at 375 degrees for about 6 minutes.

Kit Rollins, Cedarburg, Wis.

OLD FASHIONED RAISIN BARS

1 cup raisins
1 cup water
1/2 cup shortening
1/2 teaspoon soda
Pinch of salt
2 cups flour
1 cup sugar
1 teaspoon cinnamon
1/2 teaspoon cloves
1/2 cup nuts, (optional)

Boil raisins and water; remove from heat and add shortening and soda to melt. Add dry ingredients and nuts. Spread on cookie sheet and bake 20 minutes at 375 degrees. Top with a thin powdered sugar icing. Cut into bars.

Mrs. Melvin Habiger, Spearville, Kans.

CHOCOLATE NUT COOKIES

1 cup brown sugar
1/2 cup margarine, melted
1-1/2 cups flour
1 teaspoon baking powder
1/2 teaspoon baking soda
1/8 teaspoon salt
3 tablespoons cocoa
1 egg
1/2 cup milk
1/3 cup walnuts, chopped

Cream together brown sugar and melted margarine. Sift together flour, baking powder, baking soda, salt, and cocoa. Add egg to first mixture and stir. Alternately stir in dry ingredients and milk. Add walnuts. Bake at 375 degrees for about 8 minutes.

Dawn Riggs, Chicago, Ill.

MRS. FIELD'S COOKIES

2 cups butter
2 cups granulated sugar
2 cups brown sugar
4 eggs
2 tablespoons vanilla
4 cups flour
5 cups oatmeal
1 teaspoon salt
2 teaspoons baking powder
2 teaspoons baking soda
24-ounce package chocolate chips
    plus 8-ounce Hershey bar
3 cups chopped nuts

Cream butter and sugars; add eggs and vanilla. Combine dry ingredients and add to creamed mixture. Add chips and grated Hershey bar. Add

SUGAR GOLDEN PUFFS

2 cups flour
1/4 cup sugar
3 teaspoons baking powder
1 teaspoon salt
1 teaspoon nutmeg
1/4 cup oil
3/4 cup milk
1 egg

Sift together flour, sugar, baking powder, salt, and nutmeg. Add oil, milk, and egg. Stir with fork until well-blended. Drop by teaspoonfuls into 375-degree deep fat. Fry about 3 minutes. Drain on paper toweling. Roll in cinnamon and sugar or confectioners' sugar; may also apply frosting and coconut.

Diantha Susan Hibbard, Rochester, N.Y.

APPLE TREASURE COOKIES
Makes 5-6 dozen

1 cup shortening
1-1/2 cups firmly packed light brown sugar
1/4 cup molasses
3 eggs, unbeaten
3-1/2 cups sifted all-purpose flour
1/2 teaspoon salt
1 teaspoon baking powder
3 teaspoons cinnamon
1/2 teaspoon nutmeg
1/2 teaspoon cloves
1 cup roasted peanuts, chopped
1 cup finely chopped apples

Cream shortening with brown sugar until light and fluffy. Add molasses. Add eggs, one at a time. In separate bowl sift flour, salt, spices, and baking powder; add to sugar-molasses mixture; mix lightly. Stir in peanuts and apples. Drop by spoonsful onto greased baking sheets. Bake at 350 degrees for 12-15 minutes.

Peggy Fowler, Woodruff, S.C.

SOUR CREAM COCONUT COOKIES
Makes 2-1/2 dozen

1/2 cup shortening
1/2 cup dairy sour cream
1 cup sugar
1 egg
1 egg yolk
1 teaspoon vanilla
2-3/4 cups sifted flour
3/4 teaspoon salt
1/2 teaspoon baking powder
1/2 teaspoon baking soda
1/2 cup flaked coconut

Cream shortening, sour cream, and sugar well. Beat in eggs and vanilla. Gradually blend in dry ingredients which have been sifted together; add coconut. Chill the dough. Roll to 1/8-to1/4-inch thickness on a lightly floured surface. Cut cookies with floured cookie cutters. Bake on ungreased cookie sheets at 375 degrees for 8-10 minutes. Frost, if desired.

Lisa Boryszewski, Middleport, N.Y.

CRUNCHY OATMEAL COOKIES
Makes 4 dozen

1 cup flour
2 teaspoons baking soda
1 teaspoon baking powder
1/2 teaspoon salt
1 cup shortening
2 cups cornflakes
1 cup sugar
1 cup brown sugar, packed
2 eggs
1 teaspoon vanilla extract
2 cups uncooked, quick-cooking oats

Combine flour, soda, baking powder, and salt. Set aside. In large bowl, cream shortening and sugars; beat in eggs and vanilla. Add flour mixture, mixing well. Stir in oats and cornflakes. Drop by heaping tablespoonsful onto lightly greased cookie sheets. Bake at 325 degrees for 12-14 minutes.

Cool for 2 minutes on cookie sheet; remove to wire racks and cool completely.

CRANBERRY COOKIE BARS

1-1/2 cups sifted flour
1 teaspoon baking powder
1/2 teaspoon salt
1/2 cup butter or margarine
1 cup granulated sugar
1/2 cup brown sugar, packed
2 eggs
1 teaspoon vanilla
1 cup Ocean Spray fresh or frozen cranberries, chopped
1/2 cup chopped nuts (optional)

Preheat oven to 350 degrees. Grease 9x13x2-inch pan. In a bowl sift together flour, baking powder and salt. In a second bowl, cream butter and both sugars; add eggs one at a time, beating until fluffy; stir in vanilla. Blend in dry ingredients. Stir in cranberries and nuts. Spread in greased pan. Bake 30 minutes. When cool, cut into bars.

ALMOND BARS

2 cups brown sugar
1 cup white sugar
3/4 cup melted butter
3/4 cup melted lard
4-1/2 cups sifted flour
1 cup almonds, sliced
3 eggs, well beaten
1 teaspoon soda
1 scant teaspoon salt

Cream butter and lard; add sugars, and well-beaten eggs. Sift flour with soda and salt. Combine with creamed mixture; add almonds. Pack into bread pan. (I roll in waxed paper.) Chill in refrigerator 24 hours. Slice and bake until brown at 350 degrees. (I substitute margarine for both butter and lard.) This recipe has been passed down through the family for years.

J.P. Hart, Stoughton, Wis.

AUNT MINNIE'S APPLE–BUTTER BARS
Makes 3 dozen

1-1/2 cups flour
1 teaspoon baking soda
1 teaspoon salt
1-1/2 cups quick-cooking oats, uncooked
1-1/2 cups sugar
1 cup butter or margarine, melted
1-1/2 cups apple butter
1 cup chopped pecans or walnuts

Combine flour, baking soda, and salt in a large mixing bowl. Mix in oats and sugar. Pour in melted butter and mix well.

Press half of this mixture into a greased 13 x 9 x 2-inch baking pan. Mix apple butter and nuts together; spread over mixture in pan. Sprinkle with remaining crumbly mixture.

Bake at 350 degrees for 50-60 minutes or until brown. Cool before cutting into bars.

Cooking
FOR TWO

GRAPEFRUIT IN RASPBERRY PUREE
Serves 2

1 (10-ounce) package frozen red raspberries
1/4 cup sugar
2 small grapefruit

Thaw raspberries as directed on package. Place in blender container; add sugar; blend until smooth. Stir through a fine sieve to remove seeds.

Peel, then section grapefruit into a small bowl. Pour off juice to drain (drink it). Stir in about 1/3 cup raspberry purée. Cover; chill 2 to 6 hours for flavors to blend. Set out about 30 minutes before serving—it will taste sweeter.

Cover and refrigerate remaining purée to serve over vanilla ice cream—an incomparable sundae for raspberry lovers.

APPLE BROWN BETTY
Serves 2

Made the old-fashioned way.

1-1/2 tablespoons butter
1 cup soft white or raisin bread crumbs*
1 tablespoon granulated sugar
1/4 teaspoon cinnamon
Pinch cloves
Pinch allspice
1/4 cup brown sugar (preferably dark)

2 tablespoons water
2 tart apples
1/4 teaspoon vanilla
1 tablespoon butter, slivered

Preheat oven to 350 degrees. Place butter in 3- or 4-cup baking dish; melt in preheating oven. Swirl butter in dish to coat; pour remaining butter over crumbs; toss to mix; set aside. In a custard cup mix granulated sugar and spices; set aside. In a small saucepan mix brown sugar and water. Stir over medium heat until boiling (this can be done in a cup in microwave oven); set aside. Peel; core and thinly slice apples.

Assemble in layers in baking dish: half of apples, half of sugar-spice mixture, half of crumbs, then remaining apples. Add vanilla to brown sugar syrup; pour over apples. Sprinkle on remaining spiced sugar then crumbs. Top with slivers of butter.

Bake until apples are tender when pierced with cake tester, 35 to 40 minutes. Let rest 20 to 30 minutes. Serve plain or with whipped cream or ice cream sprinkled with nutmeg or cinnamon.

ORANGES IN RED WINE
Serves 2

3 juice oranges
1/4 cup dry red wine
2 tablespoons sugar
Dash cinnamon (optional)

Peel, then section oranges into a small bowl. Pour off juice to drain (I drink it). In a small saucepan combine wine, sugar, and cinnamon, if using. Stir over medium heat until sugar is dissolved and wine is hot, but not boiling. Pour over oranges; stir gently. Cover and chill about 4 hours before serving.

DEVILED EGGS

4 hard-cooked eggs
1/4 teaspoon salt
A sprinkle of black pepper
About 2 tablespoons mayonnaise
1/4 teaspoon prepared mustard (optional)
Paprika

Cut eggs in half lengthwise. Place medium-mesh strainer (not a fine-mesh sieve or the job will take forever) over a bowl. Spoon yolks into strainer and rub through with the back of a spoon. I do them a half-yolk at a time using only a small area of strainer so too much yolk isn't wasted clogging the strainer.

Add salt, pepper, mayonnaise and mustard, if using. Whip lightly with fork. If too dry, add a little more mayonnaise. Spoon into egg white cavities. Cover and refrigerate. Sprinkle on paprika just before serving.

SWEET MILK WAFFLES

An alternative mixing method — folding in beaten egg white — is also given. It makes a somewhat lighter waffle

3 tablespoons butter or margarine (see Note)
1 cup flour, lightly spooned into cup
2 teaspoons baking powder
1 teaspoon sugar
1/4 teaspoon salt
1 large egg
1 cup milk
1/4 teaspoon vanilla

Yield: 2 cups batter; two and one-half 10 by 6-inch waffles.

Spray waffle iron with Pam, release; preheat.

Melt butter in a custard cup in microwave oven or in small saucepan on stove; set aside.

Into pitcher or medium bowl measure flour, baking powder, sugar, and salt. Blend with mixer on lowest speed; set aside.

In a small bowl beat egg until light. On low speed beat in milk, vanilla, and melted butter. Add to dry ingredients; mix to blend well on low speed.

Pour over center three-fourths of preheated waffle iron. Cook until steam is no longer escaping around edge of waffle iron.

Note: If using 2% milk increase butter to 4 tablespoons.

Alternative mixing method: Melt butter. Separate egg putting white into a very clean small bowl and yolk into pitcher or medium bowl. Add milk to egg yolk. Measure flour, baking powder, sugar, and salt into small bowl; whisk to blend. Beat egg white until it will just hold stiff peaks. Transfer beater to yolk-milk mixture; beat until smooth. Add dry ingredients; beat smooth. With rubber spatula stir in melted butter, then fold in beaten egg white. This batter thickens a bit on standing, so refrigerate one hour before using if possible.

RICH BUTTERMILK WAFFLES

1/3 cup butter or margarine
1 cup flour, lightly spooned into cup
1/4 teaspoon salt
1/2 teaspoon soda
1 teaspoon baking powder
1 teaspoon sugar
2 eggs
1 cup buttermilk
1/4 teaspoon vanilla

Yield: 2-1/2 cups batter; three 10 by 6-inch waffles. Spray waffle iron with pan release; preheat.

Melt butter in a custard cup in microwave oven or in small saucepan on stove; set aside.

Measure flour, salt, soda, baking powder, and sugar into a small bowl. Blend with mixer on lowest speed; set aside.

In a pitcher or medium bowl beat eggs until light. On low speed add dry ingredients in three additions alternating with buttermilk in two additions. Blend in melted butter and vanilla.

Pour over center three-fourths of preheated waffle iron. Cook until steam is no longer escaping around edge of waffle iron.

DESSERT SOUFFLE
Two servings

Use one tablespoon dark rum, brandy or a liqueur instead of vanilla if desired.

2 large eggs
1-1/2 tablespoons butter
1-1/2 tablespoons flour
1/8 teaspoon salt
1/2 cup milk
1 teaspoon vanilla
1/4 cup sugar, divided

Separate eggs, whites into very clean medium mixing bowl, yolks into another medium bowl.

Grease or spray with pan release a one-quart straight-sided baking dish. Coat with sugar; set aside.

Preheat oven to 325 degrees.

In a small saucepan melt butter; whisk in flour and salt; cook, whisking, until boiling and bubbly. Whisk in milk; whisk over medium heat until smooth and thick. Remove from heat; whisk in vanilla or other flavoring; set aside to cool.

Beat egg whites just until peaks are soft (tips roll over) when beater is lifted. Gradually beat in half of sugar (2 tablespoons). Beat until stiff and glossy. Transfer beaters to yolks; tilt bowl so beaters are in yolks; beat about 1 minute; gradually beat in remaining sugar (2 tablespoons). On low speed beat in sauce. With a rubber spatula gently fold in egg whites. Pour into prepared dish. Bake until set—cake tester comes out dry—about 25 minutes. Immediately spoon into dessert dishes; pour on chocolate sauce.

ORANGE-FLAVORED APPLES
Serves 2

2 large cooking apples
1 tablespoon butter or margarine
1/4 cup brown sugar
1/4 cup orange juice
Pinch nutmeg

Peel; core and cut apples into eighths.

In medium-size skillet melt butter; swirl to coat bottom of skillet. Add apples. Sprinkle on sugar. Pour orange juice over apples. Cook on high heat until juice begins to boil. Stir; cover with lid ajar; reduce heat to low; cook until apples are barely tender, stirring now and then, about 8 minutes. Remove apples with slotted spoon to bowl. Add nutmeg to sauce; boil over high heat to reduce and thicken, about 1 minute; pour over apples.

Serve over vanilla ice cream, or plain, if you prefer a simple dessert.

CORN PUDDING
Serves 2

(A soft creamy pudding)

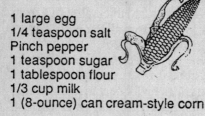

1 large egg
1/4 teaspoon salt
Pinch pepper
1 teaspoon sugar
1 tablespoon flour
1/3 cup milk
1 (8-ounce) can cream-style corn

Preheat oven to 350 degrees.
Grease or spray with pan release a small baking dish (flat-bottomed, if possible; I use a 6-inch soufflé dish). In a small bowl whisk egg to blend. Whisk in salt, pepper, sugar, flour, and milk. When smooth, whisk in corn. Pour into prepared dish. Bake until set—firm when dish is jiggled—35-40 minutes.

PUFFY FRENCH TOAST
Serves 2

4 slices bread
1/2 cup milk
1 egg
3/4 cup biscuit mix
2 tablespoons sugar
1/2 teaspoon cinnamon
1/2 cup margarine

Melt margarine in skillet on medium heat. With electric mixer, combine milk, egg, biscuit mix, sugar and cinnamon. Cut each slice of bread in half diagonally. Dip in batter; coating completely. Fry four pieces at a time until golden brown and puffy. (About 3 minutes on each side). Sprinkle with confectioners sugar and cinnamon. Serve with warm syrup. (Blueberry syrup is delicious.)

Helen Weissinger, Levittown, PA

GLAZED PARSNIPS
Serves 2

1/2 pound parsnips
1 tablespoon butter or margarine
2 tablespoons brown sugar
Salt and pepper
Pinch nutmeg
1 tablespoon whipping cream
1 tablespoon dry white wine, dry vermouth or sherry

Half-fill a medium saucepan with water; add salt; bring to boiling.
Meanwhile trim top and root ends from parsnips; pare with vegetable peeler. Cut in half lengthwise then crosswise; cut into lengthwise strips to make uniform pieces so they will cook evenly. Drop into boiling water; cover; cook until barely tender, 4 to 5 minutes. Drain; rinse under cold water to stop the cooking; drain well. If done ahead cover and refrigerate; drain again before using.
Melt butter in shallow baking dish in oven with roasting hens. Add parsnips; toss to coat with butter. Sprinkle on brown sugar, salt, pepper, and nutmeg. Dribble on cream and wine. Bake at 350 degrees (with hens) about 20 minutes, stirring once to baste.

THOUSAND ISLAND SALAD
Serves 2

A main—dish salad.

Dressing:
1/4 cup mayonnaise
1-1/2 tablespoons ketchup
1-1/2 teaspoons sweet pickle relish
1/2 green onion

Salad:
Lettuce
1/4 pound ham in bite-size pieces (I add salami if I have it)
3 hard-cooked eggs

Prepare dressing; combine mayonnaise, ketchup, and relish. With scissors, snip in green onion; mix well.
Cover plates with chunks and leaves of lettuce. Top with ham; slice on eggs; spoon on dressing.

CHILI CHEDDAR OMELET
Serves 2

4 eggs
1 tablespoon water
1/4 teaspoon seasoned salt
Butter
1 cup chili
1/4 cup grated Cheddar cheese
1/2 avocado, peeled and sliced

In small bowl, beat eggs, water and seasoned salt together. Pour mixture into well-buttered 10-inch skillet.
Cook omelet over medium heat, letting liquid egg run to edges when eggs are set; slide omelet onto serving plate. Place chili, grated cheese and avocado slices on half of omelet; fold over other half.

Susan L. Wiener, Spring Hill, Fl

CHOCOLATE SAUCE
Serves 2

So good over coffee ice cream!

1/4 cup light cream
1/4 cup sugar
1 square (or envelope) unsweetened chocolate
1 teaspoon butter
1/4 teaspoon vanilla

Measure cream; add sugar to cream in measuring cup; stir to partially dissolve sugar. Set aside.
In a small saucepan combine chocolate and butter. Stir over low heat until melted and smooth. Add cream; stir sauce over medium heat until it thickens, just as it begins to boil. Remove from heat; stir in vanilla. Serve warm or at room temperature.

Delicious
DESSERTS

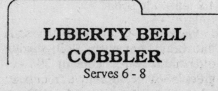

MOM'S APPLE COBBLER
Serves 8

1 stick butter or margarine
2 cups water
1/2 cup shortening
2 cups finely chopped apples
2 cups sugar
1-1/2 cups self-rising flour
1/3 cup milk
1 teaspoon cinnamon

Heat oven to 350 degrees. Melt butter in a 13 x 9 x 2-inch dish or pan. In a saucepan heat water and sugar until sugar melts. Cut shortening into flour until particles are like fine crumbs. Add milk and stir with fork only until dough leaves sides of bowl. Turn out onto lightly floured board or pastry cloth; knead just until smooth. Roll dough out into a large rectangle about 1/4 inch thick. Sprinkle cinnamon over apples and stir; sprinkle apples evenly over dough and roll up like a jelly roll. Dampen edges of dough with a little water and seal. Slice dough into 16 slices, 1/2 inch thick. Place in pan with melted butter. Pour sugar syrup carefully around rolls. (This looks like too much liquid, but the crust will absorb it). Bake for 55-60 minutes.

Cobbler Variation:

This may be made with other fresh, frozen, or canned fruits, such as blackberries, cherries, or peaches. If packed in liquid, drain and substitute for part of the sugar syrup. Always use 2 cups liquid.

Eleanor Hardman, Morehead City, N.C.

CHERRY COBBLER
6 servings

1 can (21 ounce) cherry pie filling
1 cup biscuit mix
1/2 teaspoon almond extract
1 tablespoon sugar
1/4 cup milk
1 tablespoon soft butter
2 tablespoons toasted slivered blanched almonds
Half & half or light cream

Heat oven to 400 degrees. In ungreased 1-1/2 quart casserole, mix pie filling and almond extract. Place in oven 15 minutes until hot and bubbly. Blend biscuit mix, sugar, milk and butter with fork to soften dough; beat vigorously 20 strokes. Stir in almonds. Drop dough by spoonfuls in 6 portions onto hot cherry mixture. Bake 20-25 minutes or until topping is light brown. Serve warm with light cream.

Cynthia Cardwell, Sterling, IL

LIBERTY BELL COBBLER
Serves 6 - 8

2 cups sliced strawberries
1/4 cup sugar, mixed with 1/2 cup water

6 tablespoons butter or margarine
1 cup all-purpose flour
1-1/2 teaspoons baking powder
1/2 teaspoon salt
1 cup milk
1/2 cup sugar

Blueberry Sauce:

2 pints fresh blueberries
1/4 cup water
1/4 cup sugar
1 tablespoon lemon juice
Whipped cream

Pour sugar and water mixture over strawberries and mix well. Set aside. Preheat oven to 350 degrees. Put butter in a 9 x 13-inch oven-proof baking dish and place in the oven to melt. Mix together flour, baking powder, and salt in a bowl, and stir in milk and sugar to make a batter. Remove dish with melted butter from oven and pour into the batter. Spoon drained strawberries and then the juices evenly over batter. Return dish to oven. Bake until the batter is browned and has risen up around the fruit, about 30 minutes.

To make Blueberry Sauce, rinse and pick over berries. Combine water and sugar in a saucepan and heat to the boiling point. Place 1 pint of the berries in a food processor or blender. Process, turning the machine on and off about 4 times, until berries are coarsely pureed. Add to sugar syrup with lemon juice, and bring back to a boil. Cook about 2 minutes more. Add remaining pint of whole berries, reserving a few for decoration. Serve Blueberry Sauce over warm pudding. Top with whipped cream and reserved berries.

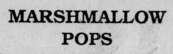

MARSHMALLOW POPS

1 (6 ounce) package semi-sweet chocolate morsels
1 teaspoon shortening
Regular sized marshmallows
Toothpicks

Melt chocolate and shortening in the top of a double boiler. Put a toothpick into each marshmallow. Dip marshmallows into the chocolate mixture, coating well.

Roll in colored coconut, sugar, candy "shot", crushed peppermint stick candy or peanut brittle, cookie crumbs or chopped nuts. These can also be decorated with colored gumdrops or colored frosting.

Banana, apple or orange chunks on toothpicks can be used instead of marshmallows.

Sue Hibbard, Rochester, NY

MIDNIGHT MINTS
Makes 36

Bottom layer:
1/2 cup margarine
5 tablespoons cocoa
1/4 cup sugar
1 egg, beaten
2 cups graham wafer crumbs
1/2 cup chopped nuts
1 cup coconut

Combine margarine, cocoa, and sugar in saucepan. Bring slowly to a boil. Stir in egg to thicken. Remove from heat; add crumbs, nuts, and coconut. Pack firmly into greased 9x9 inch pan.

Middle layer:
1/4 cup margarine
3 tablespoons milk
1 teaspoon peppermint extract
2 cups powdered sugar
Green food coloring

Combine all ingredients in bowl. Mix well, adding a few drops more liquid, if needed, for easy spreading. Tint a pretty green. Spread over first layer; chill until firm.

Top layer:
1 cup chocolate chips
2 tablespoons margarine

Melt chips and margarine in saucepan over low heat. Spread over chilled second layer. Chill and cut into squares. Keep stored in refrigerator. These squares are simply delicious and freeze well.

Gay Polier, Spillimacheen, B.C. Canada

MILLIONAIRE CANDY
Makes 4 dozen

1 package German sweet chocolate
1 package peanut butter chips
1 package butterscotch chips
1/4 bar paraffin
1 cup chopped pecans or 1 cup shredded coconut

Melt chocolate, peanut butter chips, butterscotch chips, and paraffin in top of double boiler. Add nuts; drop by spoonfuls on waxed paper; chill. When firm, may be packaged or served.

Sue Hibbard, Rochester, N.Y.

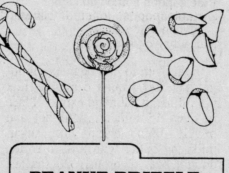

PEANUT BRITTLE
Makes 1-3/4 pounds

1-1/4 cups sugar
3/4 cup butter or margarine
1-1/2 teaspoons salt
1/4 cup Dr. Pepper
2 cups raw peanuts, shelled
1/2 teaspoon soda

Place all ingredients except soda into heavy saucepan. Boil, stirring often until temperature of 290 degrees is reached. Remove from heat; stir in soda. Pour into 15 x 10-inch pan. Cool and break into pieces.

Mrs. Bruce Fowler, Woodruff, SC

PEANUT BUTTER SWIRL CANDY

1 pound confectioners' sugar
1 stick margarine
2 tablespoons sweetened condensed milk
1 teaspoon vanilla flavoring
Peanut butter

Mix all ingredients (except peanut butter) together into a well-combined mixture and roll out on wax paper using some confectioners' sugar to keep from sticking. Spread peanut butter over dough and roll up in jelly roll fashion. Let sit 3 hours in refrigerator, then cut into 1/4 inch slices.

Peggy Fowler Revels, Woodruff, S.C.

PRALINES
Makes 20

2 cups sugar
1 teaspoon soda
1 cup buttermilk
1/8 teaspoon salt
2 tablespoons butter or margarine
2-1/2 cups (8 ounce package) pecan halves

In large (3-1/2 quart) heavy saucepan (Dutch oven) combine sugar, soda, buttermilk, and salt. Cook over high heat about 5 minutes (or to 210 degrees on candy thermometer); stir often; scrape bottom of pan. Mixture will foam up. Add butter or margarine and pecans. Over medium heat, continue cooking, stirring constantly and scraping bottom and sides of pan until candy reaches soft ball stage, (234 degrees on candy thermometer) about 6 minutes.

Remove from heat; cool slightly, about 2 minutes. Beat with spoon until thick and creamy. Drop from tablespoon onto sheet of aluminum foil or wax paper.

Check on pralines within a minute or so, should be hard enough to remove up. Do not leave on wax paper for too long as they could stick to countertop.

Jo Ann Harris, Dallas, Texas

PUDDING POPS

Serves 6

1 - 4 ounce package instant pudding mix (any flavor)
2 cups milk
6 paper cups
6 wooden sticks or plastic spoons

Pour cold milk into bowl. Add pudding mix. Beat slowly with hand rotary beater until mixture is well blended and creamy. Pour into 6 paper cups. Put a wooden stick or plastic spoon into each cup. Press a square of foil or waxed paper onto the top of the cup to cover. The handle or the stick will poke through the foil.

Freeze until firm, at least 5 hours. To serve, press firmly on the bottom of the cup to pop out.

Molly Baker, Killbuck, OH

ROCKY ROAD CANDY

1 can sweetened condensed milk
1 (12 ounce) package chocolate chips
2 cups dry roasted peanuts (salted)
1 (10-1/2 ounce) bag mini marshmallows
2 tablespoons butter

On low heat melt together milk, chocolate chips, and butter. Pour into bowl with peanuts and marshmallows; blend well. Pour into 9 x 11 inch pan; refrigerate. Cut into squares and serve. If bottom of pan is covered with wax paper, candy is easier to remove.

Judy Fisk, Aberdeen, Wash.

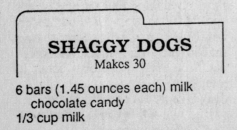

SHAGGY DOGS

Makes 30

6 bars (1.45 ounces each) milk chocolate candy
1/3 cup milk

2-1/2 cups flaked coconut
1 (10 ounce) bag large marshmallows

In small saucepan, over low heat, melt chocolate. Stir in milk to make thin syrup. Put coconut in shallow dish. Using toothpicks, dip marshmallows into chocolate syrup, then roll in coconut. Allow to sit on wax paper.

Leona Teodori, Warren, Mich.

SWEDISH ROSETTES

(Makes 6 dozen)

1 egg
2 teaspoons sugar
1 cup milk
1 cup all-purpose flour
1/2 teaspoon salt
1 tablespoon lemon extract
Salad oil
Confectioners' sugar

Beat egg slightly; add sugar; add milk. Sift flour and salt. Stir into egg mixture; beat until smooth, about consistency of heavy cream. Add lemon extract. Put enough salad oil in a 1-quart saucepan to fill about 2/3 full. Heat to 400 degrees. Dip rosette forms into hot oil to heat them. Drain excess oil on paper towel. Dip heated forms into batter to not more than 3/4 of their depth. If only a thin layer of batter adheres to the forms, dip them again until a smooth layer adheres. Plunge batter coated forms into hot oil. Cook to desired brown-ness. With fork, ease rosettes off forms onto paper towels to drain. While still warm, dip into confectioners' sugar.

SWEETHEARTS

3/4 cup butter
1 egg yolk
1/2 cup sugar
1-1/2 cup flour

Pinch of salt
Raspberry jam

Cream butter; add sugar gradually, egg yolk, flour and salt. Knead together. Cool in refrigerator for 1 hour. Break off walnut-size pieces; roll in palm of hand; place on cookie sheet. Make indentation by pressing with the thumb. Fill hollow with jam. Bake in moderate 350 degree oven until a light brown. Remove from oven; sprinkle with confectioners' sugar.

Karen Shea Fedders, Dameron, MD

TURTLES

1 pound whole pecans (arranged in clusters of 3)
1 cup white syrup
1 can Eagle Brand condensed milk

Cook syrup and milk to 248 degrees. Stir to keep from scorching. Remove from heat. Put about 1 teaspoon mixture over each cluster of pecans. Place 1 small square of Hershey chocolate bar over each cluster. When melted, smooth out chocolate.

Note: May use melted milk chocolate chips with a little paraffin wax added, in place of chocolate bar squares. Very luscious and easy to make.

Janeen Winchell, Pleasant Hill, Ill.

VALENTINE HEART TARTS

Prepare your own recipe for pastry; roll very thin. Cut with 3-inch heart-shaped cookie cutter. Cut same amount again; cut hole in center. Prick all hearts with fork tines; bake at 350 degrees for 12 to 15 minutes. Cool. To assemble: spread strawberry jelly over uncut hearts. Place the cut-out pastry heart on the top; lightly dust with confectioners' sugar.

Mrs. Gwen Campbell, Sterling, VA

BLUEBERRY CREAM DESSERT

Serves 8

Crust:
1-1/4 cups graham cracker crumbs
1/4 cup sugar
6 tablespoons margarine, melted

Filling:
1/2 cup sugar
1 envelope unflavored gelatin
3/4 cup cold water
1 cup sour cream
1 cup blueberry yogurt
1 cup whipped topping
1 cup blueberries

In a small bowl combine crumbs, 1/4 cup sugar, and butter until crumbly. Reserve 1/4 cup crumbs for topping. Press remaining crumbs into bottom of an 8 x 8-inch dish. Bake at 375 degrees for 8-10 minutes until set. Cool. In a small saucepan mix 1/2 cup sugar, unflavored gelatin, and water. Heat mixture and stir until gelatin and sugar are dissolved. Set aside. In a small bowl, combine sour cream and yogurt. Blend into gelatin mixture. Chill until partially set. Fold whipped topping into yogurt mixture. Stir in blueberries. Spoon into crust. Sprinkle with reserved crumbs. Refrigerate until set, about 3 hours.

COCONUT DESSERT CRUST

1 stick butter
1 cup flour
2 tablespoons sugar
1/2 cup pecans

Mix flour, sugar, and butter. Add nuts and pat into 9x13-inch pan. Bake about 10 minutes at 350 degrees. Cool.

1st Layer:
1 package (8 ounce) cream cheese
1 cup powdered sugar
1 small Cool Whip

Mix all together.

2nd layer:
2 packages coconut cream instant pudding

Mix with 3 cups milk (like package says).

3rd layer:
Small container Cool Whip
1 small can coconut flakes, toasted

Place coconut flakes on top of Cool Whip or whipped cream.

Ruth Rueter, Madison, IN

ECLAIR DESSERT

2 (3 ounce) packages instant French vanilla pudding
3-1/2 cups milk
1 (12 ounce) container whipped topping
Graham crackers

Mix pudding and milk at low speed, 1-2 minutes. Fold in whipped topping. Layer graham crackers in bottom of 9x13-inch pan. Pour 1/2 of the pudding mixture over crackers. Layer graham crackers again. Pour remaining pudding mixture, and layer again with crackers.

Chocolate topping:
1-1/2 cups powdered sugar
1 teaspoon vanilla
2 envelopes Nestle Choco Bake (soften by kneading envelopes before opening)
1/4 cup milk

Mix above ingredients until well blended; pour over Eclair Dessert; smooth surface, and refrigerate.

Mary Spencer, Sandusky, Ohio

LEMON CAKE DESSERT

Serves 12

1 (3-ounce) package lemon flavored gelatin
1-1/2 cups sugar
3 cups packaged biscuit mix
4 eggs
3/4 cups salad oil
3/4 cup water
1-1/2 cups sifted powdered sugar
1/2 cup lemon juice

In large mixing bowl place gelatin, 1-1/2 cups sugar, biscuit mix, egg, salad oil, and water. Beat at slow speed until ingredients are combined, then beat at medium speed for 5 minutes. Pour into greased, floured 9-inch baking pan and bake at 350 degrees for 35-40 minutes or until cake tests done. Combine powdered sugar and lemon juice. Remove cake from oven; cool 5 minutes; then pierce cake all over with fork. Pour lemon mixture evenly over top. Cool and serve with whipped cream or ice cream.

Agnes Ward, Erie, PA

RHUBARB MERINGUE DESSERT

Serves 9

1/2 cup margarine, softened
1 cup flour
1 tablespoon sugar
3 eggs, separated
1 cup sugar
2 tablespoons flour
1/4 teaspoon salt
1/2 cup half and half or light cream
2-1/2 cups cut-up rhubarb
1/3 cup sugar
1 teaspoon vanilla
1/4 cup flaked coconut

Heat oven to 350 degrees. Mix margarine, 1 cup flour and 1 tablespoon sugar. Press into ungreased 9x9x2-inch baking pan. Bake 10 minutes at 350.

Mix egg yolks, 1 cup sugar, 2 tablespoons flour, salt and half and half. Stir in rhubarb. Pour over baked layer. Bake 45 minutes.

Beat egg whites until foamy. Beat in 1/3 cup sugar, 1 tablespoon at a time, continuing to beat egg whites until stiff and glossy. Do not underbeat. Beat in vanilla. Spread over rhubarb mixture; sprinkle with coconut. Bake until light brown, about 10 minutes.

A favorite for rhubarb lovers.

Marie Franks, Millerton, PA

CORN PUDDING

Mix together:
1 can creamed style corn
1 stick margarine (melted)
1 box corn bread mix
2 eggs (beaten)
1 (8 ounce) container sour cream

Pour into a casserole dish. Bake at 350 degrees for 45 minutes.

Diane Votaw, Decatur, Ind.

NOODLE PUDDING
Serves 6

8-ounces noodles, cooked
1/2 cup sour cream
1/4 cup granulated sugar
Pinch salt
2 eggs, beaten
1/2 cup creamed cottage cheese
1/2 teaspoon vanilla
Cinnamon to taste
1/4 cup raisins
Glaze:
1/4 cup oleo or butter
1/2 cup brown sugar
1/2 cup whole pecans

Rinse noodles in cold water; drain; add remaining ingredients, mix well. Pour into baking pan, Melt oleo; sprinkle with brown sugar. Press in pecans. Bake at 350 degrees for 1 hour or until done. Let cool 10 minutes,

Edna May Jenks, Chenango Forks, NY

CREAMY RICE PUDDING
(Use 3-quart pot)

1 quart milk
3/4 cup sugar
1/2 cup rice
Salt
1 egg
1 teaspoon cornstarch
1 teaspoon vanilla
1-1/2 cups milk

To milk, add sugar, pinch of salt and rice. Bring to boil; simmer slowly for 1 hour, stirring frequently. Beat egg with cornstarch and vanilla; add 1-1/2 cups milk and mix well. Add egg-milk mixture to rice mixture; stir constantly to prevent scorching. As soon as it thickens some, remove from heat and let stand 10 minutes. (The last addition of milk makes this creamy.)

Mrs. I. T. DeHart, Middletown, PA

GRANDMA'S RICE PUDDING

1/2 cup rice (not instant)
2 cups boiling water
3 cups milk
1/2 cup sugar
1/2 teaspoon salt
1 teaspoon vanilla
Cinnamon

Cook rice in water for about 20 minutes. Add milk and simmer for 20 more minutes. Add sugar and salt and continue simmering until creamy. Do not give up, it may take awhile. Remove from heat and add vanilla. Sprinkle cinnamon over top and serve either warm or at room temperature. Very delicious!

Bernice Streed, Waukegan, IL

QUICK GLORIOUS RICE PUDDING
Serves 6

1 cup pre-cooked quick rice
1 (3 ounce) package vanilla pudding mix (not instant)
1/4 cup raisins (optional)
3 cups milk
1 egg, beaten
1/4 cup sugar
1/4 teaspoon vanilla
Cinnamon sugar

Mix all of the ingredients except vanilla. Cook over medium heat, stirring constantly, until mixture comes to a boil. Remove from heat and cool slightly. Add vanilla. Spoon into individual dessert dishes and sprinkle cinnamon sugar on top. Chill and serve cold.

Hannah V. Ismiel, Chicago, IL

SUET PUDDING
Serves 10-12
About 90 years old

1 cup suet (pressed down and run through a coarse food chopper)
1 cup raisins
1 cup dark syrup
1 cup buttermilk
1/2 cup currants (optional)
2 even teaspoons soda
Pinch salt
Flour

Add flour enough to make stiff dough. Place into greased 2-quart baking dish and steam in steamer on top of stove for at least 1-1/2 hours or until done. Serve with lemon sauce or plain cream. Re-heat by re-steaming.
Lemon Sauce:
1 cup sugar
2 tablespoons cornstarch
Pinch of salt
2 cups cold water
2 tablespoons butter or margarine
1 teaspoon lemon extract

Mix sugar, cornstarch and salt in saucepan. Stir until cornstarch is blended. Add cold water gradually, stirring well. Place on stove and bring to boil, stirring constantly until mixture thickens. Add lemon extract and butter or margarine. Serve hot over pudding.

Mrs. Opal Hamer, St. Petersburg, FL

TOMATO PUDDING
Serves 4 to 6

10-ounce can tomato puree
1/2 cup boiling water
1/2 cup brown sugar
1/2 teaspoon salt
2 cups fresh bread, cut in 1" cubes
1/3 cup butter, melted

Add sugar and salt to puree. Add water; simmer 5 minutes. Add melted butter.

Place bread in greased casserole; cover with tomato butter. Cover, or if extra crispness is desired, bake uncovered at 350 degrees for 30 minutes.

Kit Rollins, Cedarburg, WI

SWEET POTATO PUDDING

4 cups grated raw sweet potatoes
1 cup molasses (or honey)
3/4 cup milk
1 teaspoon nutmeg
1/2 cup margarine, melted
1/2 teaspoon cloves
1/2 cup chopped nuts
1/2 teaspoon salt
2 eggs, well beaten

Mix all ingredients together, except eggs. Add eggs; stir until well blended. Pour into 1-1/2 quart baking dish sprayed with non-stick spray. Bake at 375 degrees for 50-60 minutes or until done (see testing note below).

Note: You may use 1/2 cup granulated sugar and 1/2 cup syrup in place of molasses or honey.

Testing custard for doneness: Insert tip of knife blade in pie/custard/pudding about halfway between edge and center of pie. If blade comes out clean, custard will be firm all the way through when it cools. If you insert knife in center, the filling should cling like a thick cream sauce.

BLUEBERRY TORTE

Crust:
1/4 pound margarine, plus 1 tablespoon
1 cup flour
2 tablespoons sugar

Combine and press into 9-inch square pan. Bake in preheated 375 degree oven about 20 minutes, or until browned.

Filling:
1 envelope Dream Whip, prepared according to package directions
1 (8 ounce) package cream cheese, softened
1 cup powdered sugar

1 can blueberry pie filling

Allow crust to cool. Meanwhile beat prepared Dream Whip with softened cream cheese and powdered sugar. Pour over cooled crust. Top with 1 can blueberry pie filling. Chill well.

Marie Popovich, Warren, MI

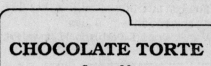

CHOCOLATE TORTE
Serves 20

1 (15-ounce) package Oreo cookies, crushed
1/3 cup melted butter
2 (3-ounce) packages instant chocolate pudding
1-1/2 cups milk
1 (9-ounce) carton Cool Whip
1 quart vanilla ice cream, softened

Mix together cookie crumbs and butter. Pat 2/3 of crumbs into a 9 x 13-inch pan. Reserve remaining 1/3 of crumbs for top. Beat together pudding and milk until very thick. Add the softened ice cream and beat together until well blended. Pour pudding mixture over the crumbs. Spread Cool Whip over the pudding mixture and top with remaining crumbs. Refrigerate overnight.

Ida Bloedow, Madison, WI

ELEGANT FINALE TORTE
Serves 12

2 cups sifted flour
2 teaspoons baking powder
1 teaspoon baking soda
1/4 teaspoon salt
1-1/2 teaspoons ground cinnamon
1/2 teaspoon ground cloves
1/8 teaspoon ground ginger
1/2 teaspoon pumpkin pie spice
2 cups firmly packed brown sugar
4 eggs
1 (1 pound) can pumpkin
1 cup finely ground graham crackers
1 cup vegetable oil
1 (6 ounce) package butterscotch morsels
1 cup chopped walnuts

Whipped cream:
1-1/2 cups heavy cream
1/2 teaspoon vanilla
2 tablespoons sugar

Into a large bowl, sift together first 8 ingredients and 2 cups sugar; set aside. In large bowl of mixer, beat eggs at high speed until foamy. Slowly mix in pumpkin, graham cracker crumbs, and oil. By hand, stir in butterscotch morsels and walnuts. Spread batter in 3 greased and waxed paper-lined, 9-inch round cake pans. Bake at 350 degrees for 25-30 minutes. Cool in pans; remove to racks. In chilled bowl beat cream, vanilla, and 2 tablespoons sugar at high speed until soft peaks form. Spread whipped cream on top of each cake layer. Stack layers, frosting-side up. Refrigerate 2-3 hours before serving.

Gwen Campbell, Sterling, Va.

STRAWBERRY REFRIGERATOR TORTE
Serves 8-12

3/4 pound "Nabisco Wafers"
3/4 cup butter
2 eggs, beaten
1 cup confectioners' sugar
1-1/2 cups whipping cream
1 quart fresh strawberries, quartered

Put "Nabiscos" thru a food chopper or crush to crumbs. Reserve 1/4 cup crumbs for topping. Stand additional whole "Nabiscos" wafers upright around and lay on bottom of torte pan. Press the crumbled "Nabiscos" in bottom of torte pan. Cream butter until light. Add eggs and sugar; beat well. Fold in whipped cream and strawberries. Pour into torte pan. Sprinkle with the remaining reserved crumbs. Chill in refrigerator 6-8 hours.

This is a very elegant dessert that could be served at a luncheon, surrounded with fresh whole strawberries for garnish.

Mrs. Edward Prinsen, Cedarburg, WI

LEMON CHEESE TORTE

Serves 8 to 10
A February party dessert

Graham cracker crumbs
3-1/2 ounce package lemon pudding
 and pie filling mix
2/3 cup sugar
1 cup light cream
2 cups creamed cottage cheese
8 ounce package cream cheese
4 egg yolks
1/4 teaspoon salt
4 egg whites, beaten to soft peaks
Cherry Glaze (recipe follows)

In 9-inch spring form pan, cover bottom only with graham cracker crumb crust. Set aside. Combine pudding mix, 2/3 cup sugar and light cream in saucepan; cook, stirring, until texture comes to full boil and is thickened, about 5 minutes. (Mix may curdle but it will smooth out when mixture boils). Remove from heat. Combine cottage and cream cheeses. Mix well; add egg yolks one at a time, mixing well after each addition. Add salt and cooked pudding; blend well. Fold in beaten egg whites and pour over crumb mixture in pan. Bake at 300 degrees for 1 hour. Cool to room temperature. Chill thoroughly. Spread on Cherry Glaze. This cake is best when chilled overnight.

Cherry Glaze:

1/2 (3-ounce) package strawberry
 flavor gelatin (4 tablespoons)
1/2 cup boiling water
1/4 cup sugar
1/2 cup juice drained from cherries
16 - 17 ounce can pitted tart cherries,
 (water pack)

Dissolve gelatin in boiling water; stir in sugar. Add juice drained from the cherries. Chill until slightly thickened. Spread well drained cherries over top of chilled Lemon Cheese Torte, pour gelatin mixture over cherries. Chill until ready to serve.

Agnes Ward, Erie, PA

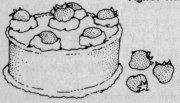

CREAM CHEESE TARTS

Makes 24-30 tarts

2 (8-ounce) packages cream cheese,
 softened
3/4 cup sugar
3 eggs
1 tablespoon lemon juice
Vanilla wafers (Nabisco 'Nilla wafers)

Beat cream cheese, eggs, sugar, and lemon juice until smooth and fluffy. Place vanilla wafers in bottom of cupcake papers and place in muffin pan. Pour cream cheese mixture on top of vanilla wafers until cups are at least half full.

Bake at 350 degrees for 20-25 minutes. (Tarts will crack across the top but will go back together as they cool). Refrigerate. Remove cupcake paper and top with cherry, blueberry, or pineapple topping.

These are miniature cheese cakes, dainty and so good!

Dorothy Smith, Sandy, UT

STRAWBERRY CHEESECAKE TARTS

Makes 6 tarts

1 package (3 ounces) cream cheese,
 softened
6 tablespoons sugar
1 teaspoon vanilla
1 ounce semi-sweet chocolate,
 melted
1/3 cup sour cream
1 cup prepared whipped topping
1 package (4 ounces) Keebler Ready-
 Crust Graham cracker tart crusts
1 pint fresh strawberries, washed,
 hulled, and sliced
1 teaspoon cornstarch
2 tablespoons cold water
1 or 2 drops red food coloring, if desired

Beat cream cheese, 2 tablespoons of the sugar, and the vanilla in small mixer bowl at medium speed until

smooth; blend in melted chocolate. Beat in sour cream until smooth. Fold in 1/2 cup of the whipped topping. Divide mixture between tart crusts, spreading evenly into each crust. Reserve 1/2 cup of the strawberries; arrange remaining slices over cream cheese mixture in each crust. Mash reserved strawberries in small saucepan. Dissolve cornstarch in the cold water; add to remaining strawberries with remaining 3 tablespoons sugar. Cook over low heat, stirring constantly until mixture boils. Boil and stir 1 minute; remove from heat. Stir in food coloring; allow to cool. Spread evenly over tarts; garnish with remaining whipped topping. Refrigerate until needed.

Peggy Fowler, Woodruff, S.C.

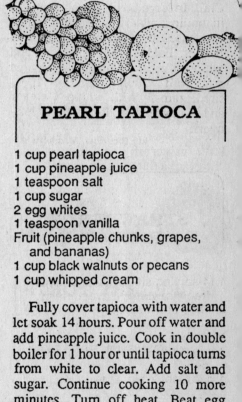

PEARL TAPIOCA

1 cup pearl tapioca
1 cup pineapple juice
1 teaspoon salt
1 cup sugar
2 egg whites
1 teaspoon vanilla
Fruit (pineapple chunks, grapes,
 and bananas)
1 cup black walnuts or pecans
1 cup whipped cream

Fully cover tapioca with water and let soak 14 hours. Pour off water and add pineapple juice. Cook in double boiler for 1 hour or until tapioca turns from white to clear. Add salt and sugar. Continue cooking 10 more minutes. Turn off heat. Beat egg whites until fluffy and stir into hot mixture. Add vanilla and mix well. Chill in refrigerator. Add fruit, as much as you like. Add bananas, as late as possible, unless you first soak them in pineapple juice. Add nuts. Just before serving, add whipped cream.

This recipe has been a family favorite for 50 years.

Mrs. Robert Combs, Fair Play, Mo.

STRAWBERRY CHIF-FON SQUARES

1/3 cup margarine
1-1/2 cups vanilla wafers, crushed
1 (3-ounce) package strawberry gelatin
3/4 cup boiling water
1 (14-ounce) can sweetened condensed milk
1 (10-ounce) package frozen sliced strawberries in syrup, thawed
4 cups mini-marshmallows
1 cup (1/2 pint) whipping cream, whipped

In a small saucepan, melt margarine; stir in crumbs. Pat firmly onto bottom of 11x7-inch baking dish. Chill. In large bowl, dissolve gelatin in boiling water; stir in sweetened condensed milk and undrained strawberries. Fold in marshmallows and whipped cream. Pour into prepared pan. Chill 2 hours or until set. If desired, garnish with whipped cream and strawberries. Refrigerate leftovers.

Ida Bloedow, Madison, Wis

STRAWBERRY PARFAIT

Serves 6

1 (4-serving size) package sugar-free strawberry-flavor gelatin
3/4 cup boiling water
1/2 cup cold water
Ice cubes
1 cup chopped or sliced strawberries
1 cup Cool Whip, thawed

Completely dissolve gelatin in boiling water. Combine cold water and ice cubes to make 1-1/4 cups. Add to gelatin and stir until slightly thickened; remove any unmelted ice. Measure 3/4 cup and add strawberries; pour into 6 individual parfait glasses. Blend whipped topping into remaining gelatin and spoon into glasses. Chill until set, about 1 hour. (50 calories per serving)

Ida Bloedow, Madison, Wis.

QUICK AND EASY STRAWBERRY PARFAIT

Serves 4

1 (1-1/4 ounce) envelope pudding mix
2 cups milk
2 pints strawberries

Prepare pudding as directed. Cover surface with waxed paper. (This can be done ahead of time). Before serving, beat pudding with spoon until light and fluffy. Reserve 4 strawberries cut crosswise. In 4 parfait glasses alternate layers of pudding and strawberries. Add berries.

This is such a delicious and easy dessert, even your children can make it!

Susan Wiener, Spring Hill, Fla.

STRAWBERRY YUM-YUM

Serves 4

1 envelope unflavored gelatin
1/4 cup water, cold
1-1/2 cups fresh strawberries
1 teaspoon sugar
1 tablespoon lemon juice
1/8 teaspoon salt
1/4 cup ice water
1/4 cup non-fat dry milk

In the cold water, soften gelatin. Dissolve gelatin by placing over hot water. Mash strawberries; add salt, lemon juice, and sugar. Blend in softened gelatin. Chill until mixture begins to thicken. Combine dry milk and ice water together. Beat with mixer on high speed until stiff; fold into gelatin. Pour into a 1-quart wet mold. Chill. (23 calories per serving)

Dorothy Shepard, Campton, Ky.

DRUMSTICK TREAT

2 cups vanilla wafers (crushed)

1 cup crushed Spanish peanuts
1/2 cup melted butter or margarine
1 8-ounce package cream cheese
1/3 cup peanut butter
1 cup confectioners' sugar
4 cups whipped topping
2 small packages instant chocolate pudding
3 cups milk
1 small chocolate candy bar

Mix vanilla wafers, 2/3 cup peanuts, and margarine together. Pat in a 9x13-inch pan. Bake in oven, 350 degrees, for 10 minutes. Cool. Mix cream cheese, peanut butter, and confectioners' sugar until smooth. Fold in 2 cups whipped topping. Layer over crumb crust and refrigerate. Meanwhile, mix pudding and milk together. Pour over layers in pan; refrigerate until set. Spread remaining 2 cups whipped topping over pudding mixture. Top with remaining peanuts. Grate chocolate bar over top. Cover and place in freezer. This may be served directly from freezer or after setting at room temperature for about 15 minutes.

Ida Bloedow, Madison, Wis.

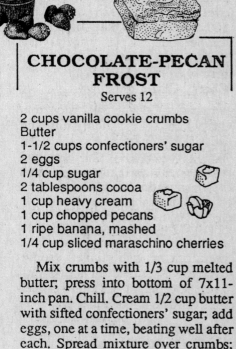

CHOCOLATE-PECAN FROST

Serves 12

2 cups vanilla cookie crumbs
Butter
1-1/2 cups confectioners' sugar
2 eggs
1/4 cup sugar
2 tablespoons cocoa
1 cup heavy cream
1 cup chopped pecans
1 ripe banana, mashed
1/4 cup sliced maraschino cherries

Mix crumbs with 1/3 cup melted butter; press into bottom of 7x11-inch pan. Chill. Cream 1/2 cup butter with sifted confectioners' sugar; add eggs, one at a time, beating well after each. Spread mixture over crumbs; chill. Mix sugar with cocoa; stir into heavy cream. Whip; fold in pecans, bananas, and cherries. Pile over butter layers; freeze.

Elizabeth S. Lawson, Delbarton, W.V.

PINK AND WHITE ASPIC

Serves 4

1 envelope unflavored gelatin
1/2 cup cold water
1 (10-1/2-ounce) can condensed tomato soup
1 teaspoon grated onion
Crisp salad greens
1 cup creamy cottage cheese (topping)

Sprinkle gelatin on cold water to soften. Place over low heat. Stir until gelatin is dissolved. Remove from heat. Combine with soup and onion. Pour into 1-quart or 4 individual molds that have been rinsed with cold water. Chill until firm. Unmold. Serve on salad greens with a topping of cottage cheese.

BLACK CHERRY SPARKLE

1 (2-pound) can pitted black cherries
2 tablespoons butter
1-1/2 tablespoons cornstarch
2 tablespoons sugar
1/2 teaspoon almond extract
8 slices plain pound cake

Drain cherries; set aside juice. In saucepan, melt butter; add juice from cherries; mix well. Add cornstarch and sugar; stir until smooth. Heat, stirring constantly, until clear and thickened; remove from heat. Add cherries and almond extract. Put cake on individual plates; pour sparkling cherry sauce over slices.

Gwen Campbell, Sterling, VA

COCO-NUTTY BANANAS

Serves 6-8

6 firm bananas
1/4 cup orange juice
1/2 cup light brown sugar
1 cup fresh coconut, grated
1/2 cup blanched, slivered almonds
1 teaspoon powdered cardamom
1/4 cup melted butter

Preheat oven to 400 degrees. Peel bananas; cut in half lengthwise, then in half across, making each banana into 4 pieces. Arrange in a buttered baking dish. Pour orange juice over bananas. Sprinkle sugar, coconut, almonds, and cardamom over bananas; pour butter over all. Bake for 25 minutes.

Agnes Ward, Erie, PA

CHERRY AMORETTO CREAM

2 envelopes unflavored gelatin
1 cup cold water
2 tablespoons lemon juice
1/4 teaspoon salt
21-ounce can cherry pie filling
1 pint whipping cream
1/4 teaspoon almond extract
2 tablespoons Amoretto liqueur
1/4 cup sugar

Sprinkle gelatin over cold water in saucepan; let stand 3 - 4 minutes. Stir over low heat until gelatin is completely dissolved, about 5 minutes. Add sugar, lemon juice and salt. Stir to combine. Stir in 1-1/2 cups cherry pie filling. Chill until mixture begins to thicken slightly. Fold in whipped cream and 1 tablespoon sugar if desired. Pour into 2-quart mold; chill until firm.

Sauce:
Combine Amoretto liqueur with remaining cherry pie filling; cook slowly 2 - 3 minutes. Cool slightly. To serve, unmold dessert onto serving plate and top with sauce.

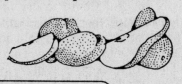

EASTER EGG TWIST

1 - 1 pound loaf frozen white bread dough
1 tablespoon grated orange peel
1/2 teaspoon anise seed
6 eggs
1 tablespoon water
Food coloring
Vanilla icing

Thaw dough according to package direction. Sprinkle orange peel and anise seed on flattened dough piece; work in well. Divide dough in half; roll each piece into a 24 inch rope.

On a greased baking sheet, loosely twist ropes and shape into a circle, sealing the ends. Place 5 eggs between ropes in the twist. Cover and let rise until double in size.

Beat one egg with water and brush the loaf. Bake in preheated oven at 350 degrees for 30-35 minutes. Cool on rack. Brush eggs with food coloring. Drizzle with your favorite vanilla icing.

Diantha Susan Hibbard, Rochester, NY

EASY CHEESE STRUDEL

2 packages (8 roll size) crescent rolls
2 (8-ounce) packages cream cheese, softened
2 egg yolks
1 egg white
3/4 cup sugar
1 teaspoon vanilla
1 teaspoon lemon juice

Pat 1 package of crescent rolls into ungreased 8-inch square casserole dish; seal edges together. Combine remaining ingredients; beat until smooth. Spread cheese mixture over crescent rolls. Place other package of crescent roll dough on top of cheese mixture. Bake at 350 degrees for 20 minutes or until lightly browned. Cool.

Glaze:
1 cup confectioners' sugar
1 teaspoon vanilla
3 tablespoons milk

Mix ingredients together for glaze.
Deborah M. Mucháy, Cleveland, OH

PEACH DELICIOUS

1 (13-ounce) box yellow cake mix
1-1/2 cups fresh peaches, thinly
    sliced
2 tablespoons sugar
1 teaspoon cinnamon

Glaze:
2 tablespoons sugar
1/4 teaspoon grated lemon rind
1 cup dairy sour cream

Grease a 9x12-inch baking pan.
Prepare cake mix according to package directions. Spread batter in pan.
Arrange peach slices in rows over
cake mix. Mix sugar and cinnamon;
sprinkle over peaches. Bake in 350-
degree oven for about 30-35 minutes.

For glaze, blend sugar and lemon
rind into sour cream; spread evenly
over cake. Return cake to oven for 3-
4 minutes. Cool and cut into squares.
Frozen or drained canned peaches cut
into thin slices may be used.

Betty L. Perkins, Hot Springs, Ark.

GOLDEN FROST PEACH ROLL

1-1/2 cups all-purpose flour
1/4 teaspoon salt
3 teaspoons baking powder
2 tablespoons sugar
1/4 cup vegetable shortening
1/2 cup peach nectar
Sliced sweet peaches to cover roll
1 tablespoon nutmeg
Whipped topping to cover roll
1 tablespoon grated orange zest
    (rind)

Sift together flour, salt, and baking
powder. Add sugar; work in shortening; moisten with the peach nectar.
Turn onto a floured board; roll into
rectangular shape about 1/2-inch
thick. Spread generously with peaches
and nutmeg. Roll up; place on a
greased jelly-roll baking sheet. Bake
at 350 degrees for 40 minutes. Place
gently on rack to cool. When completely cool spread generously with

whipped cream; sprinkle grated orange zest over topping. Refrigerate at
once.

Gwen Campbell, Sterling, Va.

PUMPKIN SWIRL SQUARES
Makes 2 dozen

1 (16-ounce) can pumpkin
1-3/4 cups sugar
1/2 cup oil
3 eggs
2 cups flour
2 teaspoons baking powder
2 teaspoons cinnamon
1 teaspoon baking soda
1 (8-ounce) package cream
    cheese, softened

Combine pumpkin, 1-1/2 cups
sugar, oil, and 2 eggs, mixing until
well-blended. Add combined dry
ingredients. Mix well. Combine cream
cheese, remaining sugar, and egg,
mixing until well-blended. Spoon
pumpkin mixture into greased and
floured 15x10x1-inch jelly roll pan.
Spoon cream cheese mixture over
pumpkin batter. Cut through batter
with knife several times for marble
effect. Bake at 350 degrees, 25 to 30
minutes or until wooden pick placed
in center comes out clean. Cool. Cut
into squares.

Joy Shamway, Freeport, Ill.

EASTER GRUNTIES
Serves 4

2 cups blueberries, washed and
    drained
1/2 cup sugar
1 cup water
1 cup unbleached all-purpose flour
2 teaspoon baking powder
1/2 cup half-and-half
1/2 cup raisins
Whipped cream for garnish

Mix blueberries, sugar, and water
in a saucepan. Bring to a boil and
cook over low heat for 10 minutes.

Stir the flour, baking powder, and
half-and-half together and add to blueberries. Stir *only* enough to mix.
Cover tightly; cook for 15 minutes
longer. (During the cooking, keep
heat high enough only to keep berries
bubbling.) Remove from heat and
add raisins. Serve warm; garnish with
whipped cream.

Marie Musaro, Manasquan, N.J.

EASTER GOODIES

Crust:
1 cup flour
2 tablespoons brown sugar
1/2 cup butter

Combine flour and brown sugar.
Cut in butter until mixture is the
consistency of fine crumbs. Pack into
bottom of a 9-inch square pan. Bake
at 350 degrees for 15 minutes.

Filling:
2 eggs
1-1/2 cups brown sugar, packed
1 cup flour
1/2 teaspoon baking powder
1/2 teaspoon vanilla
1 cup chocolate chips
1 cup coconut
1/4 cup chopped maraschino
    cherries, optional

Beat eggs until light. Add brown
sugar, gradually beating constantly.
Sift flour and baking powder; add to
egg mixture, then add vanilla. Fold in
chocolate chips, coconut, and cherries. Pour into the partially baked
crust and bake at 350 degrees for
about 40 minutes. Cool; cut into 9 (3-
inch) squares and serve.

Agnes Ward, Erie, Pa.

EASY PEACH CRUMBLE

Serves 4

1 (29 ounce) can sliced peaches, drained
3/4 cup firmly packed brown sugar
1/2 cup all-purpose flour
1/2 teaspoon cinnamon
1/4 cup butter or margarine, softened

Place peaches in lightly greased 9-inch pie plate. Combine sugar, flour, cinnamon; add butter and cut into mixture until it resembles coarse crumbs. Sprinkle over peaches. Bake in preheated 375 degree oven for 25 minutes.

Mrs. Bruce Fowler, Woodruff, SC

EGGNOG CREAM PUFFS

Makes 24

24 small cream puffs, 2-1/2 t inches in diameter
1/4 cup cold water
2 tablespoons unflavored gelatin (2 envelopes)
2-1/2 cups dairy eggnog
2 tablespoons rum or 1 teaspoon rum extract
1 teaspoon vanilla
1 cup whipping cream
1/4 cup chopped red candied cherries
6 squares German's sweet chocolate, finely chopped

Soften gelatin in cold water. Heat 1 cup eggnog over low heat to simmering. Add gelatin and stir until dissolved. Remove from heat. Add remaining 1-1/2 cups eggnog, rum, and vanilla. Chill until partially set. Whip cream until stiff. Fold into eggnog mixture. Fold in cherries and chocolate. Chill until mixture mounds when dropped from a spoon. To serve, split cream puffs and fill with eggnog filling. Garnish as desired.

FRUIT FRITTERS

Makes 18

1 cup sifted all-purpose flour
2 tablespoons sugar
2 teaspoons baking powder
1/4 teaspoon salt
1 beaten egg
2/3 cup milk
2 tablespoons butter, melted
3 to 4 apples, pared, cored and sliced crosswise into rings, or 18 thin pineapple slices.

Sift together flour, sugar, baking powder, and salt. Mix together egg, milk, and butter. Stir into dry ingredients; blend until smooth but do not overbeat. Batter should be heavy enough to coat fruit. (If necessary, add more milk and flour.)

Dip fruit rings into batter, one at a time, then fry in deep hot fat (375 degrees) for 3 minutes, turning once. Drain on paper towels. Serve hot with powdered sugar or cinnamon-sugar sprinkled over top.

Alice Bates, Mineola, NY

GOOD PUFFY FRITTERS

Serves 4

Any fruit or vegetable such as 1 can corn, peaches, apples or mushrooms, drained
1 cup flour
1-1/2 teaspoons baking powder
1/2 teaspoon salt
2 eggs, well beaten
1/3 cup milk

Sift together flour, baking powder and salt. Beat egg with milk. Stir remaining ingredients into egg mixture. Beat until smooth and well blended. Fold in desired vegetables or fruit. Drop by tablespoonfuls into deep oil at 375 degrees; fry until golden brown. Drain on paper towel. Remove with a slotted spoon.

Ruth Muldoon, Baldwin, Long Island, NY

FROZEN REFRESHER

1 (13 ounce) can evaporated milk

1 package unsweetened Kool-Aid (any flavor)
3/4 cup sugar
1 (4-1/2 ounce) container Cool Whip
3/4 to 1 cup chopped pecans
1 (8-1/4 ounce) can crushed pineapple, drained

Pour milk into bowl and place in freezer until partially frozen. Remove from freezer and beat on high speed until fluffy and thick, about 2 or 3 minutes. Add Kool-Aid, sugar, Cool Whip, pecans, and crushed pineapple. Beat to mix well.

Pour into 9-inch square pan and freeze until firm.

Lynn Roark, Dayton, TX

FRUIT SHERBET

Juice of 3 oranges
Juice of 3 lemons
3 ripe bananas, mashed
1 (#2 can) crushed pineapple, undrained
3 cups sugar
3 cups water
1 pint cream (evaporated milk may be substituted)
1 pint milk

Mix in order given, stir until sugar is dissolved. Pour into gallon-size ice cream freezer, freeze as directed.

Audrey L. Reynolds, Lumberport, WV

HAWAIIAN HASH

1 can pineapple chunks or fresh pineapple, diced
1 cup avocado (peeled and diced)
1/4 cup maraschino cherries, sliced
1-1/2 cups miniature marshmallows
1 large bowl Cool Whip
2 sliced bananas
1 can or package coconut, flaked

Drain pineapple; mix in a large bowl the pineapple, avocado, cherries, and marshmallows until well-combined. Refrigerate covered, until well-chilled, about 1 hour.

Fold in Cool Whip just before serving. Stir in bananas and 1 cup coconut. Spoon into dessert bowls; sprinkle with rest of coconut.

Kimberly Ritchey, Mars, PA

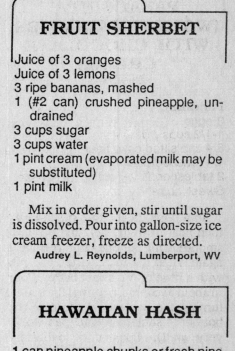

Foreign & EXOTIC

GSUSZTATOTT PALACSINTA (WALNUT PANCAKES WITH CHOCOLATE CREAM)
Serves 6-8

Pancakes:
3 eggs
1-1/2 cups milk
3/4 cup sifted cake flour
1/4 teaspoon salt
2 tablespoons vegetable oil (Crisco)
Sweet butter

In a bowl, beat eggs; stir in milk, then beat in flour, salt, and oil until smooth. Chill for one hour, then beat again. Heat a 7-inch skillet, and rub with a little of the sweet butter. Pour in about two tablespoons of the batter, turning the pan quickly to coat the bottom (a stick-free sauté pan works very well). Cook until delicately browned on both sides. Turn out onto a napkin and stack while preparing the balance of the pancakes. Keep warm (in oven warmed to 250 degrees and then shut off).

Filling:
1-1/2 cups walnuts
1/2 cup superfine sugar
1 teaspoon cinnamon
1 teaspoon vanilla extract
3/4 cup whipping (heavy) cream

Pulverize the nuts in a food processor or electric blender. Mix in the sugar, cinnamon, vanilla extract, and only enough of the cream to make a spreadable mixture.

Sauce:
3/4 cup sugar
1 cup milk
8 ounces unsweetened chocolate

Combine sugar and milk in a saucepan; cook over low heat, stirring constantly, until sugar dissolves. Add chocolate and continue stirring over very low heat until chocolate melts and mixture is smooth.

Spread some of the nut mixture on each pancake, and fold over. Serve the chocolate sauce in a separate dish to be spooned individually as desired.

The above recipe was served at a fine hotel in Austria when I traveled there in 1970.

Eleanor J. Froehlich, Rochester Hills, Mich.

PRESSNAKO (RUSSIAN COOKIE)
Makes 4 dozen

These cookies, although quite plain in ingredients, make a very tasty and satisfying cookie. Brought over from the old country, they continued to use those ingredients that were inexpensive and readily available. Not too sweet, one Pressnako (press cookie), will still quench your appetite for something sugary and "sinful."

1/2 pound butter
3/4 cup sugar
3 eggs, beaten
1-1/2 tablespoons baking powder
1/2 teaspoon salt
3-1/2 cups flour
1/8 cup heavy cream

Melt butter; add sugar and eggs. Mix together baking powder, salt, and flour in separate bowl. Add egg mixture to flour and mix well (this will be coarse and thick). Add cream to mixture and mix until pliable enough to knead. Knead for 5 minutes on lightly floured board until well-mixed and satiny. Shape into walnut-size balls. On floured board, roll out to 1/4-inch thickness. Place on cookie sheet and bake at 400 degrees until golden brown, 10-15 minutes.

Roberta Rothwell, Palmdale, Calif.

RISI BISI (RICE AND PEAS)
Serves 6

3 cups cooked rice (which has been cooked in chicken broth)
2 cups cooked peas (sautéed briefly in several tablespoons butter)
Salt and pepper to taste
2 tablespoons freshly grated Parmesan cheese (optional)

Combine hot cooked rice, peas, and butter from pan in a bowl. Season with salt and pepper to taste. Pack into a well-greased 6-cup ring mold. Carefully invert onto platter. Sprinkle with the grated cheese. Fill center of mold, *if desired*, with any colorful vegetable.

Risi Bisi also may be heated in a casserole dish, baked at 350 degrees for about 20 minutes.

Joan Ross, Amenia, N.Y.

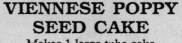

VIENNESE POPPY SEED CAKE

Makes 1 large tube cake

1/2 pound butter, softened
4 beaten egg yolks
4 stiffly beaten egg whites (not dry)
1-1/2 cups sugar
1 teaspoon baking soda
1/2 pint sour cream
2 cups flour
2 teaspoons vanilla
2-1/4 ounces poppy seeds

Cream butter; gradually beat in sugar until fluffy. Stir in poppy seeds and vanilla with beaten egg yolks. Add sour cream that has been mixed with baking soda to creamed mixture, *alternately* with flour, ending with flour. Fold in the stiffly beaten egg whites. Pour into an ungreased 9- or 10-inch tube pan. Bake in a 350-degree oven for 1 hour or until it tests done. Cool on rack 15 minutes. Loosen and remove from pan. Completely cool on rack. This moist cake needs no frosting and freezes well.

Joan Ross, Amenia, N.Y.

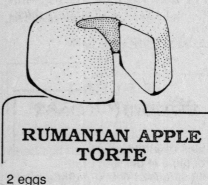

RUMANIAN APPLE TORTE

2 eggs
1/2 cup sugar
1/2 cup sifted all-purpose flour
1/2 teaspoon baking powder
1/4 teaspoon salt
1 cup chopped apples
1/2 cup chopped walnuts

Beat eggs until light, gradually add sugar and beat until fluffy. Sift dry ingredients and add to mixture. Add apples and nuts; blend well.

Bake in greased 8x8-inch pan at 325 degrees for 40 minutes. There is no shortening in this recipe. Delicious!

Mildred V. Schuler, Beaver Falls, Pa.

DUTCH TEA CAKES (KLETSKOPPEN)

This recipe is more than 400 years old and originated in the Dutch city of Leyden.

1-1/2 cups brown sugar
2 tablespoons water
1/4 cup butter
1 teaspoon cinnamon
1 cup ground almonds
1 cup flour

Mix sugar and water to make a thick paste. Add butter, cinnamon, almonds, and flour. Shape into small rounds, about 1 inch in diameter, on a baking sheet greased with unsalted fat. Place at least 2 inches apart. Bake about 15 minutes in 350-degree oven. Remove from oven; let stand 30 seconds and lift from baking sheet with spatula. If wafers become too hard to remove easily, return to oven for a minute, then remove.

Agnes Ward, Erie, Pa.

POTATO DUMPLINGS (GERMANY)

Serves 6–8

3 pounds medium potatoes
2 medium eggs
1 cup unsifted all-purpose flour
1/2 cup packaged dry bread crumbs
1/4 teaspoon nutmeg
1/4 cup chopped parsley
Salt
Dash of pepper

Cook unpeeled potatoes, covered, in boiling water just until tender—about 30 minutes. Drain; cool slightly; peel.

Put potatoes through ricer. Spread on paper towels to dry well. Turn potatoes into large bowl. Lightly toss with 2-1/2 teaspoons salt and the dash pepper. Make a well in center; break eggs into it.

Sift 3/4 cup flour over eggs. Then add bread crumbs, nutmeg, and parsley. With hands, work mixture until it is smooth and holds together. Shape into approximately 18 egg-size balls. Roll in remaining flour.

Meanwhile, in large pan, bring about 2 quarts lightly salted water to boiling point; reduce heat. Drop in at one time just enough potato balls to fit comfortably in pan. Boil gently, uncovered, 2 minutes after they rise to surface. With slotted spoon, transfer dumplings to paper towels; drain. Serve hot.

Judie Betz, Eureka, Calif.

PUACKI (POLISH DOUGHNUTS)

2 cups milk
1 scant cup butter
2 packages dry yeast
5 eggs
1-1/4 cups sugar
1-1/2 teaspoons vanilla extract
1/2 teaspoon lemon extract
1/2 teaspoon salt
8-10 cups flour
1 stick butter

Dissolve yeast in 2 tablespoons sugar and a little warm water. Scald milk; add butter to it and let cool. Beat eggs, sugar, salt, and the two extracts until very light in color, at least 7 minutes. Add flour, a little at a time; beat after each addition. This is not a sticky dough. Let rise in bowl until double, then roll out 1/2-inch thick and cut 2-inch rounds with a biscuit cutter. Let rise again, until double. Fry in hot oil (deep-fat fry) until brown on one side; turn and brown on the other; lift out of fat and drain on a brown paper sack. Melt butter; dip doughnuts in butter then shake in a paper sack with some sugar. Doughnuts are ready to eat. These can be frozen before you dip in melted butter and shake in sugar.

Kathleen Dwyer, Saginaw, Minn.

DUTCH APPLE CAKE

3 cups flour
2 cups sugar
1 cup oil
2 teaspoons vanilla
3 teaspoons baking powder
1/2 cup orange juice
4 eggs

Mix all above ingredients together in bowl with electric mixer. Pour half of batter into greased and floured tube pan. Layer half of apple mixture into batter, and then spread on rest of batter. Pour rest of apple mixture on top. Bake in preheated 350 degree oven for 1 hour and 10 minutes until golden brown. Cool 1 hour in pan before removing.

Apple Mixture:
4 or 5 apples, thinly sliced
2 teaspoons cinnamon
5 tablespoons sugar

Toss together in bowl until apples are coated.

Mrs. Joseph E. Yokitis, Sinking Spring, PA

PALACINKY (THIN PANCAKES)

2 eggs
Pinch of salt
3 tablespoons sugar
2 cups milk
2 cups flour
1/4 cup butter for pan
Jam

Beat together eggs, salt, sugar, milk, and flour until smooth. Heat a frying pan; brush with butter. Pour in a thin layer of batter and spread by tilting the pan. Pancakes must be very thin, almost transparent. Fry on both sides to a golden brown. Spread with jam, roll up, and dust with vanilla bean flavored powdered sugar.

Palacinky is the name for thin pancakes, usually served around the holidays—very similar to crepe suzettes.

BUCHE DE NOEL (FRENCH YULE LOG)
Serves 8

Spongecake:
4 eggs
2 egg yolks
3/4 cup granulated sugar
1 teaspoon vanilla
1 cup sifted all-purpose flour
1/2 teaspoon baking powder
3 tablespoons unsalted butter, melted
Confectioners' sugar
Raspberry preserves

Mocha Butter Cream Frosting:
1/4 cup butter or margarine
2 cups confectioners' sugar (divided)
1 teaspoon vanilla extract
1-1/2 tablespoons instant coffee powder
2 ounces bittersweet chocolate, melted
2 to 4 tablespoons heavy cream

To make cake, line greased jelly roll pan (15-1/2x10-1/2) with wax paper. Grease and dust lightly with flour. Set aside. In large bowl, put eggs, egg yolks, sugar, and vanilla. Beat at high speed for 8 minutes. Mixture will triple in volume and be creamy. Fold in sifted flour and baking powder gently with slotted spoon, lifting to aerate. Fold in melted butter. Do not over-fold. Pour batter into prepared pan. Bake at 350 degrees for 20-25 minutes. Remove from oven.

While cake is still in pan, cut off crisp edges. Invert pan on towel dusted with confectioners' sugar. Remove wax paper at once. Roll both cake and towel together. Cool on rack, seam side down. Unroll carefully and fill with preserves. Roll again. Frost.

To make frosting, blend butter, 1 cup confectioners' sugar. Add coffee, dissolved in vanilla. Add chocolate and heavy cream. Add remaining 1 cup confectioners' sugar until desired consistency.

ENCHILADAS

1 pound ground beef
1 onion, chopped
2 teaspoons salt
1/4 teaspoon pepper
2 teaspoons chili powder
1 dozen corn tortillas
2 cups sauce (recipe follows)
1-1/2 cups sharp grated cheese

Brown meat and onion; add seasonings. Dip each tortilla in warm oil. On each one, spoon 2 tablespoons sauce, a generous tablespoon of filling and a sprinkling of cheese; roll up and place close together in large pan. Pour remaining sauce and cheese over top. Bake at 350 degrees for 15-20 minutes.

Sauce:
1 (No. 2-1/2) can tomatoes
1 medium onion, chopped
2 teaspoons chili powder
1/8 teaspoon oregano
1 (6-ounce) can tomato paste
1 garlic clove, minced
1/2 teaspoon salt
1/4 teaspoon cayenne pepper

Combine above ingredients. Simmer about 1 hour until slightly thickened.

Jean Baker, Chula Vista, Calif.

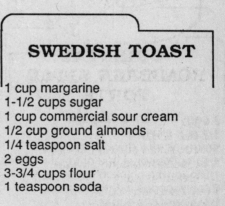

SWEDISH TOAST

1 cup margarine
1-1/2 cups sugar
1 cup commercial sour cream
1/2 cup ground almonds
1/4 teaspoon salt
2 eggs
3-3/4 cups flour
1 teaspoon soda

Mix all ingredients and pour into two greased and floured loaf pans. Bake in 350-degree oven for 45 minutes. Cool. Slice and place slices on cookie sheet. Place in oven again for 13-15 minutes until lightly browned, or slice as you want and use your toaster. Then spread the toast with butter and eat. Delicious!

Sandra Young, Victoria, Texas

SLEEK GREEK SALAD
Serves 6

1/2 pound cooked shrimp
1/2 pound feta cheese (rinsed, patted dry, and crumbled)
4 green onions, sliced
2 teaspoons fresh chopped oregano (or 3/4 teaspoon dried)
2 teaspoons fresh chopped basil (or 3/4 teaspoon dried)
1/4 cup sliced ripe olives
3 tomatoes (peeled, cored, and chopped)
1 (12-ounce) package uncooked spaghetti

In a 3-quart bowl combine the shrimp, cheese, onions, seasonings, olives, and tomatoes. Let stand at room temperature for 1 hour. Cook spaghetti in 5 quarts water until tender; drain. Toss the salad ingredients with the hot pasta and serve immediately.

This is a warm main-dish salad that is rich-tasting even though it is low in calories.

Sharon Vircks, Auburn, Wash

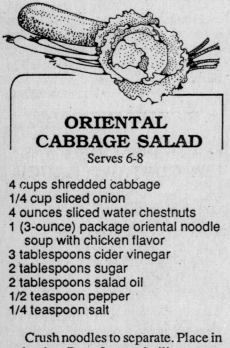

ORIENTAL CABBAGE SALAD
Serves 6-8

4 cups shredded cabbage
1/4 cup sliced onion
4 ounces sliced water chestnuts
1 (3-ounce) package oriental noodle soup with chicken flavor
3 tablespoons cider vinegar
2 tablespoons sugar
2 tablespoons salad oil
1/2 teaspoon pepper
1/4 teaspoon salt

Crush noodles to separate. Place in colander. Pour 2 cups boiling water over noodles to soften slightly. Combine drained noodles, cabbage, onions, and water chestnuts in large bowl.

For dressing mix together vinegar, sugar, oil, pepper, salt, and seasoning packet from soup mix. Mix well and pour over cabbage; toss. Chill a few hours before serving.

Loretta M. Brown, Birdsboro, Pa.

GATEAU AUX POIRES (PEAR CAKE)
Serves 8

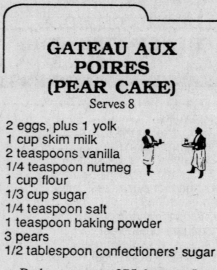

2 eggs, plus 1 yolk
1 cup skim milk
2 teaspoons vanilla
1/4 teaspoon nutmeg
1 cup flour
1/3 cup sugar
1/4 teaspoon salt
1 teaspoon baking powder
3 pears
1/2 tablespoon confectioners' sugar

Preheat oven to 375 degrees. In a mixing bowl, beat together eggs, egg yolk, skim milk, vanilla, and nutmeg. Sift flour with sugar, salt, and baking powder; gradually add liquid ingredients. Pour batter into a deep 9-inch pie dish.

Peel pears; cut in half lengthwise, removing the cores and seeds. Place pears in a circle in the batter, cut sides down and with the stem ends toward center. Do not allow the bottom ends to touch the sides of the dish. The rounded sides of the pears will be above the batter level.

Place in the oven and bake for 35 minutes or until top is a deep golden brown and pears are tender when pierced with a small, sharp knife. The batter will have puffed. Pear Cake should be eaten warm or cool. Sprinkle with confectioners' sugar before serving.

Suzan L. Wiener, Spring Hill, Fla.

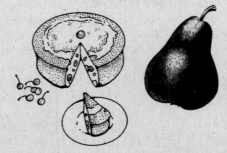

HELADO DE MANGO (MANGO SHERBET)
Serves 6

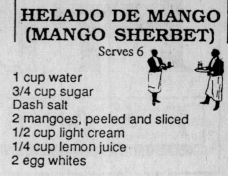

1 cup water
3/4 cup sugar
Dash salt
2 mangoes, peeled and sliced
1/2 cup light cream
1/4 cup lemon juice
2 egg whites

In saucepan combine water, 1/2 cup sugar, and salt. Cook 5 minutes; cool. In blender combine mangoes and cream, blending until smooth. Stir in cooled syrup and lemon juice. Place in freezer until partially frozen. Beat egg whites to soft peaks; gradually add 1/4 cup sugar, beating to stiff peaks. Place partially frozen mixture into chilled mixing bowl; break into chunks. Beat until mixture is smooth. Fold in beaten egg whites. Freeze until firm.

Kenneth McAdams, El Dorado, Ark.

CZECHOSLOVAKIAN COOKIES
Makes 2-1/2 dozen

1 cup butter
1 cup sugar
2 egg yolks
2 cups flour, sifted
1 cup walnuts, chopped
1/2 cup raspberry or strawberry jam

Cream butter until soft. Gradually add the sugar, creaming until light and fluffy. Add egg yolks and blend well. Gradually add flour and mix thoroughly. Then fold in nuts. Spoon half the batter into a buttered 8-inch square cake pan; spread evenly. Top with jam. Cover with remaining cookie dough. Bake in a moderately slow 325-degree oven for 1 hour or until lightly browned. Cool and cut into 1x2-inch bars.

This cookie recipe is over 100 years old and is also called Kolacky.

Ella Evanicky, Fayetteville, Texas

Fruits
FANTASTIC

COUNTRY BAKED APPLES
Serves 5

5 large baking apples, peeled and cored
1/2 cup brown sugar
1 teaspoon cinnamon
1 teaspoon nutmeg
1 cup apple jelly
1-1/4 tablespoons butter or margarine
1/2 cup apple juice

Place apples in an 8-inch square baking dish. Combine next four ingredients; spoon about 1 tablespoon of mixture into apple cavity; dot each apple with butter. Bring apple juice to a boil; pour juice into baking dish. Cover; bake at 350 degrees for 40 minutes.

Gwen Campbell, Sterling, Va.

BAKED BANANAS
Serves 4

4 large bananas
Butter
1/2 cup pineapple juice
1/4 cup brown sugar
1/4 teaspoon cinnamon
1/4 teaspoon allspice
1/2 cup sherry
3 tablespoons rum

Preheat oven to 450 degrees. Peel bananas and place in buttered baking dish after splitting them lengthwise. Place pineapple juice, brown sugar, spices, and sherry in saucepan. Heat and pour over bananas. Dot with butter and bake for about 15 minutes, basting often. Remove from oven; sprinkle with rum and serve at once.

Suzan L. Wiener, Spring Hill, Fla.

GINGERED BAKED FRUIT
Serves 8

1 (20-ounce) can pineapple chunks, drained
1 (16-ounce) can pear halves, drained
1 (16-ounce) can peach halves, drained
1 (16-ounce) jar maraschino cherries, drained
1/4 cup butter or margarine
3/4 cup firmly packed brown sugar
1 tablespoon ground ginger

Combine fruit in a 1-1/2-quart casserole. Melt butter; add sugar and ginger, stirring until smooth. Pour ginger mixture over fruit. Bake at 325 degrees for 30 minutes.

Mrs. Bruce Fowler, Woodruff, S.C.

APRICOT FOOL
Serves 4

1 (8-3/4-ounce) can apricot halves, drained
1-1/2 teaspoons lemon juice
1/4 teaspoon almond extract
1 cup heavy or whipping cream
2 tablespoons confectioners' sugar
2 tablespoons sliced, toasted almonds

In blender at medium speed, blend apricots, lemon juice, and extract until smooth. In small bowl, with mixer at medium speed, beat cream and sugar until stiff. Fold in apricot mixture just enough to marble. Spoon into 4 dessert dishes. Sprinkle with almonds.

Dorothy Garms, Anaheim, Calif.

CHERRY FRITTERS
Serves 4

1 cup flour
1/2 teaspoon salt
1 teaspoon baking powder
1 tablespoon melted butter
1 egg
1/3 cup milk
1/4 cup drained cherries
2 tablespoons sugar

Mix dry ingredients. Beat egg; add melted butter. Combine with milk and add to dry ingredients. Fold in cherries. Drop by small teaspoon into 1-1/2 or 2 inches of hot fat. Fry 2 or more minutes until brown. Drain and dust with confectioners' sugar. Fresh peaches, apricots, apples, or pineapple may be used instead of cherries.

Lucy Dowd, Sequim, Wash.

PEACHES IN CUSTARD SAUCE
Serves 6

1 (1-pound) can sliced cling peaches
1-2/3 cups evaporated milk
1 (3-1/2-ounce) package instant vanilla pudding mix
1/2 cup water
1/8 teaspoon nutmeg

Drain peaches well. Cut peaches in chunks. Place evaporated milk and water in mixing bowl. Add nutmeg and pudding mix. Beat slowly with rotary beater until smooth. Stir in peaches. Chill thoroughly before serving.

Mrs. Albert Foley, Lemoyne, Pa.

Meat
DISHES

CHERRY PORK CHOPS
Serves 6

6 pork chops, cut 3/4-inch thick
1/4 teaspoon salt
1/4 teaspoon pepper
1/2 can cherry pie filling (1 cup)
2 teaspoons lemon juice
1/2 teaspoon instant chicken bouillon granules
1/8 teaspoon ground mace

Trim excess fat from pork chops. Brown pork chops in hot skillet with butter or oil. Sprinkle each chop with salt and pepper. Combine cherry pie filling, lemon juice, chicken bouillon granules, and ground mace in cooker. Stir well. Place pork chops in Crockpot. Cover. Cook on *low* for 4-5 hours. Place chops on platter. Pour cherry sauce over meat.

COUNTRY ROAST AND VEGETABLES
Serves 6-8

1 roast, thawed
Several potatoes, canned sliced or whole
Several carrots
Green beans, corn (optional)
1 onion, sliced
1 cup water
1/4 teaspoon salt
1/4 teaspoon pepper
3 tablespoons butter or margarine
1/4 cup flour (optional)

Place roast in Crockpot. Add peeled potatoes, carrots, beans, corn, sliced onion, and butter. Add water and flour for gravy. Sprinkle with salt and pepper. Cook on *low* for 6-12 hours, *high* for less than 6 hours.

TENDER MEATBALLS IN MUSHROOM GRAVY
Serves 4-6

1 pound hamburger
4 slices soft white bread
1 teaspoon salt
1/4 teaspoon pepper
1 tablespoon minced onion
1 can mushroom soup
1/3 cup water

Pull apart bread into small, dime-size pieces. Combine hamburger, bread, salt, pepper, and minced onion in large mixing bowl. Using a spoon, scoop out rounds of meat, or shape into several round, 2-inch balls by hand.

Brown meatballs in a hot skillet using a small amount of butter or oil. Turn them occasionally so all sides are browned. Place meat in cooker. Add soup and water. Cook on *low* for 6 to 12 hours, *high* for up to 6 hours.

CORNED BEEF AND CABBAGE

2 medium onions, sliced
1 (2 1/2-to 3-pound) corned beef brisket

1 cup apple juice
1/4 cup packed brown sugar
2 teaspoons orange peel, finely shredded
2 teaspoons prepared mustard
6 whole cloves
6 cabbage wedges

Place onions in crockpot. Trim away any fat that might be present on the corned beef brisket. If needed, cut brisket to fit into Crockpot; place on top of onions. In a bowl combine apple juice, sugar, orange peel, mustard, and cloves; pour over brisket. Place cabbage on top of brisket. Cover; cook on *low* setting for 10-12 hours or on *high* setting for 5-6 hours.

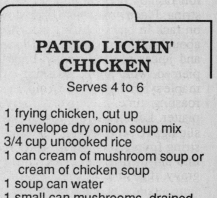

PATIO LICKIN' CHICKEN
Serves 4 to 6

1 frying chicken, cut up
1 envelope dry onion soup mix
3/4 cup uncooked rice
1 can cream of mushroom soup or cream of chicken soup
1 soup can water
1 small can mushrooms, drained
1/2 teaspoon salt
1/4 teaspoon pepper

Season chicken; brown slightly in frying pan. Mix remaining ingredients together; place in 9 x 13-inch baking dish. Arrange chicken on top. Cover with foil; bake one hour at 350 degrees. Remove foil and bake 20 minutes longer.

MAPLE-GLAZED TURKEY BREAST
Serves 6-8

1 (16-ounce) package cornbread mix
1 (4-pound) whole boneless turkey breast
1 pound hot Italian sausages, casings removed
1 large egg
1 teaspoon fennel seed, crushed
1 tablespoon maple syrup

Prepare cornbread mix according to package directions. Cool. Crumble enough cornbread to make 3 cups crumbs. Set remaining cornbread aside for other use. Reserve crumbs.

Prepare turkey breast: Heat oven to 325 degrees. Place turkey breast, skin-side down, on work surface. Press out flat. Using meat mallet or dull side of heavy knife, pound breast to uniform 3/4-inch thickness. Set aside.

Prepare stuffing: In 12-inch skillet over medium heat, cook sausage meat about 10 minutes, or until well browned, stirring frequently to break up meat. Drain well. Place in large bowl along with cornbread, egg, fennel seed and 1/2 cup water. Toss to mix well.

To assemble, spoon stuffing evenly over turkey breast. Starting at one side edge, carefully roll breast, jelly-roll fashion. Fasten with skewers or string. Place breast seam side down, on rack in open roasting pan. Roast about 1-1/2 hours until cooked through and juices run clear when breast is pierced with knife, brushing with maple syrup during last 10 minutes of roasting time. Remove to serving platter. Let stand 10 minutes before slicing. To serve, remove skewers or string from turkey breast. Cut breast into 3/4-inch slices. Serve with pan gravy, if desired.

CLASSIC SWISS STEAK
Serves 4-6

1 round steak
2 cups flour
1/4 teaspoon salt and pepper
2 tablespoons butter or shortening
1 (4-ounce) can tomato sauce
1 sliced onion
1 sliced green pepper

Cut steak into serving portions. Combine flour, salt, and pepper in medium-size bowl. Roll cut steaks in flour mixture, coating both sides. Melt shortening or butter in hot skillet. Brown meat on both sides, but do not

PORCUPINE MEATBALLS

1 package beef-flavored Rice-A-Roni (you can use chicken, Spanish, or turkey)
1 pound hamburger
1 egg beaten
Dash of steak seasoning
Small onion, chopped
2-1/2 cups hot water

Combine Rice-A-Roni ingredients with ground beef, egg, and steak seasoning. Shape into meatballs. Brown on all sides in skillet. Combine contents of beef seasonings packet with hot water. Pour over meat; cover and simmer 30 minutes. Serve over mashed potatoes, rice, egg noodles, or spaghetti.

Theresa Guillaume, Mosinee, WI

RICH SALMON ROMANOFF
Serves 4

1 cup green onion, chopped finely
1 clove garlic, minced
2 tablespoons butter or margarine
1-1/2 cups creamed cottage cheese
2 cups dairy sour cream
1/4 teaspoon liquid hot sauce
1/4 teaspoon salt
1 (15-1/2-ounce) can salmon (reserve liquid)
1-1/2 cups medium noodles
1 cup cheddar cheese, shredded

In a skillet, sauté onion and garlic in butter until onion is transparent; empty into large mixing bowl. Stir in cottage cheese, sour cream, hot sauce, and salt. Stir in salmon liquid. Flake and add salmon; mix lightly. Cook noodles, drain; stir into salmon mixture. Turn into a greased ovenproof baking dish; sprinkle with shredded cheese. Bake at 325 degrees, 30 minutes, or until cheese has melted, casserole is bubbly, and baked to a golden brown.

Gwen Campbell, Sterling, Va.

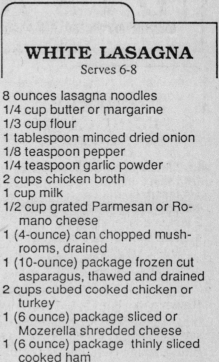

WHITE LASAGNA
Serves 6-8

8 ounces lasagna noodles
1/4 cup butter or margarine
1/3 cup flour
1 tablespoon minced dried onion
1/8 teaspoon pepper
1/4 teaspoon garlic powder
2 cups chicken broth
1 cup milk
1/2 cup grated Parmesan or Romano cheese
1 (4-ounce) can chopped mushrooms, drained
1 (10-ounce) package frozen cut asparagus, thawed and drained
2 cups cubed cooked chicken or turkey
1 (6 ounce) package sliced or Mozerella shredded cheese
1 (6 ounce) package thinly sliced cooked ham
1/2 cup grated Parmesan or Romano cheese

Cook noodles as directed on package; drain. In saucepan melt butter or margarine; blend in flour, onion, garlic powder, and pepper. Add chicken broth and milk; cook and stir until bubbly. Stir in the first 1/2 cup grated cheese and mushrooms. In 13x9x3-inch baking dish layer half the noodles, all of the asparagus, chicken, and mozzarella, and 1/3 of milk mixture. Top with ham, remaining noodles, and remaining milk mixture. Sprinkle with remaining grated cheese. Bake in 350-degree oven for 35 minutes. Let stand 10 minutes before cutting.

This recipe is a great way to use turkey leftovers. At family dinners, I make one pan of traditional lasagna and this one. The white lasagna is always the most popular.

Connie Blommers, Pella, Iowa

CHICKEN 'N NOODLES
Serves 4

4 tablespoons butter, divided
1 cup sliced fresh mushrooms
1/2 cup sliced carrots
1 cup light cream
1/4 teaspoon pepper
1/8 teaspoon nutmeg
1/2 cup grated Parmesan cheese
1/2 cup frozen peas
2 cups cooked chicken, diced
6 ounces broad noodles, cooked
   according to package directions
Additional Parmesan cheese (optional)

In large skillet on medium heat with 2 tablespoons of the butter, cook mushrooms and carrots until tender or until liquid is evaporated. Stir occasionally. Add cream, remaining butter, pepper, and nutmeg. Bring to simmer; gradually stir in cheese. Add peas and chicken; heat through. Toss chicken mixture with cooked noodles. Serve; sprinkle with additional cheese, if desired.

Easy "top-of-the-range" dish. Good way to use leftover chicken.

Anna Y. Bodisch, Coplay, Pa.

SAN DIEGO RATATOUILLE
Serves 6

2 (6-1/2-ounce) cans shrimp
1 large eggplant, cut into 1/2-inch
   cubes
1/4 teaspoon salt
2 green bell peppers, remove seeds
   and cut into chunks
2 fresh tomatoes, cut into 1/2-inch
   cubes
2 large onions, sliced and separated
   into rings
1 (29-ounce) can tomatoes, drained
1/2 cup chopped fresh parsley
1 tablespoon garlic salt
2 tablespoons basil, crumbled

Spread cubed eggplant in single layer on paper towel. Sprinkle with salt and let stand 20 minutes. Pat dry with paper towel. Mix all ingredients, except shrimp, in large skillet; simmer, uncovered, slowly for 25-30 minutes, or until volume is reduced. Stir in shrimp; continue simmering until mixture is very thick. Serve hot or cold. (140 calories per serving)

Nancy M. Butts, San Diego, Calif.

CRAB AND VEGETABLE FRITTATA
Serves 6

1 can crabmeat or 8 ounces fresh or
   frozen crabmeat
2 tablespoons butter or oleo
2/3 cup chopped onion
1/4 cup sliced mushrooms
1/4 teaspoon black pepper
1/2 cup non-fat milk
1 clove crushed garlic
1 cup chopped asparagus
1-1/2 teaspoons salt
3 eggs
1/2 cup grated Parmesan cheese

Drain and slice crab. Melt butter in large skillet. Add garlic, onion, asparagus, and mushrooms; sauté until tender. Add salt and pepper. Cook, covered, 5 to 7 minutes. Beat eggs, milk, and cheese. Combine crab and all ingredients in buttered casserole. Bake at 350 degrees for 20 minutes or until brown. Garnish with parsley.

1966 Queen Carole Cota Gelfuso

BAKED HALIBUT WITH CHEESE SAUCE
Serves 4

2 halibut fillets (1-1/2 pounds)
1/2 teaspoon butter or margarine
1/4 pound grated cheddar cheese
1 egg, well-beaten
1-1/2 teaspoons salt, divided
1/4 teaspoon pepper, divided
1/4 teaspoon dry mustard
1 cup milk
4 sprigs parsley

Put halibut fillets in greased baking pan. Sprinkle with 1 teaspoon of the salt, 1/8 teaspoon pepper, and 1/2 teaspoon melted butter. Bake in very hot 450-degree oven until fish can be flaked with a fork. Mix grated cheese, beaten egg, dry mustard, 1/2 teaspoon salt, and 1/8 teaspoon pepper. Scald milk and slowly stir it into cheese mixture. Then cook this slowly in double boiler until smooth, thick sauce is made. Put fish on warm platter; pour on cheese sauce and garnish with parsley. Serve immediately.

Suzan L. Wiener, Spring Hill, Fla.

SAVORY SPANISH TUNA LOAF
Serves 6-8

2 (12-1/2-ounce) cans tuna, drained
   and flaked
1-1/2 cups fresh bread crumbs
1/2 cup mayonnaise
1/4 cup celery, chopped
1/4 cup onion, chopped
1/4 cup bell pepper, chopped
3 tablespoons fresh lemon juice
2 eggs
2 tablespoons paprika
Spanish Sauce (recipe follows)

Combine all ingredients except Spanish Sauce. Place in a greased shallow baking dish; shape into loaf; dust with paprika across top of loaf. Bake at 350 degrees for 40 minutes or until golden brown. Serve with Spanish Sauce.

Spanish Sauce:
Makes 2 cups
1 (14-1/2-ounce) can stewed
   tomatoes
2 teaspoons cornstarch
3 tablespoons fresh lemon juice
1 teaspoon Worcestershire sauce
1/4 teaspoon sugar
1/8 teaspoon liquid hot pepper
   sauce

Combine tomatoes and cornstarch; add remaining ingredients. Over high heat bring to a boil; reduce heat; cook 5 minutes.

Gwen Campbell, Sterling, Va.

OVEN-FRIED CHICKEN PARMESAN
Serves 3-4

1/2 cup (2 ounces) grated Parmesan cheese
1/4 cup flour
1 teaspoon paprika
1/2 teaspoon salt
Dash of pepper
2-1/2- to 3-pound broiler-fryer, cut up
1 egg, slightly beaten
1 tablespoon milk
1/4 cup margarine, melted

Combine cheese, flour, and seasonings. Dip chicken in combined egg and milk; coat with cheese mix-cook. Place browned meat in Crock-pot. Add tomato sauce, onion, and green pepper. Cook on *low* for 6 to 12 hours, or on *high* for up to 6 hours.

DEVILED CHICKEN WITH CORN BREAD TOPPING
Serves 4

1 onion, chopped
3 tablespoons butter or margarine
1/4 cup flour
1 tablespoon chicken bouillon granules
1 cup milk
1/2 cup light cream
1 teaspoon Worcestershire sauce
1 tablespoon prepared mustard
1/4 teaspoon fresh lemon juice
4 cups cooked chicken, diced
2 cups frozen mixed vegetables, thawed
Salt and pepper to taste
1 package corn bread mix

Sauté onion in butter until soft; blend in flour and chicken bouillon granules. Stir in milk and cream; add Worcestershire sauce, mustard, and lemon juice; cook until mixture thickens. Add chicken, mixed vegetables, salt and pepper. Turn into 1-1/2-quart casserole. Prepare corn bread mix according to package directions. Carefully spoon corn bread mixture over top. Bake at 375 degrees for 30

minutes or until corn bread has risen and is golden brown.

Gwen Campbell, Sterling, VA

ORIENTAL RAINBOW CHICKEN
Serves 4

2 tablespoons vegetable oil
1 tablespoon toasted sesame oil
1 small slice ginger root, cut into threads
1 tablespoon garlic, minced
2 whole chicken breasts, cut into 1-1/2-inch pieces
1 yellow pepper, cut into threads
1 red pepper, cut into threads
1 green pepper, cut into threads
1/2 pound fresh snow peas
1/2 pound fresh broccoli florets
1 cup green onion, sliced diagonally
2/3 cup teriyaki sauce
1 tablespoon cornstarch

Heat a wok or heavy skillet; add vegetable oil, toasted sesame oil, ginger threads, and garlic; stir-fry 10 seconds until fragrant. Add chicken; stir-fry 3 minutes. Add rainbow vegetables; stir-fry, stirring constantly, for 3 minutes. Combine teriyaki sauce and cornstarch; pour over chicken/vegetable mixture. Allow to thicken. Remove to a warmed platter; serve with cellophane noodles or hot rice.

Gwen Campbell, Sterling, Va.

YOGURT MARINATED CHICKEN

1 broiler chicken, cut into serving-size pieces
2 tablespoons lemon juice
1 cup plain yogurt
1/4 inch fresh ginger, minced
2 cloves garlic, minced
1/2 teaspoon ground cardamom
1/2 teaspoon chili powder
1/2 teaspoon cinnamon

Combine all the ingredients and marinate the chicken overnight. Bake at 375 degrees for 40-45 minutes, basting occasionally.

This chicken has a mild flavor and is very moist. It is just as delicious served cold as well.

Lillian Smith, Montreal, Quebec, Canada

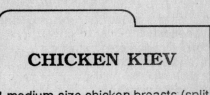

CHICKEN KIEV

4 medium-size chicken breasts (split lengthwise, skinned and boned)
Salt
1 tablespoon chopped green onion
1 tablespoon chopped parsley
1/4 pound (1 stick) butter or margarine
2 beaten eggs
Flour and dry bread crumbs

Place each piece of chicken (skinned and boned) between two pieces of waxed paper. Pound with wooden mallet to form cutlets not quite 1/4 inch thick. Peel off paper and sprinkle with salt. Place a piece of butter at each end of cutlet. Sprinkle with parsley and onion. Roll meat as for jelly roll, tucking in sides and ends. Dust each roll with flour and dip in beaten egg, then roll in bread crumbs. Chill thoroughly at least one hour. Fry in hot fat about 15 minutes or until golden brown. Serve with mushroom sauce, if desired.

Karin Shea Fedders, Dameron, Md.

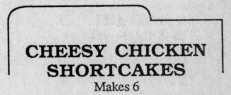

CHEESY CHICKEN SHORTCAKES
Makes 6

1/3 pound processed soft cheese
1/3 cup chicken broth
1-1/2 cups cubed cooked chicken
6 baking powder biscuits
Butter or margarine
Parsley (for garnish)

In the top of a double boiler melt cheese. Add chicken broth gradually, stirring constantly until sauce thickens. Add chicken. Split hot biscuits; spread with butter. Put biscuits together with a filling of hot chicken-cheese mixture; add parsley.

Suzan L. Wiener, Spring Hill, Fla.

SALMON CIRCLE LOAF

Serves 6 to 8

2 cups or a pound salmon, flaked and deboned
1-1/2 cups cooked tomatoes
1-3/4 cups stale bread crumbs
2 tablespoons melted margarine
1 egg, well beaten
1 tablespoon lemon juice
1 teaspoon salt
1/4 teaspoon pepper

Mix ingredients lightly. Pour into well-greased circular mold. Bake in 425 degree oven for 20 minutes. Turn out onto round platter. Fill center with buttered peas and surround with tiny, whole beets.

Margaret Packard, Turner, ME

SHRIMP BARCELONA

Serves 6
259 calories per serving

1/2 cup finely chopped onions
2 cloves garlic, crushed
3 tablespoons vegetable oil
1 pound peeled, deveined raw shrimp
1 can (15-ounce) tomato sauce
1/4 cup sherry
1 cup fresh mushrooms, sliced, or use 1 (4-ounce) can sliced mushrooms
1 cup chopped green peppers
2 tablespoons snipped parsley
1 teaspoon chili powder
1/2 teaspoon salt
1/2 teaspoon thyme leaves, crushed
1/8 teaspoon ground black pepper
3 cups hot cooked rice

In large skillet cook onions and garlic in oil until tender crisp. Add remaining ingredients except rice. Simmer 10 minutes, or until shrimp are pink and vegetables are tender crisp. Serve over beds of fluffy rice.

CRAB BARBECUE ON RUSKS

1 package (4 ounce) Holland round rusks (Zwieback)
1 package (3 ounce) cream cheese (more if desired)
1 pound crabmeat
1/3 cup bottled barbecue sauce
1/2 cup salad dressing or mayonnaise
12 thick tomato slices
6 slices sharp Cheddar slices

Spread 12 rusks with cream cheese. Combine crabmeat with barbecue sauce and salad dressing. Heap crab mixture on rusks. Top each with a slice of tomato. Cut cheese slices in 4 strips and cross over tomato. Bake in moderate oven at 350 degrees until cheese melts, about 15 minutes.

Karin Shea Fedders, Dameron, MD

TUNA BAKE ITALIAN STYLE

Serves 6

8 ounce package macaroni, cooked and drained
7 ounce can tuna, drained and flaked
15 ounce can tomato sauce
1/2 cup grated Parmesan cheese
1 tablespoon parsley flakes
1 teaspoon instant minced onion
1/2 teaspoon mixed Italian seasoning
1 chicken bouillon cube
1/4 cup boiling water
1 cup shredded Mozzarella cheese (4 ounces)

Combine macaroni, tuna, tomato sauce, Parmesan cheese, parsley, onion, and Italian seasoning. Dissolve bouillon cube in boiling water; add to macaroni mixture. Turn into greased 2-quart casserole. Bake in 350 degree oven for 30 minutes. Sprinkle with Mozzarella cheese. Continue baking 3 to 5 minutes or until cheese in melted.

A good family dish.

Barbara Beauregard-Smith, South Australia

BARBECUED SPICY SHRIMP

Serves 4

2 pounds raw, medium shrimp
1 cup olive oil
1/4 cup chili sauce
1 teaspoon salt
1 teaspoon oregano
1/2 teaspoon bottled red pepper sauce
2 garlic cloves, mashed
3 tablespoons lemon juice

Shell and devein shrimp, leaving tail attached. In bowl, mix shrimp with remaining ingredients until well blended; marinate at room temperature one hour. Spear shrimp on skewers; grill 8 inches above gray coals 5 minutes per side.

Annie Cmehil, New Castle, IN

CRAB RANGOON

1/2 pound fresh crab, drained and chopped
8 ounces cream cheese, room temperature
1/2 teaspoon Worcestershire sauce
1/4 teaspoon garlic salt
3 dozen wonton wrappers
3 cups cooking oil

Combine crab, cream cheese, Worcestershire sauce and garlic salt; mix until well combined. Place 1/4 teaspoon of filling in center of wonton wrapper (a large amount will only crack a wonton wrapper). Moisten top 2 ends of triangle and seal together with fork. Heat oil to 350 degrees; deepfry rangoon until golden brown. Dip in sweet and sour sauce and Chinese hot mustard. Uncooked crab rangoons may be frozen and deep-fried directly from the freezer.

They really taste just like those found on a Chinese Pu Pu Platter. We love them as a snack or with a meal.

Jane Weimann, Woostock, CT

SPOONBREAD CHICKEN PIE

Serves 8

Chicken Filling:
6 tablespoons butter
1/4 cup chopped celery
6 tablespoons flour
2-1/2 cups chicken broth
1 teaspoon onion salt
1/2 teaspoon pepper
1 tablespoon dried parsley
3 cups chopped cooked chicken

Spoon Bread:
3 eggs
1 cup self-rising cornmeal mix
2 cups boiling water
1 cup buttermilk

Melt butter in saucepan. Sauté celery in butter. Add flour and stir well. Add chicken broth and stir until mixture thickens. Add onion salt, pepper, and parsley. Stir in chicken. Pour into 3 quart casserole and bake at 400 degrees for 10 minutes.

While casserole bakes, prepare spoon bread. Beat eggs; add cornmeal, boiling water, and buttermilk. Stir well after each ingredient is added. Pour mixture on top of hot chicken mixture and return to oven at 400 degrees. Continue to bake 30-40 minutes, or until brown.

Mrs. Terry A. Cobb, San Jose, Calif.

MEXICALI CHICKEN

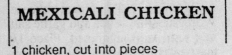

1 chicken, cut into pieces
1/2 cup shortening
1 small onion, chopped
1 clove garlic, mashed
2 stalks celery, chopped
1/2 green pepper, chopped
1 cup catsup
1 cup water
2 tablespoons brown sauce
2 tablespoons Worcestershire sauce
1 teaspoon salt
1/2 teaspoon cumin

Brown chicken pieces in shortening. Remove from pan and place in 9 x 13-inch baking dish, skin side down. Add onion and garlic to pan in which chicken was cooked; stir over low heat until onion is wilted. Add remaining ingredients; bring to a boil. Pour over chicken pieces in baking dish. Bake uncovered in 350 degree oven for 30 minutes. Turn chicken pieces over and continue to cook uncovered for another 30 minutes or until tender.

Good served with rice, cornbread, and green salad.

Eleanor V. Craycraft, Santa Monica, Calif.

PICKLED CHICKEN GIZZARDS

1 quart chicken gizzards
1 cup water
1 cup cider vinegar
1 sliced onion
4 tablespoons pickling spice
1 tablespoon sugar

Cut chicken gizzards in half and cook thoroughly. Place in a quart jar and pour remaining ingredients over gizzards. Place a tight lid on jar and let set at least 8 hours, turning several times.

Lucy Dowd, Sequim, Wash.

CHICKEN LIVERS

1/2-3/4 pound chicken livers
1/4 cup all-purpose flour
1 teaspoon salt
1/8 teaspoon pepper
1 teaspoon oregano, crushed
2 tablespoons vegetable oil
Lemon juice

Dredge livers in flour mixed with salt, pepper, and oregano. Heat oil in skillet. Add livers; fry 10 minutes, turning frequently. Squeeze fresh lemon juice over top before serving.

Marcella Swigert, Monroe City, MO

TURKEY MEATBALLS

1-1/2 to 2 pounds uncooked turkey
1 cup Italian style bread crumbs
1 teaspoon fennel seed
1/2 to 1 teaspoon crushed red pepper
1/2 teaspoon salt
1/2 cup finely chopped onion
Few shakes garlic powder
2 eggs (or 1/2 cup Egg Beaters)

Mix ingredients well; form into meatballs. Bake at 375 degrees on a cookie sheet sprayed with non-stick cooking spray for 20 minutes, turning once. Add to spaghetti sauce, continue to simmer until sauce is done.

Peggy F. Revels, Woodruff, SC

TURKEY FRIED RICE

1 cup diced roasted turkey
1 tablespoon soy sauce
1/4 cup oil
1 cup uncooked rice
2 cups chicken bouillon (2 teaspoons instant bouillon or 2 bouillon cubes dissolved in 2 cups boiling water)
2 tablespoons chopped onion
1/4 cup sliced celery
1/4 cup minced green pepper
1 egg slightly beaten
1/2 cup finely-shredded head lettuce or Chinese cabbage

Pour soy sauce over turkey and let stand while starting to prepare rice. Heat oil in large skillet and add rice. Fry, stirring frequently, until rice is golden brown. Add bouillon and turkey. Cover and simmer until rice is almost tender and liquid is absorbed. Add onion, celery, and green pepper; cook uncovered a few minutes. Push rice to side of skillet and add egg. Stir slightly and cook until almost set. Then combine with rice mixture. Stir in cabbage or lettuce and serve immediately.

Corena J. Bennington, Whitestown, Ind.

MOCK CHICKEN - FRIED STEAK

Serves 8

1 beaten egg
1 cup corn flake crumbs
1/4 cup milk
1 teaspoon onion powder
1 teaspoon chili powder
1/2 teaspoon salt
1 pound beef
2 tablespoons cooking oil

Combine egg, 1/2 cup corn flake crumbs, milk, onion, chili powder, and salt; add ground beef and mix well. Shape into 8 patties. Coat with remaining corn flake crumbs. Cook in hot oil over medium heat for about 3-5 minutes on each side or until done.　　Sharon Crider, Evansville, WI

CHICKEN CACCIATORE

Serves 4
159 calories per serving

4 chicken breasts, skinned
2 small green peppers, minced
1 clove garlic, minced
2 tablespoons chopped pimentos
1 bay leaf
1/8 teaspoon thyme
1 tablespoons dried parsley
1 cup mushrooms, chopped
2 cups stewed tomatoes

Combine all ingredients; simmer 45 minutes. Serve over cooked rice.
Betty Peel, Milford, OH

GOOEY CHICKEN

8-ounce bottle Russian dressing
10-ounce jar apricot preserves
1 package onion soup mix
2-1/2 to 3 pound chicken, cut up
Seasoned salt and freshly ground pepper to taste

Combine dressing, preserves and onion soup mix in bowl. Pour into 9 x

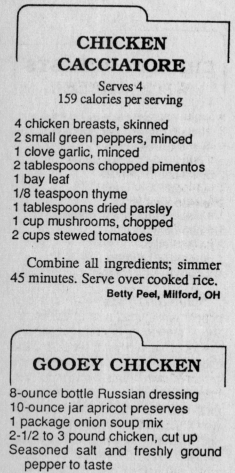

13-inch baking dish. Sprinkle chicken with seasoned salt and pepper. Place chicken, skin side down, in baking dish. Bake at 375 degrees for 45 minutes, basting occasionally. Turn chicken over and baste. Bake for 35 minutes more, basting occasionally.

An excellent main dish (when doubled) for a buffet dinner, served with wild rice and a green salad.
Frances K. McKinney, Macon, MO

BANDIT WINGS

12-14 chicken wings
1/2 teaspoon salt
1/8 teaspoon pepper
8 tablespoons margarine
2 tablespoons vegetable oil
1/2 cup taco sauce
1/4 cup barbeque sauce
1/4 cup French dressing
1/8 teaspoon red pepper sauce
1/8 teaspoon Worcestershire sauce

Preheat oven to 300 degrees. Snip off wing tips at 1st joint. Cut apart two remaining parts at joint. Sprinkle with salt and pepper. Heat 2 tablespoons oleo and oil in large skillet. Cook half the wings until golden brown. Repeat with remaining wing parts. Melt remaining 6 tablespoons oleo in saucepan. Blend in remaining ingredients. Arrange wings in shallow baking pan, brushing enough sauce over wings to coat evenly. Bake until hot, 5-8 minutes. Arrange wings on platter. Pour remaining sauce into bowl and serve as a dip.
Dorothy Sorensen, Muskego, WI

CHICKEN SHEPHERD'S PIE

Serves 4

1 (2-1/2 pound) broiler-fryer, cut up
1 stalk celery, cut up
5 peppercorns
4 large potatoes, pared and quartered
1 teaspoon salt
1 (10-ounce) package frozen mixed vegetables

1/4 cup minced onion
1/3 cup milk
3 tablespoons butter or margarine

Cook chicken in water to cover, with celery and peppercorns, until tender, about 45 minutes. Strain and reserve 2 cups broth. Cool chicken. Skin; bone; and cut up enough chicken to make 2 cups. Cook potatoes in large saucepan with salt and water to cover, until tender, about 30 minutes. Combine chicken broth, mixed vegetables, onion, and a sprinkle of salt in a large saucepan. Bring to a boil. Lower heat and simmer 5 minutes. Stir in chicken. Heat milk and margarine in a small saucepan. Drain and mash potatoes. Beat in hot milk mixture until potatoes are fluffy. Stir 1-1/2 cups mashed potatoes into the chicken mixture to thicken. Spoon into a 10-inch pie plate, quiche dish, or 6-cup shallow dish. Pipe remaining potatoes around edge of chicken mixture. Bake in a 400 degree oven for 20 minutes or until mixture is bubbly and potatoes are browned. Garnish with parsley, if desired.

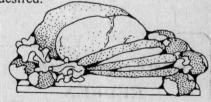

BUFFALO CHICKEN WINGS

15-20 chicken wings
Flour, salt and pepper
1 stick butter
1 tablespoon white vinegar
1/4 cup hot sauce (not Tabasco), more or less according to taste

Dredge wings in flour, salt and pepper. Deep fry until brown and crisp, about 12 minutes. (Wings may also be pan fried or baked). Keep hot.

Melt butter in saucepan. Add vinegar and hot sauce to taste. Put hot wings in a large bowl and pour sauce over wings. Toss until wings are well coated with sauce.
Barbara Reed, Wyandanch, NY

CHICKEN SKILLET RATATOUILLE

Serves 8

1 small eggplant, pared and diced
1 small zucchini, pared and diced
1 onion, pared, halved, and thinly sliced
1 clove garlic, minced
2 cups canned tomatoes, undrained, broken up
Salt and pepper to taste
1/2 teaspoon oregano
1 pound chicken fillets, cut in cubes (2 skinless boneless breasts)

Spray a large non-stick skillet with cooking spray. Combine all ingredients, except chicken. Cover and simmer for 10 minutes, stirring frequently until vegetables are tender-crisp.

Meanwhile, cut chicken into cubes. Cook and stir in skillet, uncovered, until nearly all the liquid is evaporated, and chicken cubes are white, about 4 minutes. Good with cooked rice.

Sylvia Zindman, Oceanside, NY

BAKED CHICKEN REUBEN

4 whole chicken breasts, halved and boned
1/4 teaspoon salt
1/8 teaspoon pepper
1 can (16 ounce) sauerkraut; drained
4 slices (4 x 6 inches square) natural Swiss cheese
1-1/4 cups bottled Thousand Island Salad Dressing. (Can use Weight Watchers for less calories)
1 tablespoon chopped fresh parsley

Place chicken in greased baking dish. Sprinkle on salt and pepper. Add sauerkraut over chicken; top with cheese. Spoon dressing evenly over cheese. Cover and bake in 325 degree oven about 1-1/2 hours. Sprinkle with chopped parsley to serve.

Roselyn Finan, Fort Wayne, IN

CHICKEN-ASPARAGUS-CHEESE BAKE

Serves 6

1 pound fresh asparagus, cut up and cooked, (or 1 package frozen cut-up asparagus, cooked)
2 cups sliced cooked chicken
1/2 teaspoon each marjoram and sage
1 cup unsifted Gold Medal flour
2 teaspoons baking powder
1 teaspoon salt
2 eggs, beaten
1/2 cup milk
1 cup grated Cheddar cheese
Cheese Sauce

Heat oven to 350 degrees (moderate). Line 11-1/2 x 7-1/2 x 1-1/2" baking dish with layer of asparagus. Place chicken atop asparagus. Sprinkle herbs over chicken. Stir flour, baking powder, and salt together in mixing bowl. Beat eggs, milk, and cheese; add to flour mixture. Beat batter well and pour over chicken, spreading evenly. Bake 25 to 30 minutes. Cut into squares and serve hot with Cheese sauce.

EASY CHICKEN MUSHROOM BAKE

2-1/2 to 3 pounds frying chicken, cut up or quartered
1-1/4 cups (10-1/2-ounce can) condensed cream of mushroom, celery or chicken soup
1/4 cup milk
1/2 cup (4-ounce can) drained mushroom stems and pieces
1/2 cup (1 envelope) dry onion chicken mix

Preheat oven to 375 degrees. Arrange chicken pieces in 13 x 9-inch pan. In medium mixing bowl, combine remaining ingredients; mix well. Pour over chicken. Bake at 375 degrees for about 1 hour until tender. Serve mushroom mixture as gravy.

Barbara Beauregard-Smith, Northfield, South Australia

LO-CAL CHICKEN DIVAN

Serves 4, 235 calories per person

2 large chicken breasts, split and remove skin
3/4 cup sherry wine
3/4 cup lo-cal Caesar dressing
1 tablespoon dried parsley flakes

Place chicken in a nonstick shallow baking pan or lightly oil a shallow baking dish. Vigorously mix the wine, salad dressing and parsley together until well blended. Pour over the chicken. Bake 50 minutes in a preheated 350 degree over, basting occasionally. Serve the chicken with cooked frozen broccoli or you favorite vegetable. Pour the sauce the broccoli.

Mrs. Norma DesRoches, Warwick, RI

CHICKEN BREASTS WITH CHEESE

3 whole chicken breasts, skinned, boned, halved, and flattened
Salt and pepper
1/2 cup butter or margarine
2 tablespoons parsley
1 teaspoon marjoram
2 teaspoons thyme
1/4 pound mozzarella cheese
1/2 cup flour
2 beaten eggs
1 cup bread crumbs
1/2 cup dry white wine

Sprinkle chicken with salt and pepper and spread on half the butter. Blend remaining butter with parsley, marjoram, and thyme; set aside. Cut cheese into 6 sticks. Place one in the center of each breast. Roll up and tuck in ends. Roll breasts in flour and eggs; then roll in bread crumbs. Place in well buttered baking pan. Melt butter and herb mixture; pour evenly over breasts. Bake 30 minutes. Then pour wine into baking pan. Bake 25 minutes longer, basting frequently.

Leona Teodori, Warren, Mich.

MANDARIN CHICKEN

3 pounds chicken pieces
1/2 cup graham wafer crumbs
1 teaspoon salt
1/2 teaspoon garlic powder
1/2 teaspoon paprika
1/2 teaspoon pepper
2 eggs
1 tablespoon milk

Combine crumbs and spices in a plastic bag. Mix eggs and beat well with 1 tablespoon milk. Dip chicken pieces one at a time into egg mixture and then shake in the bag of crumbs and spices. Place chicken on lightly greased baking sheet. Bake at 425 degrees for 20 minutes. Turn and bake another 15 minutes or until done.

Mandarin Orange Sauce:

1 can mandarin oranges, drained (284 ml can), reserve liquid
2 tablespoons cornstarch
1 tablespoon sugar
1 teaspoon ketchup

Combine reserved mandarin juice with enough water to make 1 cup of liquid. Pour juice mixture into sauce pan. Add cornstarch, sugar, and ketchup, bring to a boil. Cook 2 minutes, stirring constantly. Add mandarin orange sections. Pour sauce over hot chicken on serving platter. Serve with white rice and broccoli.

Lynne Hurlburt, Welland, Ontario, Canada

BAKED CHOP SUEY
Serves 8

2 cups diced, cooked chicken
2 tablespoons margarine
1-1/2 cups chopped onion
1-1/2 cups chopped celery
1 cup chopped green pepper
3 tablespoons chopped pimiento
1/2 cup *uncooked* long grain rice
1 can mushroom soup
2 cups milk
2 tablespoons soy sauce
1 (3-ounce) can chow mein noodles

Sauté vegetables in margarine until golden. Add remaining ingredients, except noodles. Turn into

greased 13 x 9-inch casserole; cover. Bake in 350 degree oven for 1 hour, stirring occasionally. Add more milk, if needed. Sprinkle noodles on top and return to oven, uncovered, for 5 minutes.

Margaret Hamfeldt, Louisville, Ky.

WORKING GIRL'S CHICKEN

4 chicken legs
4 chicken breasts
1 teaspoon salt
1/2 teaspoon pepper
1/8 teaspoon garlic powder
1 can cream of mushroom soup
1 soup can milk

Season chicken with salt, pepper, and small amount of garlic powder. Dilute soup with milk. Place chicken in buttered casserole dish. Cover with soup. Bake at 400 degrees for 1 hour or until tender.

Donna Flick, Kalamazoo, MI

EASY PINEAPPLE CHICKEN

1 pound chicken breasts, cubed
1 can pineapple chunks
1 green pepper, cut in strips
1 red pepper, cut in strips
1 carrot, sliced thin
1/4 cup vinegar
2 teaspoons sugar (or substitute)
1 tablespoon cornstarch
2 tablespoons soy sauce
3/4 cup chicken broth

Bring broth to a boil; add chicken cubes. Simmer 10 minutes, stirring occasionally. Add undrained pineapple, green and red pepper slices, carrot slices, vinegar and sugar; bring to boil.

Stir cornstarch into soy sauce until smooth; stir into chicken mixture. Bring to boil, stirring constantly. Lower heat, cover and simmer 10 minutes. Serve with rice.

Helen Keillor, Berwyn, Canada

JEWELED CHICKEN SQUARES
Serves 6

1 cup chopped onion
1 cup chopped celery
1 tablespoon butter
2 tablespoons flour
1 cup double strength chicken broth *or* 1 cup chicken broth and 1 teaspoon chicken bouillon powder *or* 1 cube—dissolved in hot broth.
1 cup milk
3/4 teaspoon poultry seasoning
1/8 teaspoon pepper
2 cups chopped, cooked chicken
2 cups cooked rice
4 eggs, beaten
1 (8-ounce) can jellied cranberry sauce, diced
1/2 cup buttered soft bread crumbs

Sauté onions and celery in butter. Blend in flour. Add broth, milk, and seasonings. Cook until thickened. Add chicken and rice. Blend in eggs. Fold in cranberry sauce. Turn into greased shallow 2-quart casserole, sprinkle with crumbs. Bake 350 degrees for 30 minutes until firm in center. Cut into squares.

Ann Sterzer, Lincoln, Neb.

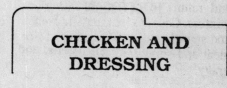

CHICKEN AND DRESSING

3/4 cup minced onion
1-1/2 cups chopped celery
1 stick butter
9 cups soft bread, cubed
2 teaspoons salt
1/2 teaspoon sage
1/2 teaspoon pepper

In a large skillet, cook and stir onion and celery in butter until onion is tender. Stir in about 1/3 of the bread cubes. Turn into large bowl. Add remaining ingredients. Add enough chicken broth to make mixing easy. Spoon over chicken. Bake in a 375 degree oven for 1 hour

Marcella Swigert, Monroe City, MO

STUFFED PORK ROAST

Serves 6-8

1 (4-5 pound) rolled pork roast
2 teaspoons poultry seasoning
   (divided)
2 teaspoons salt (divided)
3/4 teaspoon pepper (divided)
3 cups bread crumbs
3/4 cup chopped celery
1/2 cup chopped onion
1/2 cup butter or margarine

Season roast with 1 teaspoon poultry seasoning, 1 teaspoon salt, and 1/2 teaspoon pepper. Combine remaining ingredients for stuffing. Fill roast cavity with stuffing. Skewer edges. Place fat side up on roasting pan. Bake at 350 degrees for 1-1/2 to 2 hours, or until roast tests done.

well on all sides in hot fat in deep skillet or Dutch oven. Add chopped onion and saute until lightly browned and tender. Add 1-1/2 cups water, salt, pepper, parsley, and bay leaf; bring to boil. Cover and simmer until meat is tender, 3 to 4 hours, adding more water if necessary. Discard parsley and bay leaf. Add vegetables and cook 20 to 30 minutes or until tender. Remove meat and vegetables from skillet; keep warm. Measure drippings, add water to make 2 cups and return to skillet. Stir in flour mixture. Cook and stir until thickened and smooth; adjust seasonings. Slice meat and serve with vegetables and gravy.

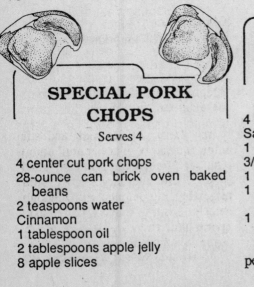

SPECIAL PORK CHOPS

Serves 4

4 center cut pork chops
28-ounce can brick oven baked
   beans
2 teaspoons water
Cinnamon
1 tablespoon oil
2 tablespoons apple jelly
8 apple slices

In skillet, brown chops evenly in oil, about 10 minutes each side; drain chops on paper towels. Pour beans into 2-quart casserole; place chops on top of beans. Bake at 350 degrees for 45 minutes. In small bowl, combine jelly and water. Baste chops with mixture; arrange apple slices on top. Sprinkle with cinnamon. Return to oven and continue baking for another 15 minutes.

Judy M. Sax, San Antonio, TX

CRANBERRY CHOPS

Serves 6

6 pork chops, 1/2 inch thick
2 tablespoons butter
2 tablespoons oil
1 cup chopped onions
1/3 cup chopped carrots
1-1/4 cups chicken broth
2 tablespoons sugar
2 tablespoons red wine vinegar
1/2 cup cranberries

Trim chops, if necessary. Heat butter and oil in a heavy frypan. Brown chops on both sides; set aside. Sauté onions and carrots until brown and tender. Return chops to pan. Add chicken broth. Cover; cook 20 minutes until pork is done. Remove chops and keep warm. Add sugar, vinegar, and cranberries. Cook until cranberries pop. Heat chops in sauce before serving.

Petty Fowler Revels, Woodruff, S.C.

PORK CHOPS WITH HAWAIIAN RICE

Serves 4

4 lean pork chops
Salt and pepper
1 cup uncooked rice
3/4 cup chopped green pepper
1 (15 ounce) can tomato sauce
1 (13-1/4 ounce) can pineapple tidbits, undrained
1 tablespoon vinegar

Sprinkle chops with salt and pepper. Brown well on both sides in skillet, and pour off fat. Add 1 cup water, remaining ingredients, and salt to taste. Mix well. Simmer, tightly covered, for 45 minutes or until rice is tender.

Beverly Brannon, Vidor, TX

PORK CHOP BAKE

Serves 4

4 pork chops
4 potatoes, peeled and sliced
2 onions, sliced
1 can lima beans
1 teaspoon sage

Parboil potatoes. In a lightly greased hot skillet, sear pork chops. In 2-quart baking dish, layer lima beans, potatoes and onions.

Lay pork chops on top; season with sage. Cover and bake at 350 degrees for 1 hour.

Note: Canned corn, sweet potatoes or apples can be substituted for lima beans.

June Harding, Ferndale, MI

BBQ PORK CHOPS

6 servings, 2 chops each

12 pork chops
3 medium onions cut in slices and
   separated into rings
2 cups tomato juices
2 tablespoons vinegar
1 teaspoons dry mustard
1 tablespoon Worcestershire sauce
1/2 cup finely chopped onion
1/2 teaspoon chili powder
1/2 teaspoon salt
Dash pepper

Brown chops on both sides. Arrange in roaster or large casserole. Cover each chop with sliced onion rings.

Sauce:
Combine all sauce ingredients together in medium size saucepan. Bring to boil. Simmer slowly for 10 minutes. Pour over chops in roaster, cover. Bake in 350 degrees oven for 30 minutes. Remove cover and bake for 15 minutes more.

Carole Vtilleux, Ontario, Canada

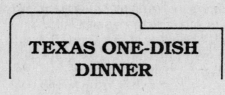

PIZZA MEATBALLS

1 cup ground beef
1 cup dried bread crumbs
1/2 cup milk
2 tablespoons instant minced onion
1 teaspoon garlic salt
1/2 teaspoon pepper
1/2 (8-ounce) package Mozzarella cheese cut into 12 bite size cubes
3 tablespoons flour
2 tablespoons salad oil
12 to 15-1/2 - ounce jar pizza sauce
4 cups hot cooked rice
Parsley for garnish

About 45 minutes before serving: In medium brown with fork, mix well first 6 ingredients; shape mixture into 12 large meatballs with 1 cube of cheese in center of each, making sure that cheese is completely covered with meat mixture. On waxed paper, coat each meatball lightly with flour. In 12-inch skillet over medium heat, in hot salad oil, cook meatballs until browned on all sides. Spoon off fat. Add pizza sauce to meatballs in skillet; heat to boiling. Reduce heat to low; cover and simmer 10 minutes. Serve on rice

Mrs. Judy M. Sax, San Antonio, TX

PIZZA PORCUPINE BALLS

Serves 2-4

1 pound hamburger
1/4 to 1/2 cup uncooked rice
1/2 cup water
1/3 cup onion
1 teaspoon salt
15-1/2-ounce jar pizza sauce
1/8 teaspoon garlic powder
1/2 teaspoon celery salt
1/8 teaspoon pepper
2 teaspoons Worcestershire sauce
1 cup grated Mozzarella cheese
1/2 teaspoon chili powder

Mix meat, rice, water, onion, salts, garlic powder, pepper and Worcestershire sauce. Shape mixture into balls; place into ungreased baking dish. Mix together chili powder and

pizza sauce; pour over balls. Bake at 350 degrees for 45 minutes, covered with foil. Uncover; bake 15 minutes longer.

Melanie Knoll, Marshalltown, IA

TEXAS ONE-DISH DINNER

2 pounds ground beef
1 chopped onion
1/2 cup chopped celery
1/4 teaspoon black pepper
1/2 teaspoon salt
1 (8 ounce) package noodles
1 can niblets corn
1 can tomato soup
1/2 cup grated Cheddar cheese

Brown beef, onion, celery, salt, and pepper. Cook noodles and drain. Place half the noodles in buttered casserole. Cover with meat mixture. Add corn and tomato soup. Add remaining noodles and top with grated cheese. Bake at 350 degrees for 25 minutes.

Peggy Fowler Revels, Woodruff, SC

HAMBURGER CHOP SUEY

2 pounds ground beef
2 tablespoons oil
1-1/2 cups chopped onion
1-1/2 cups chopped celery
1 can water chestnuts, drained and sliced
1 can bean sprouts, drained
2 (10-1/2 ounce) cans cream of mushroom soup
1-1/2 cups warm water
1/2 cup rice (not instant)
1/4 cup soy sauce

Brown beef in oil. Drain off fat. Combine beef with rest of ingredients in large bowl. Mix well. Pour into 9x13 inch pan. Cover and bake in 350 degree oven for 1 hour, or until vegetables are done. Serve over heated chow mein noodles.

Mrs. Laddie Jirovsky, Hooper, NE

DELICIOUS SLOPPY JOES WITH CHEESE

1 large onion, chopped
2 cloves fresh garlic, chopped
1 pound ground beef
1/2 teaspoon seasoning salt
1 tablespoon margarine
2 teaspoons Worcestershire sauce
2 tablespoons brown sugar
2 tablespoons vinegar (white)
1-12 ounce bottle chili sauce
1/2 cup diced Cheddar cheese

Saute onion and garlic in melted margarine, lightly. Set aside. Brown ground beef, drain well.

Put meat in pot with all ingredients, except cheese. Cook slowly on top of stove, stir occasionally. Cook 30-45 minutes. During the last few minutes, add cheese, until melted. Serve on rolls. ENJOY.

Camille Mucha, Santa Monica, CA

CHEESY CORNED BEEF LASAGNA

Serves 6-8

8 ounce package lasagna noodles
1-10 ounce package cream style corn
1-12 ounce can corned beef
2 - 10-1/2 ounce cans of condensed cream of chicken soup
1/2 cup chopped onions
1/2 cup chopped ripe olives
2 tablespoons chopped green pepper
2-1/2 cups of shredded American cheese

Cook noodles according to package directions; drain. Cook corn according to package directions. Crumble corned beef into a large bowl. Add soup, onions, olives, and green pepper. Stir in corn. Place 1/4 cup of sauce in a greased 11 x 7 inch baking dish. Alternate 3 layers of noodles, sauce and cheese, ending with cheese. Bake at 350 degrees for 45 minutes. Let stand 10 minutes before cutting.

Joy B. Shamway, Freeport, IL

L'ORANGE FILLET OF SOLE

1 pound sole fillets
1 cup sour cream
2 green onions, chopped
4 ounces small shrimp
6 ounces orange juice
Grated Parmesan cheese

Place half the sole in a greased baking dish. Cover with half the sour cream and half the green onions. Sprinkle with all of the shrimp. Repeat layers of sole, sour cream and onions. Pour orange juice over entire surface; sprinkle with Parmesan cheese. Bake at 350 degrees for 30 minutes.

Lillian Smith, Quebec, Canada

PEPPER STEAKS
Serves 4-5

1 pound boneless round stead (1/4-inch thick)
1/2 cup all purpose flour
3 tablespoons cooking oil
1 large green pepper, cut in strips
1 medium onion, sliced
1 cup diced celery
1 (16-ounce) can tomatoes
1 clove garlic, pressed
1/2 cup water
1-1/2 teaspoons salt
1/4 teaspoon pepper
1 (8-ounce) package broad egg noodles

Cut steak into strips 1/8-inch wide (it will be easier to cut if partially frozen). Dredge with flour. Add the prepared vegetables, water, and seasonings. Cover and cook over low heat for about 30 minutes. Add more water if necessary; stir occasionally. Meanwhile, cook noodles as directed on package. Drain in colander. Serve steak and sauce over noodles.

Great with a fresh green salad and hot rolls.

Marjorie W. Boxla, Greenfield, Ohio

CHICKEN-FRIED STEAK
Serves 4-6

1-1/2 pounds beef round steak, 1/2-inch thick
1 egg
1 tablespoon milk
1 cup fine cracker crumbs
1/4 cup salad oil

Using a meat mallet, pound steak to 1/4-inch thickness. Cut into serving-size strips. In a pie pan, beat together egg and milk. In another pie pan, place cracker crumbs. Dip meat into egg mixture. Dredge in cracker crumbs.

In large heavy skillet, heat oil. Add coated meat and cook over medium heat until browned on both sides, turning once. Reduce heat and cook, covered, for 45-60 minutes or until meat is tender. Add salt and pepper to taste. Serve immediately.

Annie Cmehil, New Castle, Ind.

STIR-FRY BEEF WITH VEGETABLES
Makes 5 cups

1 pound boneless round steak (3/4-inch thick)
1/2 cup diagonally sliced carrots
1/2 cup diagonally sliced celery
1/2 cup diagonally sliced green onions
1/2 cup broccoli buds
1/2 cup red pepper, sliced
1/2 teaspoon ground ginger
2 tablespoons butter or margarine
1 (10-3/4-ounce) can condensed beefy mushroom soup
1-1/2 cups water
2 (6-ounce) packages frozen pea pods
1 tablespoon cornstarch
1 tablespoon soy sauce
1 teaspoon brown sugar
1/2 teaspoon salt

Freeze meat 1 hour to firm (makes slicing easier); slice into *very* thin strips. In skillet, cook carrots, celery, and onion with ginger in butter until *just* tender; push to one side. Add meat; cook

until color *just* changes (about 3 to 4 minutes). Add remaining ingredients. Cook, stirring until thickened. Serve over rice with additional soy sauce.

Mary Linger, Jacksonville, Fla.

COUNTRY FRIED STEAK

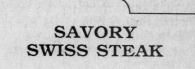

2-1/2 pounds ground beef
3/4 cup evaporated milk
3 tablespoons flour
1 tablespoon salt, pepper
Onions, chopped

Mix all together. Roll out onto floured board until 1/2 inch thick. Cut into squares; brown in skillet. May brown meat with chopped onion for additional flavor. Put in oblong cake pan. Make gravy from drippings. Pour over meat squares; bake at 350 degrees for 20-25 minutes.

Evelyn L. Pore, Kittanning, PA

SAVORY SWISS STEAK

2 pounds round steak
1/4 cup flour
3 tablespoons shortening
1 (12-ounce) can vegetable juice cocktail
1/8 teaspoon pepper
1/4 teaspoon seasoning salt
1 clove garlic, minced
1/2 cup chopped onion
1 (3-ounce) can chopped mushrooms, drained
Few drops hot pepper sauce, optional

Cut steak into 6 equal serving pieces. Coat meat with flour; brown in melted shortening over medium heat. Add vegetable juice cocktail, pepper, seasoning salt, garlic, and onion. Cover and let simmer 1-1/2 hours; add mushrooms and hot pepper sauce, if desired. Cover and simmer an additional 15 minutes until done. This can also be baked in a covered casserole, in 325 degree oven for 1-1/2 to 2 hours. Enjoy!!

Camille Mucha, Santa Monica, Calif.

CORNBREAD CHICKEN BAKE

1 (3-pound) chicken, cooked and boned
1/2 cup margarine
1 cup chopped onion
1 cup chopped celery
Salt and pepper to taste
3 tablespoons flour
3 cups chicken broth

Place chicken in bottom of 13x9x2 inch pan. Sauté onion and celery in 1/2 cup margarine until tender. Blend in 3 tablespoons flour, salt, and pepper. Spoon over chicken. Spoon Cornbread Topping (recipe follows) over casserole. Slowly pour chicken broth over topping. Bake at 350 degrees for 35-40 minutes.

Cornbread Topping:
1 cup flour
1/2 cup cornmeal
1 tablespoon baking powder
2 teaspoons sugar
1/2 teaspoon salt
1/4 teaspoon sage
1/2 teaspoon thyme
1/2 teaspoon pepper
1 tablespoon shortening
3 eggs, slightly beaten
1 cup buttermilk

Combine dry ingredients; cut in shortening, add eggs and buttermilk.
Loretta Alsobrooks, Benton, Il

CHICKEN AND RICE

1 stick margarine
1 cup uncooked rice
1-1/3 cups water
Dash of garlic salt
1 can cream of mushroom soup
1 can cream of celery soup
1 can cream of chicken soup
Chicken parts

Melt margarine. Combine with remaining ingredients, except chicken. Place in casserole. Put chicken pieces on top. Cover and bake at 300 degrees for 3 hours *or* 350 degrees for 1-1/2 hours.
Winnie Dittmer, Canfield, Ohi

BROILED CHICKEN BREAST
Serves 1

1 (4-ounce) boneless skinned chicken breast
1 tablespoon lemon juice
1 teaspoon coarse garlic (in jar)
1/4 teaspoon poultry seasoning
Salt, pepper, and paprika to season

Marinate chicken breast in lemon, garlic, and seasonings at least an hour. Broil chicken 6 minutes on each side, putting a little more paprika on as you turn it over. (180 calories per serving)
Marilyn Holmer, Belvidere, Ill.

PEACHY CHICKEN
Serves 4-6

1 ready-to-cook chicken (broiler-fryer), 2-1/2 - 3 pounds, cut up
2 tablespoons melted butter or margarine
1 teaspoon salt
1/2 cup peach syrup (from canned peaches)
1 cup tomato catsup
1 tablespoon lemon juice
2 teaspoons Worcestershire sauce
1 tablespoon instant minced onion
1/4 teaspoon powdered ginger
1 tablespoon brown sugar
1 cup sliced canned cling peaches

Line a 13x9x2-inch baking pan with heavy-duty foil, leaving an overhang of foil on sides of pan. Brush the chicken pieces with melted butter (or margarine) and sprinkle with salt, then arrange in single layer in foil-lined pan, skin side up. Blend peach syrup, catsup, lemon juice, Worcestershire sauce, instant minced onion, powdered ginger, and brown sugar, heat to boiling point. Pour sauce over chicken in baking pan. Cover tightly with foil (overhang on side of pan) and bake in a hot (400-degree) oven for 30 minutes. Uncover; broil 6 inches from heat for 10 minutes, or until chicken is browned and glazed, turning and basting with sauce while broiling. Add sliced peaches and brush with sauce last 5 minutes of broiling.
Mrs. L. Mayer, Richmond, Va.

CHICKEN PIE
Serves 6

4 cups bite-sized cooked chicken pieces
1 (10-3/4 ounce) can cream of chicken soup
1 (13-3/4 ounce) can chicken broth
1-1/2 cups flour
2 teaspoons baking powder
1-1/2 cups buttermilk
1 (10-ounce) package frozen mixed vegetables
1 stick butter (not margarine), melted

Heat oven to 350 degrees. Place chicken in lightly greased 13x9x2 inch pan. Mix soup and broth together well and pour over chicken. Arrange mixed vegetables over top. Mix flour and baking powder in a bowl. Add buttermilk and melted butter. Stir to form a thin dough and pour evenly over chicken mixture.

Bake, uncovered, about 1 hour until crust rises to top and browns.

To Make Buttermilk: Mix 1-1/2 cups milk with 1-1/2 tablespoons vinegar or lemon juice; let stand 5 minutes.

Pauline Dean, Uxbridge, Mass.

OVEN FRIED PARMESAN CHICKEN

2 fryers, cut up
2 eggs, beaten with 2 tablespoons water
1-1/2 cups corn flake crumbs
1/2 cup Parmesan cheese
1-1/2 teaspoon s salt
1 teaspoon onion salt
1 stick butter, melted

Wash and dry chicken. Dip in egg mixture. Combine corn flakes, Parmesan cheese, and seasonings. Dip egg-coated chicken into corn flake mixture and place in foil-lined pan. (Put half of butter under chicken and the remainder over chicken). Bake at 375 degrees for 1 hour.

Mildred Sherrer, Bay City, Texas

Micro-
MAGIC

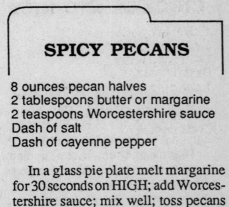

BRUSSELS SPROUTS AND CARROTS `A LA SLENDER

Serves 4-5

1 pound brussels sprouts
2 tablespoons water
5 small carrots, sliced 1/4 inch thick
1/2 cup undiluted (low-sodium) cream of mushroom soup
1/2 teaspoon thyme
1/4 cup low-fat or skim milk
1 teaspoon lemon juice
1/4 teaspoon celery seed

Trim stem ends from sprouts; cut an "X" on bottom of each. Place in 1-1/2 quart microwave casserole with water and carrots. Microwave, covered, on HIGH 7-9 minutes (or until tender-crisp). Drain.

In small microwave bowl, combine soup, thyme, milk, lemon juice, and celery seed; microwave, uncovered, 1 minute. Stir until smooth. Add to drained vegetables and toss to coat. Microwave, covered, 1 minute on HIGH. (68 calories per serving)

Dorothy Sorensen, Muskego, Wis.

TACO RICE CASSEROLE

Serves 5-6

1 pound ground beef
1 medium onion, diced
1 green pepper, diced
1 envelope of dried taco mix
1 cup converted rice
1 (16-ounce) can whole tomatoes, with liquid
1 teaspoon garlic salt
2-1/2 cups shredded cheddar cheese
Parsley flakes

In a 2-quart casserole cook ground beef with onion and green pepper; microwave for 4 minutes on HIGH; drain. Add taco mix, rice, tomatoes with liquid, and garlic salt; microwave, covered, 7 minutes on HIGH, then 18 minutes on 70% power. Add shredded cheddar cheese; combine thoroughly; top with parsley flakes; return to microwave for 3 more minutes on 70%.

BROCCOLI-RICE QUICHE

Serves 6

2 cups hot cooked rice
1/2 cup (2 ounces) shredded cheddar cheese
1 egg, beaten
1 tablespoon margarine
1/2 teaspoon salt
1 (10-ounce) package frozen chopped broccoli
1 (4-ounce) can sliced mushrooms, drained
1 (2-ounce) jar sliced pimiento, drained
2 eggs, beaten
1/2 cup (2 ounces) shredded cheddar cheese
5 drops hot pepper sauce
1 teaspoon lemon juice
1/2 teaspoon salt
1/8 teaspoon dried oregano

Combine hot rice, 1/2 cup cheese, 1 egg, margarine, and salt. Mix until cheese and margarine are melted. Press rice mixture into bottom and up side of 9-inch microwave-safe quiche or pie plate. Set aside. Place broccoli in 1-quart microwave-safe casserole. Cover with casserole lid.

Microwave (HIGH) 5-6 minutes or until just about tender, stirring once. Squeeze out excess liquid. Add mushrooms, pimiento, 2 eggs, 1/2 cup cheese, pepper sauce, lemon juice, salt, and oregano. Mix well. Spoon into rice crust. Cover with waxed paper. Microwave (MEDIUM - 50%) 10-12 minutes or until set, rotating dish once. Let stand 5 minutes before cutting into wedges.

Tips: If rice is cold, microwave about 2 minutes to heat. With full power, microwave 6-7 minutes during medium-heat cooking time, rotating dish twice. (170 calories per serving)

C. Childers, Gray Court, S.C.

SPICY PECANS

8 ounces pecan halves
2 tablespoons butter or margarine
2 teaspoons Worcestershire sauce
Dash of salt
Dash of cayenne pepper

In a glass pie plate melt margarine for 30 seconds on HIGH; add Worcestershire sauce; mix well; toss pecans to coat. Microwave for 4-6 minutes on HIGH; stir twice. Sprinkle lightly with salt and dash of cayenne pepper.

HERBED CHICKEN

2 chicken breast halves, skinned
1/2 teaspoon dried rosemary
1/2 teaspoon marjoram
1 teaspoon dried minced onion
2 tablespoons lemon juice
Freshly ground pepper

Arrange chicken, rib side up, in 9x9 inch microwave glass baking dish; sprinkle with half the quantities of rosemary, marjoram, onion, lemon juice, and pepper. Cover with waxed paper; microwave on HIGH for 6 minutes. Turn chicken over; use remaining herbs. Return, uncovered, to microwave for 6 minutes at 70% (MEDIUM HIGH). Let stand 3 minutes.

PORK AND APPLE CASSEROLE

Serves 5

5 ounces uncooked egg noodles (about 3 cups)
1 tablespoon cooking oil
1 pound boneless pork, cubed
1 tablespoon flour
1 cooking apple, sliced
1 small onion, sliced
1 clove garlic, minced
1/2 cup sliced celery
1/4 cup water
1/4 teaspoon salt
Dash pepper
1/2 cup sour cream

Cook noodles as directed on package; drain and set aside. Heat oil in glass casserole over medium-high heat; coat pork with flour; add pork to casserole and brown. Add apple, onion, garlic, celery, water, salt, and pepper. Cover and microwave on 30% (low) for 8-10 minutes; stir once. Stir in sour cream. Serve over noodles. This is also good over boiled and/or baked potatoes.

SAVORY BRUNCH CASSEROLE

Serves 6

2 tablespoons butter or margarine
1-1/2 tablespoons flour
Dash of pepper
1 cup milk
1 cup (4 ounces) cubed American cheese
2 tablespoons butter or margarine
1 cup cubed ham
1 small onion, chopped
1/4 cup chopped green pepper
1/4 teaspoon dill weed
6 eggs, beaten

Microwave on HIGH 2 tablespoons butter in 2-cup measuring cup for one minute or until melted. Blend in flour and pepper, gradually stir in milk. Microwave on HIGH uncovered 2-3 minutes or until mixture boils and thickens slightly; stir once or twice. Stir in cheese until melted; set aside. Combine 2 tablespoons butter, ham, onion, and green pepper into 1-1/2 quart casserole and microwave on HIGH uncovered 3 to 3-1/2 minutes or until onion is tender. Stir in cheese sauce; fold in eggs until well blended. Return to microwave and cook 5-7 minutes or until just set. Stir twice while cooking. May substitute mushrooms for green pepper.

DIVINE MASHED POTATO CASSEROLE

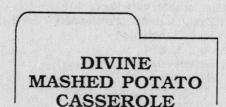

10 servings instant mashed potatoes
1 (3-ounce) package cream cheese
1 cup sour cream
1-1/2 teaspoons chives, optional
1/2 teaspoon garlic salt
2 tablespoons margarine
Paprika

Prepare potatoes as package directs; omit butter. Soften cream

cheese for one minute on 70%. Mix into potatoes; add sour cream, chives, and garlic salt.

Top with margarine and paprika. Microwave for 8-9 minutes on HIGH.

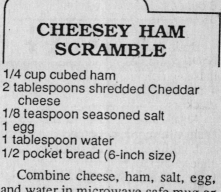

CHEESEY HAM SCRAMBLE

1/4 cup cubed ham
2 tablespoons shredded Cheddar cheese
1/8 teaspoon seasoned salt
1 egg
1 tablespoon water
1/2 pocket bread (6-inch size)

Combine cheese, ham, salt, egg, and water in microwave safe mug or dish; beat with fork. Microwave on HIGH, uncovered, 1-1/2 to 2 minutes or until egg is just about set, stirring twice. Place pocket bread half on napkin; microwave 10-15 seconds. Spoon egg mixture into bread.

SCRAMBLED SAUSAGE

Serves 9

12 ounces bulk pork sausage
6 eggs
1 cup milk
1-1/2 cups (6 ounces) shredded Cheddar cheese
1 cup herb-seasoned croutons

Crumble sausage into 8" baking dish, microwave on HIGH uncovered for 5-6 minutes, or until meat is no longer pink, stir twice while cooking. Break into small pieces and drain. Add eggs, milk, 1 cup cheese, and croutons to sausage, blend well. Cover with wax paper; microwave on HIGH for 5-6 minutes. Stir, then microwave on MEDIUM HIGH (70%) for 7-8 minutes or until center is just about set. Sprinkle with remaining cheese. Let sit covered for 5 minutes, cut into squares.

CRAB CANAPES

7-1/2 ounce can crabmeat
2 tablespoons sliced green onions
1/2 cup mayonnaise
1 teaspoon lemon juice
6 ounces sliced Swiss cheese
36 crackers

Drain crabmeat well. In small bowl, combine crab, onions, mayonnaise, lemon juice. Cut cheese into 1/4 inch slices, then into pieces to fit the crackers.

Arrange crackers on a tray. Top each with cheese slice then divide the crab filling in portions over the cheese. Place 12 canapes on round plate and microwave on **HIGH** for 1 - 1-1/2 minutes.

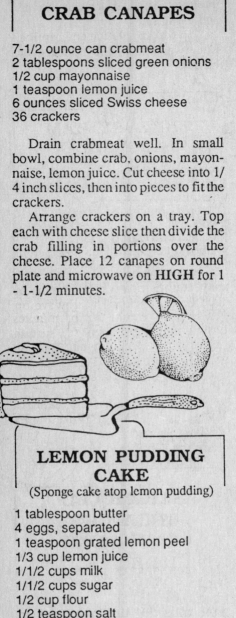

LEMON PUDDING CAKE
(Sponge cake atop lemon pudding)

1 tablespoon butter
4 eggs, separated
1 teaspoon grated lemon peel
1/3 cup lemon juice
1/1/2 cups milk
1/1/2 cups sugar
1/2 cup flour
1/2 teaspoon salt
Nutmeg

In glass mixing bowl, microwave butter for 30 seconds to 1 minute or until melted. Separate eggs, adding yolks to butter, and placing whites in another bowl. Beat egg whites until they form soft peaks. Set aside. Using same beaters, beat egg yolks until slightly thickened and lemon colored. Blend in lemon peel and juice. In a 2-cup glass measure, heat milk until steaming hot, approximately 2-1/2 to 3 minutes. Add sugar, flour, and salt to egg yolk mixture. Blend in milk, gradually, while beating at low speed, just until smooth. Mixture will be very thin. Fold into egg whites. Pour into greased 8-inch square baking dish. Microwave at 50% (MEDIUM), uncovered, 12-13 minutes or until top of cake is set. Rotate dish 3 times; sprinkle with nutmeg.

ORANGE ZUCCHINI CAKE

1 cup oil
2 cups packed brown sugar
1-3 teaspoons grated orange peel
4 eggs
1/3 cup orange juice
2 cups shredded zucchini
2-2/3 cups flour
2 teaspoons baking powder
1 teaspoon cinnamon
1/2 teaspoon salt and nutmeg
1/4 teaspoon cloves and cinnamon
1 tablespoon sugar

Beat together oil, brown sugar, and orange peel. Add eggs, one at a time, beating well after each. Blend in juice and zucchini. Add flour, baking powder, 1 teaspoon cinnamon, salt, nutmeg, and cloves; mix until just blended. Grease a 10-12 cup microwave-safe tube pan. Combine 1 tablespoon sugar and 1/4 teaspoon cinnamon; sprinkle pan with this mixture; coating all surfaces; shake out excess. Spoon batter evenly into pan. Microwave on MEDIUM HIGH (70%), uncovered, for 15 minutes; rotate pan once. Then microwave for 4-5 minutes or until no longer doughy. Let stand 10 minutes. Invert onto serving plate.

PUMPKIN SPICE CAKE

2 eggs
1 cup packed brown sugar
1/2 cup sugar
3/4 cup oil
1 cup cooked or canned pumpkin
1 teaspoon vanilla
2 cups flour
1 teaspoon salt
1/2 teaspoon baking powder
1/2 teaspoon soda
1/2 teaspoon cinnamon

1/4 teaspoon nutmeg
1/4 teaspoon ginger
1/4 cup milk

Beat eggs until foamy; add sugars and oil; beat. Blend in pumpkin and vanilla; stir in remaining ingredients until smooth. Do not overbeat. Pour batter into 12 x 8-inch baking dish, greased only on bottom; microwave on HIGH for 9-1/2 to 10-1/2 minutes, or until cake springs back when touched. Cool; frost.

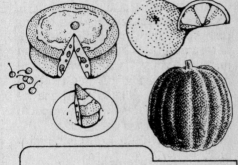

PUMPKIN RAISIN CAKE

1/4 cup margarine
1/3 cup sugar
2 eggs
1 can pumpkin
1 teaspoon vanilla
1-1/4 cups flour
1/2 teaspoon baking powder
1/2 cup raisins
1/2 teaspoon baking soda
1/2 teaspoon salt
1 teaspoon cinnamon
1/2 teaspoon nutmeg
1/4 teaspoon allspice
1/8 teaspoon ground allspice
1/8 teaspoon ground cloves
1/3 cup milk

In large glass bowl, microwave margarine on HIGH for one minute. Blend in sugar; add eggs, one at a time, beating well after each. Blend in pumpkin and vanilla; add flour, baking powder, soda, salt, cinnamon, nutmeg, allspice, cloves, and milk, beating until smooth. Stir in raisins. Grease bottom of 8-inch square dish; microwave 6-1/2 to 7 minutes on HIGH or until no longer doughy. Rotate dish, if necessary, 2-3 times. Serve warm or cold. Allow cake to stand 5-10 minutes to assure complete cooking.

Party
FARE

CARAMEL APPLES
Serves 6

6 wooden skewers
6 medium-sized apples, stems removed
1 cup sugar
3/4 cup white corn syrup
1 (14-ounce) can sweetened condensed milk
1/8 teaspoon salt
1/4 cup butter or margarine
1 teaspoon vanilla

Insert wooden skewer into stem end of each washed and thoroughly dried apple; set aside. In heavy saucepan, combine sugar, corn syrup, condensed milk, and salt. Mix well. Cook over medium heat, stirring gently, but constantly, to 230 degrees on candy thermometer, or until small amount dropped into cold water forms a soft ball (about 3 minutes). Remove from heat. Cool slightly. Stir in butter and vanilla. Working quickly, dip apples in caramel to coat well. Place apples stem side up on buttered waxed paper to harden.

CHEESE WAFERS

1/4 pound butter
1/4 pound grated sharp cheddar cheese
2 cups flour
1/2 teaspoon salt
Dash of cayenne pepper

Cream butter and cheese together. Add flour, salt and pepper; mix well.

Form into 1-inch roll. Chill thoroughly; cut into thin slices. Bake at 350 degrees for about 8 minutes or until light brown.
Marcella Swigert, Monroe City, Mo.

FRIED CHEESE

4 slices cheddar cheese, 3/4-inch thick
Salt
1/2 cup flour
1 egg, beaten
2/3 cup bread crumbs
1 cup shortening

Sprinkle cheese with salt. Dip slices in flour, then in egg, and finally in bread crumbs. Fry quickly in hot shortening until golden brown.
Edna Askins, Greenville, Texas

CHICKEN LIVER PATÉ

6 ounces chicken livers
2 ounces chicken gizzards
1/2 teaspoon salt
Dash cayenne pepper
1/2 cup rendered chicken fat
1/4 teaspoon nutmeg
1 teaspoon dry mustard
1/8 teaspoon cloves
2 tablespoons finely-minced onion

In a saucepan bring livers and gizzards to a boil. Simmer until tender. Drain and put through finest blade of food processor. Mix paste with remaining ingredients. Blend well; pack mixture into a crock, and refrigerate until well chilled.
Alice McNamara, Eucha, Okla.

DIP DIP HOORAY

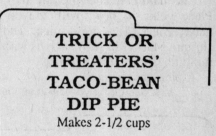

1 (16-ounce) can refried beans
1 (8-ounce) carton sour cream
1 (8-ounce) carton avocado dip
1 bunch green onions, (4 or 5)
1 cup black olives, chopped
2 cups Cheddar cheese, grated
1-1/2 cups tomatoes, chopped
1/2 cup green chilies

Spread refried beans in bottom of 9x13 casserole. Layer remaining ingredients in order listed. Cover and refrigerate until ready to serve.

TRICK OR TREATERS' TACO-BEAN DIP PIE
Makes 2-1/2 cups

2 (10-1/2 ounce) cans bean dip
1 (1-1/4 ounce) package taco seasoning mix
6 scallions, finely chopped
1 cup mayonnaise or salad dressing
1 cup dairy sour cream
1 (4-1/2 ounce) can sliced olives, drained
Corn chips or tortilla chips

In large mixing bowl, combine bean dip and taco mix. Spread mixture in a 10-inch pie plate. Sprinkle chopped scallions over mixture: Blend together mayonnaise and sour cream. Spread over onions. Sprinkle sliced olives over top. Chill. Serve with corn chips.

CREAMY SHRIMP MOLD

1 tablespoon unflavored gelatin
1 can cream of celery soup
1 (8-ounce) can shrimp
1 (8-ounce) package cream cheese
1 onion, chopped
1 cup celery, finely chopped
1 cup mayonnaise

Dissolve gelatin in 3 tablespoons water. Heat celery soup until creamy smooth; add gelatin. Combine remaining ingredients; pour in soup mixture; pour into mold. Chill until set. Serve with assorted crackers.

Marcella Swigert, Monroe City, Mo.

SHRIMP DEVILED EGGS

8 eggs, hard-cooked
1/2 cup mayonnaise
2 teaspoons mustard
1 tablespoon lemon juice
1 can shrimp pieces, drained and rinsed well

Cut hard-cooked eggs in half. Place yolks in bowl with mayonnaise, mustard, lemon juice, and shrimp. Mash. Fill white halves with mixture. Chill before serving.

A pleasant change!!

Mrs. George Franks, Millerton, Pa.

HAM NIBBLES
Makes 2-1/2 to 3 dozen balls

2 eggs, well beaten
2 cups ground cooked ham
1 (7-ounce) can whole-kernel corn, drained
1/4 cup mayonnaise
1 teaspoon prepared mustard
2 cups cheese cracker crumbs

In a mixing bowl, combine eggs, ham, corn, mayonnaise, mustard, and 1 cup of cracker crumbs. Shape into 1-inch balls. Roll in remaining crumbs. Deep-fry at 375 degrees for 2-3 minutes or until golden brown. Drain on paper towels.

Joy B. Shamway, Freeport, Ill.

POPCORN NUT LOG

6 ounces (3/4 cup) unpopped popcorn
1/4 pound butter or margarine
1 cup (6 ounces) semisweet chocolate chips
1 (10-1/2-ounce) package miniature marshmallows
2 cups Spanish peanuts
2 cups chopped pecans or almonds

Pop corn and place in large bowl. Melt margarine, chocolate chips, and marshmallows together in top half of double boiler. Pour melted chocolate sauce over popped corn, adding mixed nuts gradually. Mix until entire mixture is coated with chocolate sauce. Spoon mixture into half-gallon paper milk carton, packing tightly. Place in refrigerator for one hour. Cut lengthwise along all four corners of carton and peel carton away. Slice and serve.

Edna Askins, Greenville, Texas

PEANUT CLUSTERS

2 cups chocolate chips
1 cup peanut butter
2 cups Spanish peanuts

Melt chocolate chips and peanut butter in top of double boiler. Add peanuts; stir and drop by teaspoons on waxed paper.

These are very good, and so simple and easy to make.

Elaine Dodd, Pasco, Wash.

FLOWERPOT CUPCAKES
Makes 36

1 package devil's food cake mix
1-1/4 cups water
1/3 cup oil
3 eggs
1/2 cup finely chopped nuts
36 ice cream cones with flat bottoms
1 can ready-to-spread frosting (flavor of your choice)

Assorted candies (decoration)

Preheat oven to 350 degrees. In large mixer bowl, combine cake mix, water, oil, and eggs; mix at low speed until moistened. Beat 2 minutes on high speed. Fold nuts into batter. Place ice cream cones on cookie sheets. Fill with batter to within 1 inch of tops of cones.

Bake at 350 degrees for 20 to 25 minutes or until cake springs back when touched lightly in center. Cool completely. Spread frosting on tops of cakes. Decorate with candy (M & M's, candy corn, etc.).

ENGLISH TOFFEE

1 cup butter (*not* margarine)
1 cup sugar
3 tablespoons water
2 teaspoons vanilla
6 ounces chocolate chips

Stir butter, sugar, and water over medium heat with wooden spoon to hard crack stage. Remove from heat and stir in vanilla. Pour onto greased pizza pan; wait 1 minute, then place chocolate on top. Let melt slightly and spread. (Can also add chopped nuts over chocolate, if desired.) Refrigerate 2 hours and then break into pieces. Tastes like Heath Bar candy.

Cheryl Santefort, Thornton, Ill.

PEANUT BUTTER FUDGE

3 cups granulated or brown sugar
1/2 cup milk
2 tablespoons margarine
3 tablespoons marshmallow fluff
3 tablespoons peanut butter
1 teaspoon vanilla

Bring sugar, milk, and margarine to a boil; let boil for 3 minutes. Then take off stove; add marshmallow fluff, peanut butter, and vanilla. Beat with spoon for a few minutes. Poor into greased pan. Let set; cut into squares.

Zenana Warren, Bloomville, Ohio

Pies
TO BAKE

FLAKY NO-FAIL PIE CRUST

Makes 3 (8- or 9-inch) crusts

1 cup lard
1/2 cup boiling water
1 teaspoon salt
3 cups all-purpose flour

Pour boiling water over lard. Stir well until white and creamy. Add salt and flour, all at once. Mix with fork 25 to 30 turns, or until moist. Shape into a ball and chill.

This crust will keep for several days. It should be taken from the refrigerator an hour or so before use, so it will be manageable.

Eleanor Hardman, Morehead City, N.C.

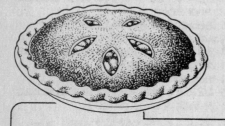

NEVER-FAIL PIE CRUST

3 cups flour
1-1/4 cups shortening
1 teaspoon salt
1 egg, slightly beaten
5 tablespoons water
1 tablespoon vinegar

Mix first three ingredients together in bowl with pastry blender. Blend liquids together; then pour into flour mixture.

Do not mix any more than necessary. Roll out dough and place in pie pan. Bake the usual oven temperature for pie recipe depending on the type you make. Single crust does not bake as long as a double crust.

Marvel Schaadt, Convoy, OH

DERBY PIE

1 (9-inch) pie shell, unbaked
1 (6-ounce) package chocolate chips
1 cup sugar
1/2 cup all-purpose flour
1/2 cup chopped pecans
3/4 stick melted butter
1 teaspoon vanilla
2 eggs

Place chocolate chips in unbaked pie shell. Beat eggs slightly. Combine with sugar and flour. Add chopped pecans, butter, and vanilla. Bake at 325 degrees for 40-45 minutes or until light brown on top.

Mrs. George Esterbrook, Rocky River,

LUSCIOUS PEACH PIE

2 (29-ounce) cans peaches
1/2 cup sugar
2 tablespoons flour
1/4 teaspoon nutmeg
Dash of salt
2 tablespoons butter
1 tablespoon lemon juice
1/2 teaspoon grated orange peel
1/8 teaspoon almond extract
Pastry for 9-inch pie

Drain peaches, reserving 1/3 cup syrup. Combine sugar, flour, nutmeg, and salt; add reserved syrup. Cook and stir until thickened. Add next 4 ingredients, then peaches. Fill pie shell; add top crust and seal. Bake in 400-degree oven for 40-45 minutes.

If you like peach pie, you'll love this!!

Barbara Miller, Pittsburgh, Pa.

CREAMY LEMON MERINGUE PIE

1 (8- or 9-inch) baked pastry shell or graham cracker crumb crust
3 eggs, separated
1 (14-ounce) can Eagle Brand Sweetened Condensed Milk (not evaporated milk)
1/2 cup Realemon lemon juice concentrate
Few drops yellow food coloring, optional
1/4 teaspoon cream of tartar
1/3 cup sugar

Preheat oven to 350 degrees. In medium mixing bowl, beat egg yolks; stir in sweetened condensed milk, Realemon, and food coloring if desired. Pour into prepared pastry shell. In small mixing bowl, beat egg whites with cream of tartar until soft peaks form; gradually add sugar, beating until stiff but not dry. Spread meringue on top of pie, sealing carefully to edge of shell. Bake 12-15 minutes or until golden brown. Cool. Chill thoroughly. Refrigerate leftovers.

Judy Taylor, Greenville, Texas

MAPLE PUMPKIN PIE

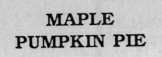

9 to 10 inch unbaked pie shell
1 cup cooked or canned pumpkin
1 tablespoon cornstarch
1/2 teaspoon cinnamon
1/2 teaspoon nutmeg
1/3 cup sugar
1-1/4 cups graham cracker crumbs
2 tablespoons sugar
1/4 cup melted butter

Combine and press into 9-inch pie pan. Bake at 375 degrees for approximately 8 minutes. Cool.

Refreshingly different! Bound to get compliments.

Mrs. George Franks, Millerton, PA

PUMPKIN CHEESE PIE

1 (8 ounce) package cream cheese
3/4 cup brown sugar
1 teaspoon cinnamon
1 teaspoon nutmeg
1/2 teaspoon ginger
1/2 teaspoon ground cloves
1/2 teaspoon salt
1/4 cup flour
3 beaten eggs
1 can pumpkin
1 cup evaporated milk
1 teaspoon vanilla

Beat cream cheese and all dry ingredients together. Add beaten eggs. Stir in pumpkin, milk, and vanilla. Pour into an unbaked pie shell. Bake at 375 degrees for 45 minutes.

Mary Linger, Jacksonville, Fla.

PUMPKIN CREAM PIE

1-3/4 cups cold milk
1 cup pumpkin

2 tablespoons sugar
1/2 teaspoon cinnamon
1/4 teaspoon cloves
1/8 teaspoon nutmeg
1 (6 ounce) package vanilla instant pudding mix
9-inch baked pastry shell

Mix together first seven ingredients, beating about 30 seconds or until smooth. Pour into baked pastry shell and refrigerate until thoroughly chilled. Simple, fast, and delicious!!

Agnes Ward, Erie, Pa.

PUMPKIN ICE CREAM PIE WITH PECAN TOPPING
Serves 8

1 quart vanilla ice cream, softened
3/4 cup canned pumpkin
1/4 cup honey
1/2 teaspoon cinnamon
1/4 teaspoon ground ginger
1/4 teaspoon salt
1/8 teaspoon nutmeg
1/8 teaspoon ground cloves
1 baked 9-inch pie crust, cooled
1/3 cup chopped pecans
Whipped cream (garnish)
Pecan halves (garnish)

Combine first 8 ingredients in mixing bowl; blend well. Pour into pie crust and sprinkle with chopped nuts. Freeze until serving time. Garnish with whipped cream and pecan halves just before serving.

PRALINE-BOTTOM PUMPKIN PIE

1/4 cup butter
1/2 cup chopped, toasted pecans
1/3 cup packed brown sugar
1 (9-inch) pastry shell, baked
1 (2-1/2 ounce) package no-bake custard mix
1/3 cup granulated sugar
2 teaspoons pumpkin pie spice

2/3 cup milk
2/3 cup evaporated milk
2 cups pumpkin

In small saucepan melt butter. Stir in the 1/2 cup pecans and brown sugar. Cook; stir until mixture bubbles. Spread over bottom of baked pastry shell. Cool to room temperature.

In 2-quart saucepan combine custard mix, granulated sugar, and pumpkin pie spice. Stir in milk, evaporated milk, and pumpkin. Cook, stirring constantly, over medium heat until mixture bubbles. Remove from heat. Cover; cool for 10 minutes.

Pour pumpkin mixture into prepared shell. Chill several hours or until firm. Garnish top with additional pecans and whipped cream. This is a different version of pumpkin pie for the holidays.

Helen Weissinger, Levittown, Pa.

CHILLED COCONUT-PEACH CHIFFON PIE

1 cup canned cling peaches, drained and diced
1 tablespoon lemon juice
1 package (3 ounce) orange gelatin
1-3/4 cups hot water and peach juice
1 cup heavy cream
1 tablespoon sherry extract
1-1/2 cups sweetened flake coconut
1 (9-inch) baked pie shell

Sprinkle peaches with lemon juice. Dissolve gelatin in hot water and peach juice. Chill until slightly thickened. Place in bowl of ice water; whip until fluffy and thick. Add 2/3 cup cream; stir mixture until thickened again. Add sherry extract, 3/4 cup coconut, and peaches. Continue stirring in the ice bath until again thickened. Turn into pie shell; chill.

Before serving, whip remaining cream; pile lightly around edge of pie; sprinkle remaining coconut on cream. Garnish with fresh mint and additional peach slices.

Gwen Campbell, Sterling, VA

KAHLUA PECAN PIE
Serves 8-10

Pastry crust (unbaked)
1/4 cup butter
3/4 cup sugar
1 teaspoon vanilla
2 tablespoons flour
3 eggs
1/2 cup Kahlua liqueur
1/2 cup dark corn syrup
3/4 cup evaporated milk
1 cup whole or chopped pecans
1/2 cup heavy cream, whipped
Pecan halves for garnish

Line 9 inch pie plate with your favorite pastry crust. Chill. Set oven at 400 degrees. Cream together butter, sugar, vanilla, and flour. Mix well. Beat in eggs, one at a time. Stir in Kahlua, corn syrup, evaporated milk, and pecans. Mix well; pour into pie shell. Bake for 10 minutes, then reduce heat to 325 degrees and bake until firm, about 40 minutes. Chill.

When ready to serve, garnish with whipped cream and pecan halves.

Linda Strader, New Ellenton, S.C.

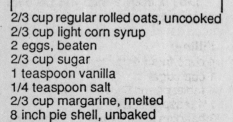

MOCK PECAN PIE

2/3 cup regular rolled oats, uncooked
2/3 cup light corn syrup
2 eggs, beaten
2/3 cup sugar
1 teaspoon vanilla
1/4 teaspoon salt
2/3 cup margarine, melted
8 inch pie shell, unbaked

Combine rolled oats, corn syrup, eggs, sugar, vanilla and salt. Mix well. Add melted butter and mix thoroughly. Pour into pastry shell; bake 1 hour at 350 degrees. Cool before serving.

Mary Linger, Jacksonville, FL

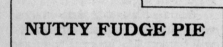

NUTTY FUDGE PIE

1 - 9 inch unbaked pastry shell

1 - 4 ounce package sweet cooking chocolate or 2 - 1 ounce squares unsweetened chocolate
1 - 14 ounce can sweetened condensed milk
1/2 cup hot water
2 eggs, well beaten
1 teaspoon vanilla
1/8 teaspoon salt
1-1/4 cup pecan or walnut halves or pieces

In a medium saucepan, over low heat, melt chocolate and butter or margarine. Stir in sweetened condensed milk, hot water and eggs; mix well. Remove from heat; stir in remaining ingredients. Spoon into prepared pastry shell.

Bake in a 350 degree oven for 40 - 45 minutes or until center is set. Cool. Chill 3 hours. Garnish as desired. Refrigerate leftovers.

Alice McNamara, Eucha, OK

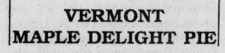

VERMONT MAPLE DELIGHT PIE

1 unbaked 10-inch pie shell
2 tablespoons melted butter
3/4 cup light brown sugar
3/4 cup maple syrup
1/4 teaspoon salt
4 large eggs (or 6 medium)
1/2 cup undiluted canned milk
1/2 teaspoon maple extract
1/2 teaspoon lemon extract
3/4 cup quick rolled oats
1/2 cup slivered almonds
Whipped topping
Maraschino cherries

Preheat oven to 400 degrees. Over low heat melt the butter, brown sugar, and maple syrup together; stir until sugar is dissolved. Add extracts and salt. Set aside to cool. Beat eggs and milk together; add to sugar mixture. Blend well. Stir in oats and nuts; pour into pie shell. Bake for 20 minutes at 400 degrees. Reduce heat to 350 degrees and bake until middle is firm, about 20-25 minutes longer. Cool on rack. Serve with whipped cream or topping; garnish with a maraschino cherry.

Pearle M. Goodwin, South Ryegate, Vt.

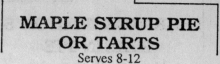

MAPLE SYRUP PIE OR TARTS
Serves 8-12

1 cup maple syrup
6 tablespoons flour
1/2 cup water
2 egg yolks, beaten
1 tablespoon butter
1/4 cup chopped walnuts
1 baked 8 inch pie shell or 12 baked medium tart shells
Walnut halves

Heat maple syrup in double boiler. Mix flour and water until smooth; stir gradually into heated syrup and cook until thickened (about 10 minutes), stirring constantly.

Mix a little of hot mixture with egg yolks; stir into remainder in double boiler and continue cooking 3 to 4 minutes. Remove from heat; stir in butter and walnuts; cool slightly. Pour into pie shell or tart shells. Top with meringue or whipped cream. Decorate with walnut halves.

Ronnie J. Heroux, Uxbridge, Mass.

APPLE BUTTER PUMPKIN PIE
Serves 8

1 cup mashed cooked pumpkin
1 cup apple butter
1/3 cup packed brown sugar
1/2 teaspoon ground cinnamon
1/4 teaspoon salt
1/4 teaspoon ground ginger
1/4 teaspoon ground nutmeg
1/4 teaspoon salt
1 teaspoon melted butter
1/2 cup milk
1-1/3 cups maple syrup
2 eggs, beaten

Sift cornstarch, spices, sugar, and salt into pumpkin; mix well. Add melted butter, milk, and maple syrup; mix well. Stir in beaten eggs. Pour into pie shell. Bake 15 minutes at 450 degrees; lower temperature to 325 degrees; continue baking 40 minutes or until done.

Fay Duman, Eugene, Ore.

BERNICE WILSON'S RAISIN PIE

Makes 2 - 9", deep pies

Crust: (For the two pies)
2 cups flour
1 cup shortening — Crisco or other vegetable
1/2 cup water
Pinch salt

Filling:
3 cups medium or small raisins
6 cups water
3/4 cup sugar
2 tablespoons corn starch
Pinch of salt
1 egg

Cook raisins with 6 cups of water until soft. Mix sugar, cornstarch, and salt; add to raisin mixture (Dampen the sugar & cornstarch mixture with a little water before adding, and wait until raisin mixture has cooled a little). Add egg, and beat, beat, BEAT! Bring mixture to boiling point; pour into crusts; cover with strips to form a lattice over the top.

Bake at 350 degrees for 1 hour.

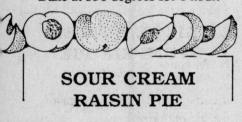

SOUR CREAM RAISIN PIE

Prepare (do not bake) and set aside pastry for 1 (9-inch) crust

Mix together:
1/2 cup sugar
2 tablespoons flour
1/2 teaspoon cinnamon
1/4 teaspoon nutmeg
1/4 teaspoon salt

Blend together:
1 egg, well beaten
1-1/2 cups thick sour cream

Add dry ingredients to sour cream mixture and blend thoroughly.

Mix in:
1-1/2 cups (about 7 ounces) dark seedless raisins

Turn into pastry shell. Bake at 450 degrees 10 minutes. Reduce heat to 350 degrees and bake 20-25 minutes longer, or until a silver knife comes out clean when inserted halfway between center and edge of filling. Remove to cooling rack to cool slightly. Serve warm.

Mildred Marshall, New Albany, Pa.

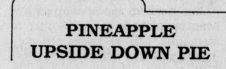

PINEAPPLE UPSIDE DOWN PIE

Pastry for 2-crust pie
1 (1 pound 4-1/2 ounce) can pineapple tidbits
Water
3 tablespoons cornstarch
3/4 cup brown sugar
2 tablespoons lemon juice
6 tablespoons butter
1/2 cup pecan halves

Drain pineapple. Add water to pineapple syrup to make 1-1/2 cups. Combine cornstarch and 1/4 cup brown sugar in saucepan. Add lemon juice and pineapple syrup mixture. Cook, stirring constantly, until mixture is thick and clear. Remove from heat and add 2 tablespoons butter, stirring until it melts. Add pineapple. While preheating oven to 425 degrees, place remaining 4 tablespoons butter in bottom of 9-inch pie pan; place in oven until butter is melted. Sprinkle with remaining 1/2 cup brown sugar and 1 tablespoon water. Arrange pecan halves, rounded side down, around bottom and sides of pie pan. Carefully line pan with pastry. Spoon in pineapple mixture. Adjust top crust; flute edges; cut vents. Place pie on square of foil in oven to catch drippings. Bake in 425 degree oven for 25 minutes. Turn out upside down on serving plate immediately. Cool on rack before cutting.

Norma L. Farrar, Sullivan, Mo.

LUSCIOUS RHUBARB MARSHMALLOW PIE

1-9 inch unbaked pie shell

3 cups rhubarb, finely diced
1-1/2 cups sugar
2 tablespoons soft margarine
1/4 teaspoon butter flavoring
Few drops of lemon juice
1/4 cup flour
3 eggs, well beaten
10 large marshmallows, cut in quarters

Mix all together and pour in an unbaked pie shell. Top with large marshmallows; each cut in 4 pieces with kitchen shears. Decorate the center and around edges of pie. This makes a pretty topping and needs no top crust. Bake at 400 degrees for 15 minutes, watch closely. Reduce heat to 375 degrees; bake for 45 minutes longer or until set and golden brown. Serve with whipped cream.

Gladys Mysak, Toledo, IA

GERTRUDE HUNGERFORD'S SPECIAL RHUBARB PIE

Line a deep 9-inch pie tin with your best pie crust.

Filling:
4 cups fresh rhubarb
1 cup sugar
4 tablespoons flour
1/4 teaspoon salt
3 heaping tablespoons of strawberry Jell-O

Use small stems of rhubarb. If you can't get those, then split thicker stems in half. Dice pieces to 1/2 inch or less.

Mix sugar, flour, salt, Jell-O. Pour over diced rhubarb; toss until pieces are thoroughly coated.

Bake 10 minutes at 450 degrees; and about 30 minutes at 350 degrees. While pie is still warm, sprinkle top crust with sugar.

When pie has cooled down somewhat, place in refrigerator so Jell-O will harden. The mixture has a nice consistency, holds its shape and cuts well when cold.

FRESH STRAWBERRY PIE

1/8 teaspoon salt
1-1/4 cups sugar
3 tablespoons cornstarch
1 cup boiling water
2 tablespoons dry strawberry gelatin
2-9 inch baked pie shells
2 quarts fresh strawberries, sliced

Mix salt, sugar, and cornstarch together. Add boiling water. Stir and cook until thickened. Add strawberry gelatin and stir in until dissolved and well blended. Pour cooked mixture into baked shells filled with sliced fresh strawberries. Chill several hours before serving. Garnish with whipped cream when serving.

Karin Shea Fedders, Dameron, MD

CHOCOLATE BUTTERSCOTCH PIE

3 cups firmly packed light brown sugar
1/2 cup butter or margarine
3 eggs
1 teaspoon vanilla extract
1/2 cup half-and-half
1 (1-ounce) square unsweetened chocolate, melted
1 (9-inch) unbaked, chilled pie shell with stand-up edge
1 cup sweetened whipping cream, whipped
Chocolate shavings

Beat sugar and butter together until creamy. Add eggs, one at a time, beating well after each addition. Add vanilla and mix well. Beat in the half-and-half; add chocolate and beat well. Pour into pie shell and bake at 350 degrees for 30 minutes. Reduce heat to 300 degrees and bake 30-40 minutes longer or until pie is set. Test for doneness, and bake longer if needed. Let cool; then decorate with whipped cream and chocolate shavings. (Note: the pie puffs up during cooking, then falls as it cools.)

If you like both chocolate and butterscotch you will love this pie!!

**Barbara Beauregard-Smith,
South Australia**

CHOCOLATE MERINGUE PIE

4 tablespoons cocoa
1-1/4 cups sugar
6 tablespoons flour
1/2 teaspoon salt
2-1/2 cups milk
3 egg yolks, slightly beaten
2 tablespoons butter or margarine
1 teaspoon vanilla

Combine cocoa, sugar, flour, salt, and milk; heat in double boiler. Cook until thickened, stirring often. Stir in beaten egg yolks. (Should stir small amount of mixture into egg yolks before adding to main mixture. This procedure helps to prevent curdling). Cook two minutes; add butter and vanilla; cool. Turn into pie shell; cover with meringue. Meringue recipe below. This is a never-fail meringue—will not fall, and slices nicely.

Meringue:
3 egg whites (room temperature)
1/4 teaspoon cream of tartar
1 tablespoon water
6 tablespoons sugar

Beat egg whites until frothy. Add cream of tartar and water; beat until whites are stiff. Add sugar gradually, beating well after each addition. Pile meringue onto pie, spreading to edge of crust. Bake in 325 degree oven for 20 minutes or until brown.

Mrs. R. D. Cramer, Big Spring, Texas

CRANBERRY ICE CREAM PIE

Serves 6-8

1 (16 ounce) can jellied cranberry sauce
1 (9 inch) baked pastry shell
1 pint vanilla ice cream

1 (4-serving size) package instant vanilla pudding mix
1/4 cup frozen orange juice concentrate, thawed
1/2 cup whipping cream

Cut cranberry sauce crosswise into 1/2 inch slices. Arrange in bottom of pastry shell, cutting to fit as necessary. In a mixing bowl, stir ice cream with wooden spoon to soften. Add dry pudding mix and orange concentrate. Mix well. Beat cream until soft peaks form (tips curl). Fold whipped cream into ice cream mixture. Spoon over cranberry slices. Sprinkle with ground nutmeg, if desired. Freeze several hours or overnight. Before serving, remove pie from freezer 10-15 minutes to soften.

DOUBLE DECKER PUMPKIN ICE CREAM PIE

1 baked graham cracker crust (see below)
1 pint vanilla ice cream
1 cup canned pumpkin
3/4 cup sugar
1/2 teaspoon nutmeg
1/2 teaspoon ginger
1/2 teaspoon cinnamon
1/2 teaspoon salt
1 cup heavy cream, whipped
1/2 cup chopped pecans

Spread slightly softened ice cream in bottom of cool pie shell. Place in freezer. Combine pumpkin, sugar, spices and salt. Fold in whipped cream. Spread over ice cream in shell. Sprinkle with pecans. Place in freezer. When frozen, wrap and return for storage.

To serve, remove from freezer a few minutes before serving.

Graham Cracker Crust:

chocolate ice cream into a layer in cookie crust and drizzle 1/4 of the sauce over top. Repeat process using vanilla and strawberry ice cream, as well as sauce. Freeze until serving time. Serve with remaining sauce.

Marcella Swigert, Monroe City, MO

BROWN-SUGAR PIE

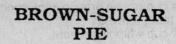

1 (9-inch) unbaked pie shell
3 eggs, beaten together
2 cups brown sugar
1/2 cup butter or margarine, soft
1/2 cup rich cream or evaporated milk

Mix cream, sugar, and beaten eggs together. Melt butter or margarine; cool a little and beat into egg mixture. Pour into the unbaked pie shell. Bake in 425-degree oven for 10 minutes, then reduce oven temperature to 350 degrees and bake 30 additional minutes or until pie filling is brown on top and shakes like jelly in the center. Rich, but oh, so good!

Sarah Drury, Brandenburg, Ky.

PEANUT BUTTER ICE CREAM PIE

Serves 8

1 quart vanilla ice cream, slightly softened
1/2 cup chunky peanut butter
1/2 cup crushed unsalted peanuts
1-1/2 tablespoons vanilla
1 (10-inch) graham cracker crust
Whipped cream and maraschino cherries for garnish

Combine ice cream, peanut butter, 1/4 cup peanuts, and vanilla in large bowl; mix well. Turn into crust and sprinkle with remaining peanuts. Freeze. Decorate with cream and cherries.

Kit Rollins, Cedarburg, WI

NO-BAKE PEANUT ICE CREAM PIE

4 cups Corn Chex cereal, crushed to 1 cup
1/4 cup firmly-packed brown sugar
1/3 cup butter or margarine, melted
1/4 cup flaked coconut

1/4 cup light corn syrup
1/4 cup peanut butter
3 tablespoons chopped salted nuts (peanuts)
1 tablespoon chopped peanuts (for topping)
1 quart vanilla ice cream, softened

Preheat oven to 300 degrees. Butter 9-inch pie plate. Combine cereal and sugar; add butter; mix well. Press this mixture evenly on bottom and sides of pie plate. Bake 10 minutes; cool. Combine next 4 ingredients. Mix with ice cream until rippled throughout. Turn into pie shell.

Sprinkle peanuts on top. Freeze 3 hours or until firm. Let stand 10-15 minutes at room temperature, before serving.

Monica Turk, Milwaukee, Wis.

"BREATH OF SPRING" PARFAIT PIE

Graham Cracker Crust:

1-1/2 cups graham cracker crumbs (about 20 crackers)
3 tablespoons sugar
1/3 cup melted butter or margarine

Combine all ingredients. Press mixture firmly and evenly against bottom and sides of pie pan. Bake at 350 degrees for 10 minutes. Cool.

Lime Parfait Pie:

1 (3-ounce) package lime gelatin
1 cup boiling water
1/4 cup frozen lemonade concentrate, thawed
1 pint vanilla ice cream

Dissolve gelatin in boiling water. Add lemonade. Add ice cream and stir until melted and smooth. Chill mixture until it begins to thicken, about 20 minutes. Pour into pie shell. Chill at least 3 hours before cutting.

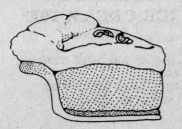

MOCHA SUNDAE PIE

Serves 6-8

Crust:

1-1/4 cups crushed chocolate wafers (about 20)
1 tablespoon sugar
1/4 cup melted butter or margarine

Filling:

1 cup evaporated milk
1 cup miniature marshmallows
1 cup semi-sweet chocolate pieces
Dash salt
1 quart coffee ice cream, softened and divided

Combine wafers, sugar, and butter. Press firmly into 9-inch pie plate. Bake in preheated 300 degree oven for 12-15 minutes. Cool, then chill. Over low heat, stir evaporated milk, marshmallows, chocolate pieces, and salt until melted and thick. Cool. Spoon half the ice cream into crust; drizzle with half the filling (chocolate sauce); spoon on remaining ice cream; drizzle with remaining filling. Freeze at least 4 hours.

Pauline Dean, Uxbridge, MA

MELT AWAY PIE

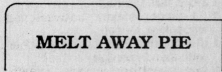

2 cups (24) crushed cream-filled chocolate cookies
1/4 cup margarine, melted
1/4 cup milk
1 (7-ounce) jar marshmallow creme
Few drops strawberry extract
Few drops red food coloring
2 cups whipping cream, whipped

Combine crumbs and margarine; reserve 1/2 cup for topping. Press remaining crumb mixture onto bottom of 9-inch spring form pan or pie plate. Chill. Gradually add milk to marshmallow creme, mixing until well blended. Add extract and food coloring; fold in whipped cream. Pour into pan; freeze until firm. Sprinkle with remaining crumbs.

A frozen pie that's quick and easy.

Barbara Nowakowski, No. Tonawanda, NY

MACAROON PIE

3 egg whites, beaten stiff
1/2 teaspoon baking powder
1 cup sugar
1 teaspoon vanilla extract
1 dozen graham crackers, rolled
    fine
1/2 cup finely cut dates
1 cup pecans, chopped
Whipped cream for topping

Beat egg whites until frothy, sprinkle baking powder over whites and continue beating until stiff. Gradually beat in sugar; add vanilla. Mix together graham cracker crumbs, dates and pecans; fold into egg white mixture. Spread in 9-or 10-inch unbuttered pie pan. Bake in 300-degree oven for 30 minutes or until set and very lightly browned. When cool, spread with whipped cream.
Mrs. J.L. Marvin, Jacksonville, FL

LEMON CHESS BUTTERMILK PIE

1/4 cup butter or margarine
1 cup sugar
1 tablespoon flour
1 tablespoon corn meal
4 eggs
1/2 cup lemon juice
1 teaspoon lemon peel (optional)
1/2 cup buttermilk

Melt butter; add sugar, flour, and corn meal. Add eggs, one at a time, beating well after each addition. Add lemon juice, lemon peel, and buttermilk. Pour into unbaked 8- or 9-inch pie shell. Bake 45 minutes at 350 degrees or until a knife comes out clean and pie is golden brown.
Mrs. P. B. Brother, Richmond, VA

FROZEN CRYSTAL LEMON PIE

3 eggs, separated
1/2 cup sugar
1/4 cup fresh lemon juice
1 teaspoon lemon zest (rind)

1/2 pint whipping cream, whipped
Crushed vanilla wafers

Beat egg yolks; add sugar, lemon zest, and juice. Cook gently until thickened; cool. Fold whipped cream into custard; fold in stiffly beaten egg whites. Crush enough vanilla wafers to cover the bottom of a freezing tray, pan, or dish. Pour lemon mixture over crumbs; cover top with crumbs. Place in freezer for at least 24 hours.

Remove from freezer 10 minutes before serving; cut into squares or slices.
Gwen Campbell, Sterling, Va.

AMISH LEMON PIE

2 tablespoons margarine, softened
1 cup sugar
3 eggs, separated
3 tablespoons flour
1/2 teaspoon salt
Juice and grated rind of one lemon
1-1/2 cups hot milk
1 (9-inch) unbaked pie shell
Cool Whip or 1/2 pint heavy whipping cream, whipped

Cream margarine and sugar; add egg yolks, beating well. Add flour, salt, lemon juice, lemon rind, and milk; blend well.

Beat egg whites until stiff; fold into lemon mixture. Pour into pie shell; bake at 350 degrees for 35 minutes. Cool; top with Cool Whip or whipped cream sweetened with 3 tablespoons sifted confectioners' sugar.

This is a very simple pie to make.
Mrs. Albert H. Foley, Lemoyne, Pa.

LEMON CHIFFON PIE

1 (8- or 9-inch) graham cracker
    crumb crust
1 (14-ounce) can Eagle Brand
    sweetened condensed milk
1/2 cup lemon juice
Few drops yellow food coloring
3 egg whites
1/4 teaspoon cream of tartar
Whipped cream or Cool Whip
    topping

Lemon slices, optional

In medium bowl, combine sweetened condensed milk, lemon juice and food coloring; mix well. In a small bowl beat egg whites with cream of tartar until stiff but not dry. Gently fold into condensed milk mixture. Turn into crust. Chill 3 hours or until set. Garnish with whipped cream and lemon slices, if desired. Refrigerate leftovers.
Aldora Hohman, Manassas, Va.

FRUIT PIZZA PIE

Crust:
Mix until light -
1 stick margarine
3/4 cup sugar
1 egg

Sift together -
1-1/2 cups flour
1 teaspoon baking powder
1/2 teaspoon salt
1/2 teaspoon vanilla

Mix together- refrigerate 1 hour. Spread on lightly greased pizza pan. Bake 350 degrees for 10 minutes or until light brown. Make glaze while dough is chilling so it can cool well.

Glaze:
1/2 cup sugar
Dash of salt
2 tablespoon cornstarch
1/2 cup orange juice
2 tablespoons lemon juice
1/4 cup water

Cook until mixture thickens (about 4 minutes). Remove from heat and let cool.

When crust is cool make filling. Mix together 1 - 8 ounce cream cheese and 1 - 8 ounce cool whip. Spread on cool crust.

Fruit:
Place grapes around outer edge, strawberries next to grapes, sliced bananas next row or two, peaches next row, fill in remaining space wiht chunk pineapple. Spoon glaze over fruit. Glaze bananas first to keep from turning dark. (KEEP REFRIGERATED).
Patricia Parsons, Shinnston, W VA

FRUIT SALAD PIE

1-1/4 cups water
3/4 cup white sugar
3 tablespoons pineapple juice
3 tablespoons maraschino cherry juice
3 tablespoons cornstarch
1/4 teaspoon red food coloring

Cook above ingredients until thick and then let cool.
Add:
2 large bananas, sliced
1/2 cup drained, crushed pineapple
1 (3-ounce) bottle maraschino cherries, drained and sliced in half

Pour into baked pie shell. Sprinkle with 1/2 cup coconut and 1/2 cup chopped walnuts. Chill; serve topped with whipped cream.

Clare R. Bracelin, Decatur, Ill.

ICE BOX CHERRY PIE

1 can red pie cherries, drained
1 cup nuts
1 can condensed milk
1/4 cup sugar
1 cup whipped cream
Juice of 2 lemons
1 graham cracker pie crust
Cool Whip

Mix milk, lemon juice, and sugar. Add cherries and nuts. Fold in whipped cream. Pour into pie crust. Top with Cool Whip. Refrigerate 4 hours or more before serving.

Monica Turk, Milwaukee, Wis.

GRAPE PIE
Serves 6-8

Pastry for 2-crust 9-inch pie
6 cups Concord grapes
1 cup sugar
1/4 cup flour
1/4 teaspoon salt

1 teaspoon lemon juice
1 tablespoon butter

Wash and peel grapes, saving skins. Cook pulp in a saucepan with no water; bring to a hard boil. Rub through a strainer or food mill to remove seeds. Mix strained pulp with the reserved skins. Mix flour, sugar, and salt; stir into grapes. Add lemon juice and butter. Pour into pastry-lined 9-inch pie pan. Top with second crust. Slip top crust and seal edges. Bake at 400 degrees for about 40 minutes or until crust is brown and pie is bubbly.

Joy Shamway, Freeport, Il

BUTTERMILK RAISIN PIE

1/4 cup cornstarch
1 cup sugar
1/4 teaspoon salt
2 cups buttermilk
1/2 cup raisins
2 tablespoons lemon juice
2 eggs, separated (use whites for meringue)
1 tablespoon butter

Cool baked 8- or 9-inch pie shell. Mix cornstarch, sugar, salt, and beaten egg yolks in top of double boiler; add buttermilk, raisins, and lemon juice. Cook over direct heat stirring constantly, until mixture boils and thickens. Remove from heat and stir in butter until melted. Cool slightly. Pour into baked pie shell. Beat egg whites until stiff. Gradually add 1/4 cup sugar; spread over pie. Bake at 350 degrees for 12-15 minutes until browned.

Helen Taugher, Nicholson, PA

RAISIN PIE

2 cups raisins (seedless or seeded)
2 cups boiling water
1/3 cup granulated sugar
1/3 cup brown sugar
2 tablespoons cornstarch
1/8 teaspoon salt
2 teaspoons grated lemon rind
1/2 teaspoon grated orange rind
2 tablespoons lemon juice
1 tablespoon orange juice
Pastry for 2-crust (9-inch) pie
2 tablespoons butter or margarine

Add raisins to water; simmer until tender (3-5 minutes). Combine sugars, cornstarch, and salt; stir into hot raisins. Cook slowly, stirring constantly, to full rolling boil; boil 1 minute. Remove from heat.

Blend in fruit rinds and juices. Pour hot filling into pastry-lined pie pan; dot top with butter. Cover with remaining pastry. Bake in 425-degree oven for 30-40 minutes. Serve slightly warm, plain, or with whipped cream.

Grace Lane, Redondo Beach, Calif.

BEST-EVER PUMPKIN PIE
Makes 2 (9-inch) pies

Pasrty for 2 1-crust pies
1-1/2 cups sifted brown sugar
1 (No. 2-1/2) can pumpkin
4 eggs
3 tablespoons butter
2 tablespoons molasses
1-1/2 teaspoons cinnamon
3/4 teaspoon ginger
1/2 teaspoon nutmeg
1 teaspoon salt
1-1/2 cups milk

Line pastry in pie plates. Add sugar to the pumpkin. Beat eggs until thick and add with butter, molasses, seasonings, and milk to the pumpkin mixture; stir. Pour pumpkin mixture into pastry-lined pans. Bake at 425 degrees for 10 minutes; reduce heat to 325 degrees and bake 25 more minutes.

Lucy Dowd, Sequim, Wash.

CRANBERRY APPLE PIE

Pastry for 9-inch two-crust pie
1 cup sugar
1/3 cup all-purpose flour
1 teaspoon apple pie spice
4 cups sliced pared tart apples
2 cups Ocean Spray fresh cranberries
2 tablespoons butter or margarine

Preheat oven to 425 degrees. Prepare pastry. In a bowl, stir together sugar, flour, and spice. In pastry-lined pie pan alternate layers of apples, cranberries, and sugar mixture, beginning and ending with sugar mixture. Dot with butter. Cover with top crust. Cut slits in crust; seal and flute edges. Bake 40 to 50 minutes. Cool.

APPLE-BUTTER CINNAMON PIE

Pastry for 9-inch pie, plus strips for lattice
1/2 cup apple butter
2 eggs, beaten lightly
1/2 cup sugar
1-1/2 tablespoons cornstarch
1-1/2 teaspoons cinnamon
1/4 teaspoon mace
2 cups milk

Combine apple butter, eggs, sugar, cornstarch, cinnamon, and mace; mix well. Add milk gradually; blend well. Pour into unbaked pie shell; top with lattice made from 1/2-inch wide strips of crust. Bake 350 degrees for 35 minutes.

Gwen Campbell, Sterling, Va.

DATE AND NUT PIE

1 unbaked 9-inch pie crust
1/2 cup butter, at room temperature
1 cup light brown sugar
4 eggs
1 teaspoon pure vanilla extract
1 teaspoon cinnamon
1/2 teaspoon nutmeg
3/4 cup whipping cream
1/2 cup chopped dates
1/2 cup raisins
1/2 cup chopped walnuts

Preheat oven to 350 degrees. Cream butter, then cream in the brown sugar, mixing until fluffy. Beat in eggs. Blend in vanilla, cinnamon, nutmeg, and cream, mixing well. Stir in dates, raisins, and nuts. Pour into pie crust. Bake in a preheated oven for about 45 minutes or until the surface is crisp and lightly browned.

This is worth the calories!
Lillian Smith, Montreal Quebec, Canada

BLUEBERRY BOTTOM PIE

2 (4-serving) packages vanilla pudding and pie filling
1-1/4 cups milk
1-1/2 cups blueberries, puréed (1 cup)
1/2 teaspoon cinnamon
1 baked 9-inch pie shell, cooled
2 teaspoons grated lemon rind
3-1/2 cups frozen whipped topping (thawed)

Combine 1 package pudding mix, 1/4 cup of the milk, the puréed berries, and cinnamon in saucepan. Cook and stir until mixture comes to a full boil. Pour into crust; chill. Prepare remaining pudding mix with milk, as directed on package for pie. Add 1 teaspoon of the lemon rind; pour into bowl and cover with plastic wrap. Chill 1 hour. Fold in 1 cup of the whipped topping and spoon over blueberry layer. Combine remaining whipped topping and lemon rind. Spoon over filling. Chill in refrigerator, at least 3 hours before serving. Garnish with blueberries, if desired.

Suzanne Dawson, Cypress, Texas

APPLESAUCE CHEESE PIE

6 graham crackers, crushed
1 tablespoon butter or margarine, melted
2 cups cottage cheese
2 eggs
1/4 cup sugar
1/4 cup flour
1 tablespoon lemon juice
1 cup thick applesauce

Mix crackers and butter; press into bottom and sides of 8- or 9-inch pie plate. Put cottage cheese through fine sieve; add eggs, one at a time, beating after each. Add sugar, flour, lemon juice, and applesauce. Beat until well blended. Pour into crumb-lined pie plate and bake in preheated 325-degree oven for 1 hour and 10 minutes or until mixture is set and lightly browned.

Kit Rollins, Cedarburg, WI

FRUIT COCKTAIL PIE

1 (1 pound, 13 ounces) can fruit cocktail, well drained
32 vanilla wafers
1/2 cup sugar
1 teaspoon vanilla
2 cups sour cream

Preheat oven to 350 degrees. Place fruit cocktail in drainer; stir. Line bottom and sides of 9-inch glass pie plate with vanilla wafers. Add sugar and vanilla to sour cream; stir. Stir fruit cocktail again to be sure it is well drained. Add to sour cream mixture, folding gently. Pour into wafer-lined pie plate. Top with additional vanilla wafer crumbs, if desired. Bake at 350 degrees for 25 minutes, or until middle is set. Cool. Chill thoroughly before serving.

Marsha Miller, Hilliard, Ohio

Salad

BOWL

CABBAGE PATCH TOMATO SLAW

4-1/2 cups finely shredded white cabbage
2 greens onions, finely chopped
10-ounce can condensed tomato soup
3 tablespoons red wine vinegar
1 clove garlic, crushed
2 tablespoons chopped fresh parsley
Salt and pepper to taste

Mix cabbage, carrots and green onions together. In separate bowl, mix tomato soup, vinegar, crushed garlic, parsley, salt and pepper. Blend thoroughly; pour over salad. Mix well; chill. Serve over cold, crisp lettuce or in chilled tomato cups.

Gwen Campbell, Sterling, VA

CRAB-SHELL SALAD

Serves 4

6 ounces cooked crab
8 ounces snow peas
4 cups cooked small pasta shells, chilled
1 green or red bell pepper, chopped
1/4 cup fresh lemon juice
1/8 teaspoon vinegar
1-1/4 teaspoons dill weed
Dressing for salad (recipe follows)

Clean snow peas; cut ends off; steam peas over boiling water for 5 minutes; drain. Mix dressing ingredients together; chill. Place crab, snow peas, pasta, and bell pepper in large salad bowl; pour lemon juice and vinegar over salad; sprinkle with dill weed. Pour dressing over salad; mix well; serve chilled. Serve with toast points or crisp crackers.

Dressing:
1/2 cup mayonnaise
1/4 cup sour cream
3 teaspoons mustard
1 teaspoon fresh ginger, grated

Gwen Campbell, Sterling, Va.

CALICO PASTA SALAD

Serves 6

1 (20-ounce) can pineapple chunks
4 cups cooked small shell pasta
3 cups cooked shredded chicken
1 clove garlic, pressed
1/2 cup mayonnaise
1/2 cup sour cream
1/3 cup white vinegar
1 tablespoon Dijon mustard
1 teaspoon basil
1 teaspoon marjoram, crumbled
1 red or green bell pepper, seeded and sliced
1-1/2 cups sliced celery
1/2 cup sliced green onion
1-1/2 cups sliced black olives

Drain pineapple; reserve 2 tablespoons juice. Add pasta and chicken to large bowl. For dressing, combine reserved juice with next 6 ingredients. Pour over pasta and chicken. Toss well. Add remaining ingredients; cover and refrigerate 1 hour, or overnight, which allows for the best flavors to develop.

Laura Hicks, Newport, Wash.

SIMPLE SALAD SPECIAL

1 small carton cottage cheese
1 small carton Cool Whip (4-1/2 ounce approximately)
*1 (3-ounce) package raspberry or wild cherry gelatin
1 small can crushed pineapple, drained

Mix all together and refrigerate. Use a small gelatin mold or any small dish.
*Most any flavor can be used. *Do not make* gelatin; use it in powder form in this recipe.

Sue Hibbard, Rochester, N.Y.

ORANGE TAPIOCA SALAD

1 (3-ounce) package orange or vanilla tapioca pudding mix
1/4 teaspoon orange flavoring
1 cup milk
1 (3-ounce) package orange gelatin
1 cup hot water
1 envelope whipped topping mix
1 cup mandarin oranges, drained
1/2 cup chopped pecans

Mix pudding, flavoring, and milk in saucepan. Bring to boil. Remove from heat. Add gelatin and hot water; let cool. Prepare topping when gelatin is cool. Fold into pudding mixture, along with oranges and pecans. May be put in a mold.
Note: Whipped topping may be used. This is a pretty salad, as well as tasty.

Betty Slavin, Omaha, Neb.

ORANGE SHERBERT GELATIN SALAD

Serves 8

2-3 ounce packages orange gelatin
1 cup boiling water
1 pint orange sherbert
1 can mandarin oranges, drained
1 cup heavy cream, whipped

Dissolve gelatin in boiling water; add sherbert, and mix well. When partially set, add mandarin oranges and fold in whipped cream. Pour into square pan or individual molds.

Margaret Hamfeldt, Louisville, KY

CRANBERRY SALAD MOLD

1 (3 ounce) package lemon gelatin
2 cups boiling water
1-1/4 cups sugar

Dissolve and set aside to cool, but not to set.

Add:
1 small can crushed pineapple
1 cup diced celery
1 orange, cut up
1 tablespoon grated orange peel
2 cups diced apples
3 cups ground cranberries

Pour into gelatin mold; refrigerate until ready to serve. Unmold on green lettuce leaves. Stores well, and may easily be made in advance.

Fay Duman, Eugene, Ore.

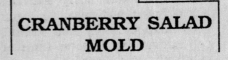

BROCCOLI ASPIC

Serves 6

1 envelope unflavored gelatin
1 can condensed consommé
Salt & pepper to taste
3/4 cup mayonnaise
3 hard-cooked eggs, sliced
Juice of 1-1/2 lemons
2 cups cooked broccoli flowerets

Soften gelatin in 1/4 cup cold consommé. Add to the rest of the consommé and heat. Stir until dissolved; add salt and pepper, if needed. Let thicken until consistency of raw egg whites. Fold in mayonnaise, sliced eggs, broccoli and lemon juice. Pour into individual molds and chill until firm.

Agnes Ward, Erie, PA

STRAWBERRY-RHUBARB SALAD MOLD

3 (3-ounce) packages strawberry gelatin
3 cups hot water
2 packages frozen rhubarb
1 quart sliced fresh strawberries
Watercress or other salad greens
1 fresh whole strawberry
Chantilly Mayonnaise (recipe follows)

Dissolve 3 packages gelatin in 3 cups hot water. Drop in 2 packages of frozen rhubarb. Stir to separate the rhubarb. When jelly begins to set, add the strawberries. Pour into individual wet molds and chill until set. Unmold on watercress. Garnish each mold with whole strawberry. Serve with Chantilly Mayonnaise.

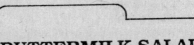

BUTTERMILK SALAD

1 (6 ounce) package apricot gelatin
1 (20 ounce) can crushed pineapple, undrained
2 cups buttermilk
1 (8 or 9 ounce) container Cool Whip

Bring pineapple to a boil in saucepan. Stir dry gelatin into pineapple and mix until dissolved. Chill until partially set. Stir in buttermilk. Chill again until partly set. Fold in Cool Whip. Refrigerate until firm.

Ruby Beheber, Ransom, IL

HOLIDAY STRAWBERRY GELATIN

1 large (6 ounce) package strawberry gelatin
2 bananas, sliced
1 can crushed pineapple with juice
1/2 cup chopped nuts
1 large package sour cream
2 packages frozen strawberries with juice

Dissolve gelatin in 1 cup boiling water; add pineapple, bananas, strawberries, and nuts. Let jell in refrigerator for about 1 hour. Pour one half mixture into 9x12 inch pan. Let jell in refrigerator about 10-15 minutes; spread sour cream on top. Pour remaining gelatin as top layer.

Refrigerate until serving; may want to garnish for the holidays.

Donna Holter, West Middlesex, Pa.

SPARKLE SALAD

1 (3 ounce) package lime gelatin
1 cup miniature marshmallows
1 cup 7-UP, heated to boiling
3/4 cup finely chopped cabbage
1/2 cup finely chopped carrots
1 cup crushed pineapple, well drained
1/2 cup chopped pecans
1 cup mayonnaise
1 cup whipped cream

Dissolve gelatin and marshmallows in 7-UP. Chill until slightly thickened. Add cabbage, carrots, pineapple, nuts, and mayonnaise. Fold in whipped cream.

Note: For convenience, use blender for cabbage and carrots.

Mrs. Charles Sharp, Newton, Kan.

SPECIAL FRUIT SALAD

1 (3 ounce) box non- instant vanilla pudding
1 (3 ounce) box non-instant tapioca pudding
1 heaping tablespoon frozen orange juice concentrate
3 (11 ounce) cans mandarin oranges
3 (15 ounce) cans pineapple tidbits
3 large bananas, sliced

Drain one can of oranges and pineapple. Use the juice and add enough water to make 3 cups of liquid. Cook puddings and orange juice with the liquid until thickened. Cool slightly and add to drained fruit.

Kristy Schemrich, Shreve, Ohio

CIDER WALDORF SALAD

Serves 12

2 envelopes Knox unflavored gelatin
2-1/2 cups cold apple cider or apple juice
1 cup apple cider or juice, heated to boiling
2 tablespoons lemon juice
1-1/4 cups chopped apple
1/2 cup diced celery
1/2 cup raisins
1/2 cup coarsely chopped walnuts

In large bowl, sprinkle unflavored gelatin over 1/2 cup cold cider; let stand 1 minute. Add hot cider and stir until gelatin is completely dissolved. Stir in remaining cold cider and lemon juice. Chill, stirring occasionally, until mixture is consistency of unbeaten egg whites. Fold in remaining ingredients. Turn into 6-1/2 cup mold or bowl; chill until firm.

Sue Hibbard, Rochester, N.Y.

FROZEN WALDORF SALAD

Serves 9-12

1 (8 ounce) can crushed pineapple
2 eggs, slightly beaten
1/2 cup sugar
1/4 cup lemon juice
1/8 teaspoon salt
2 cups unpeeled apples, diced
1 cup celery, diced
1/2 cup pecans, chopped
1/2 cup whipping cream

Drain juice from pineapple into sauce pan. Add slightly beaten eggs, sugar, lemon juice, and salt. Cook over low heat, stirring constantly, until thickened. Cool slightly. Add pineapple, apples, celery, and pecans. Mix to blend.

Whip cream. Fold into pineapple mixture. Pour into an 8-inch square dish. Freeze overnight. Before serving, place in refrigerator for about 3 hours.

Margaret Hamfeldt, Louisville, Ky.

GINGER PEAR SALAD

Serves 4-5

1 (10-1/2 -ounce) can condensed consomme
1/4 teaspoon ground ginger
Dash cinnamon
1 (3-ounce) package lemon-flavored gelatin
3/4 cup cold water
6 walnut halves
1 (1-pound) can pear halves, drained and diced
1/2 cup thinly sliced celery
1/3 cup coarsely chopped walnuts
Crisp salad greens
Sour cream

Combine consomme, ginger, and cinnamon. Bring to a boil. Add gelatin and stir until dissolved. Add water. Chill until slightly thickened. Pour a small amount into a 1-quart mold. Arrange walnut halves and several pieces of pear on gelatin. Stir remaining pears, celery, and walnuts into remaining gelatin. Spoon into

mold. Chill until firm, about 3 hours. Unmold. Serve on crisp salad greens. Garnish with sour cream.

MANDARIN ORANGE SALAD

60 Ritz crackers, crushed
1/4 pound butter, melted
1/4 cup sugar
1 (6 ounce) can unsweetened frozen orange juice, thawed
1 can Eagle Brand Sweetened Condenced Milk
1 (8 ounce) container Cool Whip
2 small cans Mandarin oranges, drained

Crush crackers finely and add melted butter and sugar to them. Press mixture firmly into 9x13x2 inch baking dish. Reserve some of crumb mixture for garnish.

Blend thawed orange juice and milk. Stir in Cool Whip and oranges. Fold in. Do not beat. Pour mixture over crumb crust. Top with reserved crumbs.

Refrigerate or freeze until serving. This is delicious, refreshing, and appetizing.

Patty White, Indianapolis, IN

GREEN BEAN SALAD

1 can (16 ounce) French-style sliced green beans
1 green onion
1/3 cup white vinegar
1/4 cup sugar
1/8 teaspoon garlic salt
4 tablespoons water
2 tablespoons oil

Drain beans well. Transfer to medium bowl. Use scissors to snip in green onion. Set aside.

In pint pitcher, measure vinegar. Add sugar and garlic salt; mix well. Add water and oil; beat with whisk or fork. Pour over beans; toss with fork to mix. Cover; refrigerate overnight for flavors to blend. Serve cold.

BREAD SALAD

1 large loaf sliced white sandwich bread
1 large onion, finely chopped
4 hard-cooked eggs, chopped
1 cup finely chopped celery
1 (7-ounce) can crab and 2 cans shrimp (or substitute 2 cups cooked chicken or turkey)
3 cups mayonnaise

Cut crusts from bread. Spread bread lightly with butter. Cut into small cubes. Add onions and eggs; refrigerate overnight. Add the remaining ingredients in the morning and chill 3 to 4 hours. Garnish with cucumbers, tomatoes, etc.
Mrs. Martha Mehlhoff, SD.

EGG SALAD
Makes 2 cups

4 hard-cooked eggs, chopped
1/2 cup mayonnaise
1/2 cup chopped ham
2 tablespoons sliced green onions
2 teaspoons Dijon mustard
Dash freshly ground pepper

In small bowl combine eggs, mayonnaise, ham, green onion, mustard, and pepper. Cover; chill.
Annie Cmehil , New Castle, Ind.

ORANGE SALAD
Serves 6

1 large (6-ounce) package orange gelatin
1 cup hot water
2 cups orange sherbet
1 cup mandarin oranges, drained
1 cup crushed pineapple, drained
1/2 pint whipping cream, whipped

Dissolve gelatin in hot water. Add sherbet, mixing well. Add drained oranges and pineapple. Fold in whipped cream. Congeals quickly. Chill.
Lucille Kavanaugh, Braymer, Mo.

RASPBERRY DELIGHT

1 (3-ounce) package raspberry gelatin
1 cup hot water
1 (8-ounce) can crushed pineapple and juice
1 (10-ounce) package frozen raspberries and juice
1 cup whipped topping or Cool Whip

Dissolve gelatin in hot water. Chill until syrupy. Add fruits and juices. Chill until thickened, but not quite set hard. Fold in topping, making a marbled effect. Chill.
Ann Sterzer, Lincoln, Neb.

EASY FRUIT WALDORF
Serves 6

1 (No. 2-1/2) can fruit cocktail
1/2 cup sliced celery
1/2 cup chopped walnuts
Salad greens
Cream Dressing (recipe follows)

Drain fruit cocktail well and mix lightly with celery and walnuts. Serve on salad greens and top with Cream Dressing or mayonnaise.

Cream Dressing:
Combine *equal* parts lemon juice and honey.
Lucille Roehr, Hammond, Ind.

BEAUTIFUL CHERRY SALAD

2 packages cherry gelatin
1 can cherry pie filling
2 cups hot water
1 cup sour cream

Dissolve gelatin in hot water. Cool until it starts to set. Add sour cream and cherry pie filling; pour into mold and refrigerate. (I add pie filling first and then just swirl sour cream through it.)
Marcella Swigert, Monroe City, Mo.

SUMMER FRUIT FANTASY
Serves 12

3 grapefruit
3 oranges
1 pint fresh strawberries
1 pineapple, cut into cubes to yield 2 cups cubes
2 peaches, cut into bite-size pieces
1 cup fresh blueberries
1 cup seedless grapes or remove seeds, use half green and half red
1 teaspoon orange rind
4 tablespoons orange juice
3 tablespoons sugar
3 tablespoons orange flavored liqueur

Mix all dressing ingredients and set aside. Cut grapefruit and oranges in half. Remove pulp in pieces. Hollow out shells and set aside. Cut pulp into bite-size segments. In a large bowl, combine grapefruit and orange segments. Add strawberries that have been washed, hulled, and cut in half. Add pineapple cubes, peaches, blueberries, and grapes. Toss well. Top with dressing. Toss carefully. Cover and chill 30 minutes to 12 hours. Serve in empty hollowed out grapefruit and orange shells. (You may substitute any fresh fruit available.)
Laura Morris, Bunnell, Fla.

RASPBERRY SALAD

1 large box raspberry gelatin
2 cups hot water
2 cups applesauce
2 packages frozen raspberries, partially defrosted
1 cup sour cream
1-1/2 cups miniature marshmallows
2 teaspoons cinnamon

In oblong dish, dissolve gelatin in hot water. Break up raspberries in mixture. Add applesauce and cinnamon. Refrigerate until set. Combine sour cream and marshmallows. Spread on top of chilled gelatin. Refrigerate again for 2 hours before serving.
Suzanne Dawson, Cypress, TX

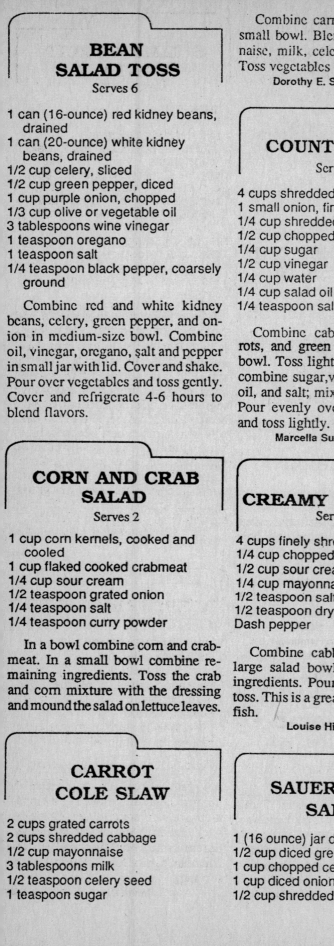

BEAN SALAD TOSS

Serves 6

1 can (16-ounce) red kidney beans, drained
1 can (20-ounce) white kidney beans, drained
1/2 cup celery, sliced
1/2 cup green pepper, diced
1 cup purple onion, chopped
1/3 cup olive or vegetable oil
3 tablespoons wine vinegar
1 teaspoon oregano
1 teaspoon salt
1/4 teaspoon black pepper, coarsely ground

Combine red and white kidney beans, celery, green pepper, and onion in medium-size bowl. Combine oil, vinegar, oregano, salt and pepper in small jar with lid. Cover and shake. Pour over vegetables and toss gently. Cover and refrigerate 4-6 hours to blend flavors.

CORN AND CRAB SALAD

Serves 2

1 cup corn kernels, cooked and cooled
1 cup flaked cooked crabmeat
1/4 cup sour cream
1/2 teaspoon grated onion
1/4 teaspoon salt
1/4 teaspoon curry powder

In a bowl combine corn and crabmeat. In a small bowl combine remaining ingredients. Toss the crab and corn mixture with the dressing and mound the salad on lettuce leaves.

CARROT COLE SLAW

2 cups grated carrots
2 cups shredded cabbage
1/2 cup mayonnaise
3 tablespoons milk
1/2 teaspoon celery seed
1 teaspoon sugar

Combine carrots and cabbage in small bowl. Blend together mayonnaise, milk, celery seed, and sugar. Toss vegetables in salad dressing.

Dorothy E. Snyder, Pine Grove, Pa.

COUNTRY SLAW

Serves 4-6

4 cups shredded cabbage
1 small onion, finely chopped
1/4 cup shredded carrots
1/2 cup chopped green peppers
1/4 cup sugar
1/2 cup vinegar
1/4 cup water
1/4 cup salad oil
1/4 teaspoon salt

Combine cabbage, onions, carrots, and green peppers in a salad bowl. Toss lightly. In a small bowl, combine sugar, vinegar, water, salad oil, and salt; mix until well blended. Pour evenly over cabbage mixture and toss lightly. Cover and chill.

Marcella Surgert, Monroe City, MO

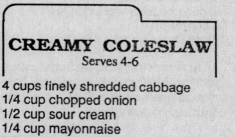

CREAMY COLESLAW

Serves 4-6

4 cups finely shredded cabbage
1/4 cup chopped onion
1/2 cup sour cream
1/4 cup mayonnaise
1/2 teaspoon salt
1/2 teaspoon dry mustard
Dash pepper

Combine cabbage and onion in large salad bowl. Blend remaining ingredients. Pour over cabbage and toss. This is a great slaw to serve with fish.

Louise Hicks, West Chicago, Ill.

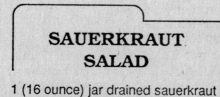

SAUERKRAUT SALAD

1 (16 ounce) jar drained sauerkraut
1/2 cup diced green pepper
1 cup chopped celery
1 cup diced onion
1/2 cup shredded carrot

1 cup sugar
1 (16 ounce) can whole kernel corn, drained
2 tablespoons oil
1/4 cup vinegar
1/4 teaspoon salt
1 (4 ounce) jar pimientos, drained

Mix all ingredients together lightly. Chill several hours before serving.

Irene Doolittle, Seffner, FL

MARINATED SALAD

Serves 8

2 cups sliced carrots
1-1/2 cups chopped celery
1 large green pepper, chopped
1 medium cauliflower
1 (1-pound) jar sweet pepper rings
8 ounces Hendrickson's Salad Dressing
1 small cucumber

Cook carrots, celery, and cauliflower until almost tender. Drain and cool. Add pepper and cucumber. Toss with salad dressing and chill for 6 hours. Serve over lettuce or spinach leaves. You may also add pasta to provide added texture and flavor.

Marcella Swigert, Monroe City, Mo.

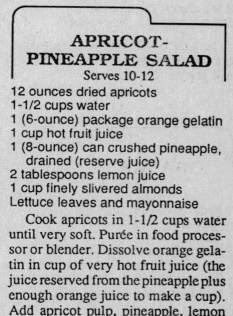

APRICOT-PINEAPPLE SALAD

Serves 10-12

12 ounces dried apricots
1-1/2 cups water
1 (6-ounce) package orange gelatin
1 cup hot fruit juice
1 (8-ounce) can crushed pineapple, drained (reserve juice)
2 tablespoons lemon juice
1 cup finely slivered almonds
Lettuce leaves and mayonnaise

Cook apricots in 1-1/2 cups water until very soft. Purée in food processor or blender. Dissolve orange gelatin in cup of very hot fruit juice (the juice reserved from the pineapple plus enough orange juice to make a cup). Add apricot pulp, pineapple, lemon juice, and almonds; stir until well-mixed. Pour into a 2-quart flat dish and chill until set. To serve, cut into squares and serve on a lettuce leaf with a dollop of mayonnaise on top.

Joy Shamway, Freeport, Ill.

SPECIAL POTATO SALAD
Serves 6

4 cups cooked, diced potatoes
1-1/2 cups sliced celery
1/2 cup chopped onion
1/4 cup sliced radishes
1 cup mayonnaise
1 tablespoon vinegar
1 teaspoon prepared mustard
1/2 teaspoon celery seed
1-1/2 teaspoons salt
1/8 teaspoon pepper
Lettuce leaves

Combine all ingredients except lettuce; refrigerate. Serve on lettuce leaves and garnish with hard-cooked eggs, tomato wedges, and sliced olives, if desired.

SOUR CREAM POTATO SALAD

1/3 cup clear Italian dressing
7 medium potatoes, cooked in jackets, peeled, sliced (6 cups)
3/4 cup sliced celery
1/3 cup sliced green onion
4 hard-cooked eggs
1 cup mayonnaise
1/2 cup dairy sour cream
1-1/2 teaspoons prepared horseradish mustard

Pour dressing over warm potatoes; chill 2 hours. Add celery and onion. Chop egg whites. Add to potato mixture; sieve yolks; mix with mayonnaise, sour cream, and horseradish mustard; fold into salad. Add salt and celery seed to taste. Chill 2 hours. Add 1/3 cup diced, pared cucumber, if desired.

Karin Shea Fedders, Dameron, Ohio

ITALIAN POTATO SALAD

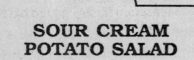

6 boiled potatoes, sliced
2 large tomatoes, diced
1 large cucumber, thinly sliced
1/2 cup onion, thinly sliced
1/2 cup celery, thinly sliced
1 bunch radishes, thinly sliced

Dressing:
1/2 cup olive oil
1/4 cup red wine vinegar
1/4 teaspoon garlic powder
1/4 teaspoon oregano
1 teaspoon salt (or salt to taste)
1/4 teaspoon black pepper

Combine all vegetables in a bowl; add dressing; toss well. Refrigerate 2 hours or more before serving.
Edna Mae Seelos, Niles, Ill.

CORNED BEEF AND POTATO SALAD
Serves 4

1-1/2 cups cold, cooked potatoes, diced
1/2 cup finely chopped celery leaves
1/4 cup sweet pickle relish, drained
1 tablespoon minced onion
1 cup chilled corned beef, cubed
1/2 cup mayonnaise
1 teaspoon prepared mustard
3 tablespoons chili sauce or catsup
Salt and pepper
Accent, to taste
2 hard-cooked eggs
Lettuce
Paprika

Combine potatoes, celery leaves, relish, onion, and corned beef. Mix mayonnaise, mustard, chili sauce or catsup, and seasonings. Add to potato mixture and toss lightly, but thoroughly. Chill well Serve on crisp lettuce and garnish with hard-cooked eggs and paprika. Recipe can easily be doubled with great success.
Agnes Ward, Erie, Pa.

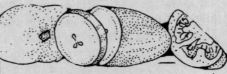

TACO SALAD

8 ounces cream cheese
8 ounces sour cream
1 package Ortega Taco Seasonings
Shredded lettuce
Chopped tomatoes
4 ounces shredded Mozzarella cheese
4 ounces sharp Cheddar cheese
Taco sauce
Black olives, sliced

Mix cream cheese, sour cream and taco seasoning together. Spread on 12-inch platter, layer remaining vegetables and cheese in order given on top. Sprinkle with taco sauce and decorate top with black olives. Serve with taco chips.
Mrs. Leah M. Daub, Milwaukee, WI

MACARONI SALAD
Serves 8-10

1 cup shell macaroni, cooked
2-1/2 cups chopped cooked ham
6 hard-cooked eggs, chopped
1/4 cup sweet pickles, finely chopped
5 or 6 green onions, thinly sliced
1/4 cup green pepper, finely chopped
1 cup salad dressing
Salt and pepper to taste
Paprika for color

Combine all ingredients in a large bowl and mix well. Chill 4 to 5 hours before serving.

This is a wonderful way to use leftover baked ham or you can also substitute turkey. Great for a buffet or potluck.

Jodie McCoy, Tulsa, Okla.

CHILLED MAIN-DISH SALAD
Serves 4

2 cups cooked beef, cut into 1/2-inch cubes
1 onion, minced
1 dill pickle, minced
1 apple, peeled and diced
2 ribs celery, diced
1 cup pickled beets, minced
1/4 cup beet liquid
1/2 cup sour cream
1 cup mayonnaise

Combine beet liquid, sour cream and mayonnaise. Pour over all ingredients; mix gently and chill before serving.

Gwen Campbell, Sterling, Va

Salad
DRESSING

ALL SEASONS SALAD DRESSING

1 can tomato soup
1 soup can oil
1 soup can vinegar
1/2 cup sugar
1 small onion, finely chopped
1 tablespoon Worcestershire sauce
1 tablespoon salt
1 teaspoon dry mustard
Dash pepper
Dash garlic powder

Blend well with mixer or blender. Let stand 24 hours for flavors to fully blend.

Susan Defendorf, Holley, N.Y.

FRENCH SALAD DRESSING

1/2 cup white sugar
1/2 cup salad oil
1/2 cup Ketchup
1/4 cup cider vinegar
1 teaspoon salt
1 teaspoon paprika
1/2 cup chopped onions (white sweet ones).

Process in blender; place in container and store in refrigerator.

Pat Linie, Havre, Mont.

FRUIT SALAD DRESSING

1/4 cup Karo light corn syrup
1/2 cup sour cream
1/2 cup mayonnaise

Mix sour cream with mayonnaise until smooth. Add Karo syrup and blend well. Spoon over a salad of assorted fresh fruits or canned fruits.

Mrs. John Walker, Shelton, Conn.

LOW-CAL DRESSING
Makes 1/2 cup

1/2 cup skim milk
1 teaspoon onion juice
1 tablespoon lemon juice
1 tablespoon minced parsley
1 tablespoon minced pimiento

Combine milk with lemon juice and flavoring agents; shake thoroughly in a small jar with tightly fitting lid. More or less lemon juice may be used according to taste.

Use at once; serve immediately. Great dressing for all types of salads.

Lucy Dowd, Sequim, Wash.

SUPER SALAD SEASONING MIX

2 cups Parmesan cheese
2 teaspoons salt

1/2 cup sesame seeds
1/2 teaspoon garlic salt
3 tablespoons celery seed
1 tablespoon instant minced onion
2 tablespoons parsley
1/2 teaspoon dill seeds
1/8 cup poppy seeds
2 teaspoons paprika
1/2 teaspoon freshly grated black pepper

Mix all ingredients together well. Use as a sprinkle on salads, baked potatoes, buttered French bread, and rolls. Also good as a garnish for potato and egg salads.

Jennie Lien, Stoughton, Wis.

TARRAGON DRESSING
Makes 3/4 cup

1/2 cup vegetable oil
1/4 cup cider vinegar
1-1/2 teaspoons sugar
1 teaspoon tarragon
1/2 teaspoon salt
1/4 teaspoon freshly ground black pepper
Dash liquid hot pepper sauce

Whisk together oil, vinegar, sugar, tarragon, salt, pepper, and hot sauce, until slightly creamy.
Note: Dressing can be made in advance. Shake or whisk before serving.

Mrs. Robert Shaffer, Middleburg, Pa.

Sauces &
TOPPINGS

BANANA BUTTER

4 large bananas
2 tablespoons juice
1-1/2 cups sugar
1/2 teaspoon cinnamon
1/8 teaspoon ground cloves

Peel bananas; cut up chunks and toss with lemon juice until well coated. Mash in blender or mixer until smooth. Put in saucepan with remaining ingredients. Bring to boil and then reduce heat; simmer gently for 15 minutes, stirring constantly. Cool.

Makes about 2-1/2 cups and keeps well for several weeks in refrigerator. A nice addition to the brunch or tea table, to be used on toast, biscuits, or English muffins. Also great to give as a last-minute gift from your kitchen.
Eleanor V. Craycraft, Santa Monica, Calif.

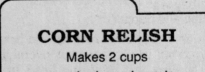

CORN RELISH
Makes 2 cups

1 cup uncooked corn kernels
2/3 cup white-wine vinegar
1/2 cup chopped red pepper
1/2 cup chopped green pepper
1/3 chopped celery
1/3 cup chopped onion
1 tablespoon mustard seed
2 teaspoons celery seed
1 teaspoon salt
1 cup sugar to taste

In a saucepan, combine all ingredients. Simmer the mixture for 15 minutes. Pack the relish into hot, sterilized jars and seal them.

HOMEMADE PANCAKE SYRUP

1 cup white sugar
2 cups brown sugar
1 cup boiling water
1 teaspoon vanilla or maple flavoring

Boil sugars and water together for 5 minutes. Let cool. Add flavoring.

PIQUANT RAISIN SAUCE
Serves 6

3/4 cup brown sugar
3/4 cup hot water
3/4 cup seedless dark raisins
3 tablespoons cider vinegar
2 tablespoons butter or margarine
1/4 teaspoon nutmeg
1/8 teaspoon ground cloves
3/4 cup any tart red jelly
1/4 teaspoon salt
1/4 teaspoon pepper
2 tablespoons cornstarch
2 tablespoons cold water

Combine brown sugar and hot water; stir until sugar dissolves. Add next 5 ingredients; simmer 5 minutes. Stir in jelly; cook until jelly melts; add salt and pepper. Mix cornstarch with cold water; stir into sauce. Cook; stirring constantly, until mixture boils, and is thickened. Serve hot over smoked pork, sliced ham, pork chops, sliced roasted pork, etc.
Gwen Campbell, Sterling, Va.

SEASONED SALT

1 cup salt
1-1/2 teaspoons oregano
1 teaspoon celery salt
2-1/2 teaspoons paprika
1 teaspoon thyme
1 teaspoon curry powder
2 teaspoons dry mustard
1/2 teaspoon garlic salt
1/2 teaspoon onion salt

Shake all together so that ingredients are well blended. Makes 1-1/4 cups. This is a great addition on fried potatoes, cottage cheese, and all types of meat.
Leota Baxter, Ingalls, Kan.

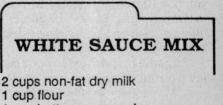

WHITE SAUCE MIX

2 cups non-fat dry milk
1 cup flour
1 cup butter or margarine

Combine dry milk and flour; cut in margarine with pastry blender. *Do not use* a mixer for this. Store in the refrigerator or freezer in an airtight container or jar.

Using this mix:

Combine 1 cup of mix and 1 cup cold water. Cook over low heat and stir with a whisk until heated and smooth in texture. You can make it thicker by adding more mix. You can also make variations by adding cheese, spices, and herbs of your choice.
Margie B. Warner, Ashville, Ohio

Soups & STEWS

CHILLY DAY BEEF HOT POT

1-1/2 pounds ground beef
3-1/2 tablespoons steak sauce
1 egg
1 (46-ounce) can vegetable-tomato juice
2 envelopes dry onion soup mix
1 (15-ounce) can red kidney beans, undrained
1 (14-ounce) can pinto beans, undrained
1 can mixed vegetables
1 cup fresh parsley, chopped

Mix ground beef with steak sauce and egg; shape into 1-inch meatballs. Heat vegetable-tomato juice to boiling. Stir in onion soup mix; cover; simmer 10 minutes. Place meatballs in simmering soup; cover; simmer 15 minutes. Stir in kidney beans, pinto beans, and mixed vegetables.

To garnish, sprinkle chopped parsley over individual servings of soup.

Gwen Campbell, Sterling, Va.

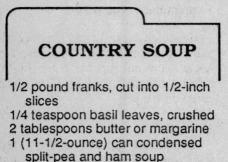

COUNTRY SOUP

1/2 pound franks, cut into 1/2-inch slices
1/4 teaspoon basil leaves, crushed
2 tablespoons butter or margarine
1 (11-1/2-ounce) can condensed split-pea and ham soup
1 (10-3/4-ounce) can condensed cream of potato soup
1 soup can water
1 (8-ounce) can tomatoes, cut up

In large saucepan, brown franks and basil in butter. Add soups; gradually stir in water. Add tomatoes. Heat; stir occasionally.

Monica Turk, Milwaukee, Wis.

COWBOY STEW
Serves 8

6 slices bacon
1 cup diced onion
1/2 cup chopped green pepper
1 clove garlic, crushed
1-1/2 pounds ground beef
2 (1-pound, 13-ounce) cans tomatoes
1 teaspoon salt
1/4 teaspoon pepper
1 tablespoon chili powder
1 (12-ounce) can whole-kernel corn, drained
1 (1-pound) can red kidney beans, drained
2 cups cubed potatoes, cooked
2 cups sliced carrots, cooked

Cook bacon until crisp; drain on paper towels; crumble and reserve. Sauté onion, green pepper, and garlic in bacon drippings until tender.

Add ground beef; cook until well-browned, breaking up with fork as it cooks. Add tomatoes, salt, pepper, and chili powder. Cover; simmer 30 minutes. Add vegetables; simmer 15 minutes. Sprinkle with bacon.

Kit Rollins, Cedarburg, Wis.

FISH CHOWDER
Serves 2

1 teaspoon butter
1/4 cup finely diced onion
1/2 pound lean white fish
1 teaspoon minced parsley
1 bouillon cube
3/4 cup milk
Salt and pepper

Place butter in small saucepan. Add onion and let cook about minute. Cut fish in 1-inch cubes and add to onion. Add 3/4 cup water, parsley, and bouillon cube. Bring to boil. Let simmer, covered, over low heat, until fish is done, about 5 minutes. Add milk and season to taste with salt and pepper. Heat thoroughly.

Suzan L. Wiener, Spring Hill, Fla.

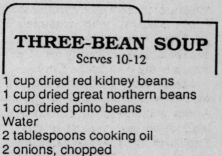

THREE-BEAN SOUP
Serves 10-12

1 cup dried red kidney beans
1 cup dried great northern beans
1 cup dried pinto beans
Water
2 tablespoons cooking oil
2 onions, chopped
1 cup chopped carrots
1 cup chopped celery
1 ham bone with ham
1 bay leaf
Salt and pepper

In large bowl, soak all the beans together in 6 cups water overnight. The next day, drain and rinse. In 5-quart Dutch oven, heat oil. Add onions, carrots, and celery; cook for a few minutes. Add 7 cups water; drain soaked beans; add with ham bone and bay leaf. Cover and bring to boil over high heat. Reduce heat to low, and simmer gently for 1-1/2 hours or until beans are tender. Remove ham bone to bowl; cool until easy to handle. Cut ham off bone; discard bone. Cut ham into bite-size pieces; return to soup. Heat through. Add salt and pepper to taste.

Leona Teodori, Warren, Mich.

FAMILY FARE CHICKEN VEGETABLE SOUP

1 cup potatoes, cut into small squares (diced)
4 cups chicken stock or broth
1 teaspoon salt
1/8 teaspoon pepper
1 cup onions, thinly sliced
1 cup carrots, diced
1 cup celery, chopped
1 cup fresh green beans, cut in 2-inch pieces
2 cups cooked chicken, diced
1 cup zucchini, sliced

In saucepan over medium heat, bring potatoes to boiling point in enough salted water to cover. Cook potatoes 5 minutes; drain and set aside. In large saucepan, heat stock to boiling. Season with salt and pepper. Add onion, carrots, and celery; simmer 5 minutes. Stir in green beans and chicken; heat soup to boiling. Add zucchini and potatoes; simmer 1 minute longer.

Gwen Campbell, Sterling, Va.

COCK-A-LEEKIE SOUP

Serves 4
(dates back to the 14th century)

1 dozen leeks
1 ounce butter
2 stalks celery, chopped
1 carrot, chopped
1-1/2 quarts chicken broth
1 cup cooked chicken, diced
Salt and pepper to taste
1 egg yolk

Wash and trim leeks. Cut into 1/2-inch-long pieces. Discard roots and tops. Fry in butter with celery and carrot. When brown, add 1 quart broth and chicken. Cover and simmer for 2 hours. Salt, pepper, and stir in egg yolk which has been blended with remaining broth. Heat thoroughly.

CREAMY ASPARAGUS SOUP

Serves 4

1 (10-ounce) package frozen asparagus
1/2 cup chicken broth
2 egg yolks
1/4 cup whole milk
1/2 teaspoon salt
1/4 teaspoon pepper
2 drops Worcestershire sauce
Parsley for garnish
Paprika for garnish

In large pan, combine asparagus and chicken broth; heat to simmer and cook, covered, for 8 minutes. Cool. Put in blender or food processor, and blend until smooth. Add egg yolks and blend well. Return asparagus mixture to pan; stir in milk, salt, and pepper; add Worcestershire sauce. Heat well, but do not boil. Top with parsley and paprika.

CREAMY TOMATO SOUP

Serves 4

1 diced potato
2 diced carrots
2 diced celery stalks
1 medium onion, chopped
2 bay leaves
1-1/2 teaspoons dried basil
3/4 teaspoon oregano
1/4 teaspoon chili powder
1/4 teaspoon pepper
1-1/2 cups stock

Place all ingredients in saucepan. Bring to a boil; reduce heat; and simmer, covered, for 10 minutes or until tender.
Then stir in:
1 (16-ounce) can undrained tomatoes
2 tablespoons tomato paste
1/3 cup tiny pasta, cooked

Simmer 5 minutes more; remove from heat and stir in 1 cup low-fat yogurt. Serve immediately.

Dorothy E. Snyder, Pine Grove, Pa.

TACO SOUP

(teenage favorite)
Makes 3-1/2 quarts

1 pound lean ground beef
2-1/2 quarts chicken stock
1 (2-1/2-ounce) package taco seasoning mix
1/2 teaspoon cumin
1/2 teaspoon salt
1/4 teaspoon pepper
2 cups green onions, thinly sliced
2 cups tomatoes, chopped
1 (18-ounce) can pitted black olives, drained and sliced
1 (14-ounce) package corn chips
4 cups iceberg lettuce, shredded
2 cups cheddar cheese, shredded

In medium-size skillet, brown ground beef. Drain well and set aside. In large skillet, combine the chicken stock, taco seasoning mix, cumin, salt, pepper, and ground beef. Bring to a boil. Reduce heat and simmer covered for 10 minutes. Add green onions, tomatoes, and black olives. Simmer another 10 minutes. Ladle into bowls; top with chips, lettuce, and cheese.

VEGETABLE BEEF SOUP

Serves 8

1 pound ground beef
1 large can tomatoes, whole
1 can tomato soup
1 small onion, chopped
2 cups water
1 can lima beans, drained
1 can whole-kernel corn, undrained
1 cup sliced carrots
1 cup potatoes, cut up
1 cup diced celery
1/4 teaspoon salt
1/4 teaspoon pepper

Combine beef, tomatoes, soup, and onion in cooker. Add water, beans, and vegetables. Add salt, pepper, and other spices of preference. Stir well. Cook at lowest setting, 4 to 6 hours.

CORNED BEEF CHOWDER
Serves 5

3 cups milk
1 can cream of potato soup
1 (10 ounce) package frozen
  Brussels sprouts, thawed
1 can corned beef, broken up

In a large saucepan, blend 1-1/3 cups milk and soup. Cut up Brussels sprouts and add to soup. Bring to boil. Reduce heat; simmer 15 minutes. Add remaining milk and beef. Heat through.

Kenneth McAdams, El Dorado, Ark.

POTATO HAM CHOWDER
Serves 6

4 potatoes
2 tablespoons margarine
1/2 cup diced onions
2 cups water
1 teaspoon salt
1/8 teaspoon pepper
4 tablespoons flour
1/3 cup water
2 cups milk
1 (12 ounce) can whole kernel corn
2 cups diced cooked ham

Peel and dice potatoes. In large saucepan, melt margarine. Add onion, and cook until tender. Add potatoes, 2 cups water, and seasonings. Cover; simmer until potatoes are done. Make a paste of flour and 1/3 cup water; add to potato mixture. Add milk and cook until slightly thickened. Stir in corn and ham. Heat thoroughly, but do not boil.

MAINE CORN CHOWDER
Makes 9 cups

5 slices bacon
2 medium onions, sliced
3 cups diced, pared potatoes
2 cups water
1 teaspoon salt
1/2 teaspoon pepper
1 (1-pound, 1-ounce) can cream-
  style corn
2 cups milk

Cook bacon in Dutch oven until crisp. Drain on paper towels. Set aside. Sauté onion in bacon drippings until soft. Add potatoes, water, salt, and pepper. Bring to a boil. Reduce heat; cover and simmer about 15 minutes until potatoes are tender. Add corn and milk. Heat thoroughly. When serving, garnish with crumbled bacon.

Helen Weissinger, Levittown, Pa.

CHILI

1 pound chunk beef
1-1/2 pounds ground beef
1 pound pork, cut into 1/4-inch
  cubes
1 large onion
1 can beer
Chili powder to taste
1 teaspoon salt
Sugar to sweeten
1 tablespoon oregano
1 (16 ounce) can kidney beans
1 (16 ounce) can butter beans
1 (16 ounce) can garbanzo beans
1 (No. 2-1/2) can tomatoes
1 (15 ounce) can tomato sauce
1 (6 ounce) can tomato paste
1 (16 ounce) can mushrooms
  (optional)
1 (16 ounce) can northern beans
1 cup beef broth made from bouillon
Garlic powder to taste
Add more tomato juice, as needed

Brown beef, pork, and onion; place in large kettle. Add all the rest of ingredients. If very thick, add water and tomato juice; simmer several hours until flavors are blended and meat is tender.

Arthur J. Gatton, Lake Mills, Wis.

LUMBERJACK CHILI

2 pounds ground beef
1 large onion, diced
1/2 green pepper, diced
4 stalks celery, diced
1 large can tomato juice
1 can whole tomatoes
2 cans red kidney beans
2 tablespoons chili powder
1 teaspoon garlic powder
1 teaspoon celery salt
1 teaspoon Italian seasoning
1/2 teaspoon pepper

Brown beef and drain well. Sauté onion, green pepper, and celery. Combine all in large saucepot with remaining ingredients. Simmer for about 1 hour. Freezes well, and is very good reheated.

Ida Bloedow, Madison, Wis.

CHI CHI CHILI

1-1/2 pounds chopped meat or
  ground chuck
1-1/2 cups onion, cut up
1-1/2 celery, chopped
2 cloves garlic
2 teaspoons salt
1 teaspoon sage
2 tablespoons chili powder
1 tablespoon paprika
1 teaspoon thyme
1 bay leaf
2 cans kidney beans or chili beans (if
  you like it hotter)
1 large can tomatos
1 small can tomato paste

Brown meat, onion, garlic and celery. Add remaining ingredients and simmer 1 to 2 hours.

Mrs. Kit Rollins, Cedarburg, WI

GOLDEN ONION SOUP
Makes 5-1/2 cups

2 cups finely chopped onion
1/4 cup butter
2 cups water
1-1/2 cups (10-3/4 ounce can)
   cream of chicken soup
2 slightly beaten eggs
1 teaspoon salt
1/4 teaspoon nutmeg
1-2/3 cups undiluted Carnation
   evaporated milk

Sauté onion in butter until tender.
Add water. Bring to boil; reduce heat
and boil gently for 20 minutes, stirring occasionally. Combine chicken
soup, eggs, salt, and nutmeg in small
bowl. Add to onion mixture. Cook
over medium heat, stirring continu-
ally, until mixture comes to a boil and
thickens. Stir in milk. Heat to serving
temperature.

Agnes Ward, Erie, Pa.

HEARTY LENTIL SOUP

1 cup lentils
Small chopped onion
1/2 can tomato sauce
Salt and pepper to taste
1 cup cooked elbow macaroni
1 package frozen cauliflower
2 tablespoons olive oil
3 cups water
1 teaspoon sugar
Grated cheese

Brown onion in oil. Add remaining ingredients, except macaroni;
cook until cauliflower is tender. Add
cooked macaroni. Before serving,
sprinkle with grated cheese.

Mrs. Rosalie Bodnovich, Long Island, NY

MEATY SPLIT PEA SOUP
Serves 8

1 pound lean ground pork
1-pound package dry split peas
2 medium potatoes, peeled,
   chopped

3/4 cup onion, chopped
1/2 cup chopped celery
2 teaspoons seasoned salt
1/2 teaspoon garlic powder
1/4 teaspoon pepper
6 cups water

Brown ground pork in skillet, stirring until crumbly; drain. Combine
with remaining ingredients in Crockpot. Cook, covered, on low for 10 to
12 hours; stir before serving.

GREAT GRANDMA'S OLD-FASHIONED SOUP

Veal shank, broken in two
Beef marrow bone
5 diced carrots
2 diced onions
5 diced potatoes
1 diced green pepper
2 or more stalks cut up celery
1 medium can tomatoes
1/8 teaspoon summer savory
1/8 teaspoon salt
Pepper to taste

Cover veal and marrow bone with
cold water; cook for several hours
until meat is nearly done. Add vegetables and seasonings. Cook until
meat and vegetables are tender. If a
more hearty soup is wanted, macaroni, noodles or a tablespoon of bar-
ley may be added.

Jennie Lien, Stoughton, WI

POTATO SOUP

6 cups potatoes
1 onion, chopped
1 small can evaporated milk
2 cups milk or half and half
2 stalks chopped celery
2 cups cream
Toasted bread cubes, for garnish

Sauté onion and celery in butter;
add broth, mushrooms, rice, and seasonings. Cover; simmer 25 minutes
or until rice is cooked. Stir in pumpkin; cook 5 minutes more. Stir in
cream; heat thoroughly. Garnish with
toasted bread cubes.

Gwen Campbell, Sterling, Va.

POTATO SOUP WITH RIVELS

2 pounds white potatoes, peeled and
   cubed
1-1/2 quarts water or chicken broth
2 stalks celery, diced
Parsley to taste
1/8 teaspoon pepper
2 eggs
1/2 cup flour

Boil potatoes in chicken broth
with celery, parsley; salt and pepper
to taste.

Rivels:

Beat the eggs and flour together
with a fork. Drizzle the mixture from
a spoon into the cooked potato soup.
Boil for about 10 minutes.

When my mother, who is now 84
years old, was a young girl of about 9
years, she used to visit her father's
sister. Her father was a Pennsylvania
Dutch descendent and lived in the
back hills of central Pennsylvania.
Her favorite dish made by this aunt
was potato soup with what she called
rivels.

Gloria E. Miller, Jersey Shore, PA

POTATO BROCCOLI CHEESE SOUP

4 or 5 baking potatoes with skins, cut
   into bite-sized pieces
1 large or 2 small onions, cut into
   small pieces
2 bunches broccoli flowerets,
   chopped into bite-size pieces
3 carrots, cut into small pieces
1-1/4 sticks butter
3 tablespoons arrowroot
1 pint milk, plus some
Grated cheese

Cook all vegetables together in
water and a little milk. Add arrowroot
to 1/4 stick melted butter; stir with
fork. Add 1 stick butter; melt. Add
milk and grated cheese; stir and heat
thoroughly.

Jean Gilliland, Valparaiso, IN

Vegetables
DELIGHT

COUNTRY-STYLE FRIED CABBAGE
Serves 4

2 tablespoons bacon fat
1 medium head green cabbage
  (about 1-1/2 pounds), shredded
Salt and pepper

Heat bacon fat in 10-inch skillet. Add cabbage. Cook over low heat, stirring frequently, until light brown. Cover and cook, stirring occasionally, until crisp-tender, about 5 minutes. Sprinkle with salt and pepper. If desired, 2 tablespoons of cream and 1-1/2 teaspoons vinegar may be added before removing from heat. Also red cabbage may be fixed the same way; just substitute vegetable oil for bacon fat.

Leota Baxter, Ingalls, Kan.

CROCK-STYLE BARBECUE BEANS
Serves 10-12

8 cups water
3 cans pork and beans
1/4 teaspoon salt
1/4 teaspoon pepper
1/4 teaspoon minced onion
1 small onion, chopped
1/2 cup brown sugar
2/3 cup syrup
3 tablespoons white sugar

Combine water, pork and beans. Add remaining ingredients and stir well. Cook on *low* for six hours, *high* for less than six hours. Stir before serving.

CRUMBED JULIENNE CARROTS
Serves 4-6

8 medium-size carrots
1 tablespoon honey
1 egg, slightly beaten
Fine cracker crumbs
3 tablespoons butter or margarine

Cook whole carrots in small amount of boiling water, with honey, until tender; drain. Cut carrots lengthwise into strips; roll carrots in egg, then in cracker crumbs. Sauté lightly in hot butter.

Gwen Campbell, Sterling, Va.

HASH BROWN DELIGHT

2 (10-ounce) packages frozen hash
  brown potatoes
2 cups sour cream
1 can cream of chicken soup
1 stick or 1/2 cup melted butter
1 tablespoon salt
1 tablespoon onion
2 cups crushed cornflakes
1/4 cup melted butter
2 cups grated cheese

Thaw hash browns. Combine sour cream, soup, and 1/2 cup butter. Add salt, onion, and cheese; mix well. Add potatoes. Place mixture in a 9x13-inch baking dish. Combine 1/4 cup melted butter and cornflakes; sprinkle on top of mixture. Bake at 350 degrees for 50 minutes or until golden brown.

Cherie Blomquist, Steamboat, Colo.

TOMATO SOUFFLE'
Serves 6

1 (1-pound, 13-ounce) can sieved
  tomatoes
2 tablespoons grated onion
1 bay leaf
1/2 teaspoon oregano
4 tablespoons butter or margarine,
  divided
1/2 cup grated Parmesan cheese,
  divided
3 tablespoons flour
1/2 teaspoon salt
Dash of pepper
4 egg yolks
4 egg whites
1/4 teaspoon cream of tartar

Combine tomatoes, onion, bay leaf, and oregano in pan; simmer, uncovered, for 30 minutes or until mixture cooks down to about 2 cups. Remove bay leaf. Grease 2-quart casserole with 1/2 tablespoon butter. Coat with 2-1/2 tablespoons Parmesan cheese. Melt remaining 3-1/2 tablespoons butter and blend in flour, salt, and pepper. Stir in tomato mixture; simmer 3 minutes, stirring constantly. Add remaining cheese. Beat egg yolks until thick; stir in tomato/cheese mixture slowly. Beat egg whites with cream of tartar until stiff; fold in tomato/egg yolk mixture. Pour into prepared casserole; place in pan of hot water. Bake at 350 degrees for 45-50 minutes, or until firm.

Kit Rollins, Cedarburg, Wis.

HARVARD CARROTS
Serves 6-8

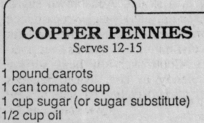

2 pounds carrots, scraped
1/2 cup sugar
1-1/2 tablespoons cornstarch
1/4 cup vinegar
1/4 cup water
1/4 cup butter or margarine

Cut carrots into 1/2-inch crosswise slices and cook, covered, in a large saucepan with a small amount of boiling salted water for 15 minutes or until tender; drain. Combine sugar and cornstarch in a small saucepan; add vinegar and water. Cook over medium heat, stirring constantly until thickened. Add sauce and butter to carrots. Cook over low heat until butter melts and carrots are thoroughly heated.

Agnes Ward, Erie, PA

COPPER PENNIES
Serves 12-15

1 pound carrots
1 can tomato soup
1 cup sugar (or sugar substitute)
1/2 cup oil
1/2 cup vinegar
1 onion, chopped
1 green pepper, chopped

Slice and cook carrots. To cooked carrots, add onion and pepper. Add remaining ingredients. Allow flavors to blend several hours before serving. This relish will keep several weeks in refrigerator.

Elizabeth Dunn, Harrisonville, NJ

DILLED BABY CARROTS
Serves 6

3/4 cup white wine vinegar
1/4 cup water
1/4 cup honey
1/2 teaspoon dried whole dillweed
1/2 teaspoon mixed pickling spices

1 teaspoon salt
1/2 pound baby carrots, scraped
Sprigs of fresh dill (optional)

Combine first 6 ingredients in large saucepan; bring to a boil. Add carrots; cover; reduce heat and simmer 10-12 minutes or until crisp and tender. Remove from heat, and pour mixture into plastic container; set container in bowl of ice water to cool quickly. Chill, Serve with slotted spoon. Garnish with sprigs of dill, if desired.

Marcella Swigert, Monroe City, Mo.

CARROT RING SOUFFLE
Serves 8

12 medium carrots, cooked and mashed
1/2 to 2 tablespoons prepared horseradish
1/2 cup mayonnaise
2 tablespoons finely minced onion
3 eggs, well beaten
1/2 teaspoon salt

Mix all ingredients together. Pour into lightly oiled ring mold. Place mold in pan of hot water; bake at 350 degrees for 40 minutes. Turn out onto serving platter; fill center with cooked frozen peas or broccoli. Serve immediately.

Marcella Swigert, Monroe City, Mo.

ROLY-POLY CARROT MARBLES
Makes 35 balls

3 ounces cream cheese, softened
1 cup shredded Cheddar cheese
1 teaspoon honey
1 cup finely shredded carrots
3/4 cup finely chopped dry roasted peanuts

Combine the first 3 ingredients and blend. Stir in carrots. Chill 1 hour. Shape into balls using 1-1/2 teaspoons mixture for each marble. Chill until firm after rolling each marble in the chopped nuts.

RICE PILAF WITH FRESH MUSHROOMS
Serves 8

4 tablespoons butter or margarine
1 large onion, chopped
1 cup sliced mushrooms
1-1/2 cups regular long grain rice
3-1/4 cups water
1 envelope (3/4 ounce) au jus gravy mix
1/2 teaspoon salt
1/2 teaspoon oregano leaves

Melt butter in a 2 quart dutch oven. Cook onion, mushrooms, and rice in butter 4-5 minutes. Stir until rice is golden brown. Add remaining ingredients. Stir to dissolve gravy mix. Cover and bake in 350 degree oven 40 minutes or until all liquid is absorbed.

NOTE: Can be cooked, covered on top of stove over medium heat for 45 minutes. Also can be frozen in "boilable plastic bags" and reheated.

Mrs. Kit Rollins, Cedarburg, WI

MUSHROOM FRITTERS
Makes 12

1 cup packaged biscuit mix
1 cup chopped fresh mushrooms
2 tablespoons sliced green onions
1 tablespoon chopped pimiento
1/4 teaspoon salt
1/4 teaspoon celery seed
1 beaten egg yolk
1/4 cup dairy sour cream
1 egg white
Cooking oil for deep fat frying

In mixing bowl combine biscuit mix, mushrooms, onion, pimiento, salt, and celery seed. Mix together egg yolk and sour cream; stir into dry ingredients just until moistened. Beat egg white to stiff peaks; gently fold into mushroom mixture.

In heavy saucepan or deep fat fryer heat oil to 375 degrees. Drop batter by tablespoons into hot oil. Fry about 2 minutes or until golden brown, turning once. Drain on rack; serve hot.

Judy Fisk, Aberdeen, Wash.

EASY POTATOES
Serves 10-12

1 can cream celery soup
1 can mushroom soup
1 large package hash brown potatoes (defrosted)
1 cup sour cream
4 tablespoons chopped bell green peppers
4 tablespoons chopped green onions
4 tablespoons chopped fresh celery
Salt & pepper

Mix together; bake 1-1/2 hours at 350 degrees. Can be made ahead.

Lorraine Schroeder, Fallbrook, CA

FOILED POTATOES
Serves 4-5

3 large baking potatoes
4-5 slices bacon, fried crisp and crumbled
1 large onion, thinly sliced
1/4 pound American cheese, cubed (or Velveeta)
1/4 pound margarine
Salt and pepper to taste

Slice peeled potatoes into a large piece of foil or a baking dish with a lid. Sprinkle with salt and pepper. Add bacon, cheese, onion slices, and dabs of margarine. Seal foil with a double fold; place on cookie sheet in oven. Bake at 350 degrees for 1 hour. Very tasty and easy clean-up when you use the foil.

Denise Winchell, Pleasant Hill, Ill.

HASH BROWNS

2 pounds frozen hash browns, partially thawed
1 can cream of chicken or mushroom soup
1 large carton sour cream
1/2 cup shredded sharp Cheddar cheese
1 stick margarine
1/2 cup chopped onion
2 cups corn flakes, crushed
Paprika

In a skillet, sauté chopped onion in 1/2 stick margarine. Mix in hash brown potatoes, cream of chicken soup, sour cream, and cheese. Place in casserole and pour 1/2 stick margarine over all. Sprinkle with crushed corn flakes and paprika. Bake at 350 degrees for 1 hour.

Donna Holter, W. Middlesex, Pa.

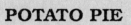

POTATO PIE

4 cups mashed potatoes
1/2 pound mozzarella cheese, cubed
1/2 pound Italian sausage, peeled
1 egg
2 tablespoons Parmesan cheese
1/4 teaspoon basil
2 tablespoons chopped parsley
Salt and pepper to taste
Flavored bread crumbs

Peel the skin from sausage, crumble into a frying pan. Cook sausage well, but not too dry; drain off fat. Mix sausage, cheeses, egg, and seasonings together well, except the bread crumbs. Put a sprinkling of bread crumbs into an oiled 10-inch pie plate. Put the filling into pie plate. Pat the top, with oil on hand, before sprinkling top lightly with a little more bread crumbs. Place in 350-degree oven; bake until golden color 30-45 minutes. Let set a few minutes for better slicing.

This is an old family recipe handed down to all the family by my grandmother. I've been using it for almost 50 years and everyone likes it. It is a very good main dish with a salad and light dessert.

Dorothy A. Lynch, Whiting, NJ

WHITE POTATO PIE

3 eggs
2 cups light cream
2 cups mashed potatoes
1 cup sugar
1 teaspoon vanilla
1/4 teaspoon salt
1 (10-inch) unbaked pie shell
Ground nutmeg

Beat eggs slightly. Stir in the cream, mashed potatoes, sugar, vanilla, and salt. Beat until smooth. Pour into pie shell. Sprinkle with nutmeg. Bake at 350 degrees for 40-45 minutes until a knife inserted off-center comes out clean. Cool completely. Sprinkle pie with toasted, slivered almonds and more nutmeg, if desired.

Fay Duman, Eugene, Ore.

CINNAMON SWEET POTATOES
Serves 4

2 tablespoons butter or margarine
2 drops imitation butter flavoring (if margarine is used)
1/4 cup brown sugar
1/2 teaspoon cinnamon
1 (1 pound, 7 ounce) can sweet potatoes in syrup

Melt margarine with butter flavoring in a skillet. Add brown sugar, cinnamon, and 1/4 cup syrup drained from sweet potatoes. Simmer for several minutes and add sweet potatoes. Cook over low heat, stirring frequently to coat sweet potatoes with glaze. Really great with turkey!

Agnes Ward, Erie, Pa.

SWEET POTATO BALLS

4 cups mashed sweet potatoes
2 tablespoons butter
1/2 teaspoon salt
1/8 teaspoon black pepper
3 tablespoons brown sugar mixed with flour
1/3 cup flour
1/4 cup chopped pecans (optional)
1/4 cup butter, melted

Mix first 4 ingredients and shape into 2-inch balls. Roll in brown sugar and flour mixture. Sprinkle with nuts and dip in melted butter. Put in greased casserole and bake 15 to 20 minutes at 350 degrees.

Betty Perkins, Hot Springs, AR

MASHED POTATOES AND TURNIP
Serves 6

4 medium potatoes
1 medium-size turnip
Salt and pepper to taste
2 tablespoons butter or margarine
1/4 cup hot milk

Pare vegetables. Slice and cook separately in boiling, salted water until tender; drain. Combine and mash. Add remaining ingredients and whip until light and fluffy.

CONVENIENT MASHED POTATOES

5 pounds potatoes
1/4-1/2 cup butter, softened
1 (3-ounce) package cream cheese (with or without chives)
1 cup sour cream
1 package dry Italian dressing mix
Bacon bits, paprika, parsley flakes, salt and pepper
Milk (enough to mash potatoes)

Boil potatoes in salted water. Drain and mash potatoes with cream cheese, sour cream, and milk. Add dry Italian dressing; mix thoroughly. Put into casserole and sprinkle top with bacon bits, paprika, parsley flakes, and pepper. Cover; chill in refrigerator until ready for oven. Heat uncovered at 350 degrees for 30-45 minutes.
This is our favorite for family gatherings. If amount is too large, divide and freeze a portion before baking.
Pat Stump, Dunnell, Minn.

PIZZA POTATOES
Serves 4

1 package (5.5 ounce) scalloped potato mix
1 can (1 pound) tomatoes
1-1/2 cups water
1/4 teaspoon crushed oregano
1 package (4 ounce) sliced pepperoni
1 cup shredded Mozzarella cheese

Heat oven to 400 degrees. Empty potato slices and seasoned sauce mix into baking dish. Heat tomatoes, water, and oregano to boiling. Pour over potatoes; stir until well mixed. Arrange pepperoni on top and sprinkle with cheese. Bake uncovered 30-35 minutes. Garnish with hot peppers if desired.

Sue Wiener, Spring Hill, FL

UNION PACIFIC POTATOES
Serves 6-8

6 medium size baking potatoes
1 onion, sliced
1 green pepper, sliced
1/4 teaspoon garlic salt
1/4 cup melted butter

Slit potatoes at 1/4 inch intervals; place onion and pepper slices in the slits. Melt butter, and to it add the garlic salt. Place potatoes in foil; pour butter mixture over potatoes. Seal foil, and place on the grill for 1 hour.

HASSELBACK POTATOES
Serves 8

8 small baking potatoes, unpeeled
1/2 cup butter
1/2 teaspoon salt
1/4 teaspoon onion salt or 1 teaspoon onion flakes
1/2 teaspoon paprika
1/4 cup shredded Cheddar or grated Parmesan cheese
2 tablespoons fine bread crumbs

Preheat oven to 350 degrees. Slice potatoes at 1/8-inch intervals, three-quarters the way through so they spread like a fan. Place each potato in square of tin foil. Drizzle with butter; sprinkle with salt, onion flakes and paprika. Seal foil around each potato and bake for 45 minutes. Combine cheese and bread crumbs; sprinkle over potatoes, leaving foil open like a cup. Bake 15 minutes more. Serve immediately.
Mrs. C. B. Williams, Richmond, VA

MUSTARD POTATO PATTIES
Makes 6-8 patties

1-1/2 cups water
1/2 cup milk
3 tablespoons butter or margarine
3/4 teaspoon salt
2 cups instant potato buds
1 tablespoon prepared mustard
Flour
Butter or margarine

Prepare potatoes by heating water, milk, 3 tablespoons butter, and salt, just to boiling. Remove from heat; stir in potatoes and mustard. Chill. Shape mixture into oval patties; dip into flour and fry in melted butter or margarine, on each side, until golden brown.

Agnes Ward, Erie, PA

BAKED CREAMED MATCHSTICK POTATOES
Serves 4

3 tablespoons butter
4 potatoes, russet or Idaho
3 tablespoons flour
2-1/4 teaspoons dry mustard
1/2 teaspoon paprika
1-3/4 cups half-and-half
Salt and pepper to taste
2 cups Cheddar cheese, grated

Peel and wash potatoes; cut into thin slices; cut across slices to make matchstick pieces. Cook potatoes about 3 minutes until almost tender. Place in a buttered casserole (ovenproof); set aside. In saucepan, melt butter; stir in flour until smooth. Whisk in mustard, paprika, and half-and-half. Bring to a gentle boil, stirring constantly; simmer 2 minutes. Add salt and pepper. Pour sauce over matchstick potatoes; sprinkle cheese on top. Bake 350 degrees for 30 minutes, or until potatoes are crisp and golden brown.

Gwen Campbell, Sterling, Va.

DIETETIC SCALLOPED POTATOES

(Milk restricted)

3/4 cup nondairy powdered coffee creamer
3 tablespoons flour
1 teaspoon salt
1/4 teaspoon paprika
Dash of garlic powder
2 tablespoons onion flakes
5 or 6 peeled and thinly sliced potatoes
3 tablespoons butter or margarine
1-1/2 cups boiling water

Combine creamer, flour, salt, paprika, garlic powder, pepper, and onion flakes. Arrange potatoes in layers, followed by alternate layers of creamer mixture and butter. Pour boiling water over potatoes. Bake at 350 degrees for 1 to 1-1/2 hours, until potatoes are done.

Mrs. James. Williams, Brainerd, MN

TILLIE'S ASPARAGUS SCALLOPED POTATOES

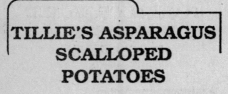

6 medium potatoes, pared and thinly sliced
1 teaspoon minced onion
2 cups milk
2 tablespoons flour
3 tablespoons butter or margarine
1 teaspoon salt
1/4 teaspoon black pepper
3 hard-boiled eggs, chopped
1/2 teaspoon lemon juice
1/2 cup American cheese, grated
1 can cream of asparagus soup

Place sliced potatoes in 2-quart casserole. Add onion, chopped eggs, salt and pepper. Set aside. In saucepan, cook flour, butter and milk until thickened. Cook over low heat stirring constantly. Add lemon juice, American cheese and cream of asparagus soup. Mix together; pour over potatoes. Bake at 350 degrees for 1 hour.

Sarah M. Burkett, Centralia, IL

SWISS STYLE SCALLOPED POTATOES

Serves 8

5 medium potatoes, thinly sliced
1/4 teaspoon salt
1/4 teaspoon pepper
4 tablespoons butter
1/4 teaspoon garlic salt
1-1/2 pounds sliced fresh mushrooms
1 cup grated Swiss cheese
1/2 cup minced parsley
3 green onions, minced
1 pint heavy cream

Mix potatoes, salt; pepper. Blend butter and garlic salt, and coat a 3 quart casserole generously. Put in one layer of potatoes and one layer of mushrooms. Sprinkle with cheese (reserve some for topping), parsley, and onion. Continue repeating layers until all ingredients are used. Finish with a layer of potatoes. Pour cream over all; sprinkle with cheese and bits of butter. Bake in moderate 375 degree oven for 1 hour, or until potatoes are done.

Susan L. Wiener, Spring Hill, Fla.

AU GRATIN POTATOES

Serves 4-6

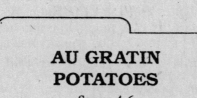

1 1/2 cups hot milk
1/2 medium onion
3/4 cup Swiss cheese (cut in cubes)
2 tablespoons flour
2 tablespoons margarine
4 medium potatoes (peeled and sliced thinly)

Put milk, onion, cheese, flour, and margarine in blender. Cover and process or grind until smooth.

Layer half of potatoes in 2 quart casserole dish. Pour half of milk mixture over potatoes. Add remaining potatoes. Pour remaining milk mixture over top. Bake uncovered at 325 degrees for about 1-1/2 hours.

June Harding, Ferndale, MI

POTATO PUDDING

Serves 8

1/2 pound bacon, diced
2 medium onions
6 large baking potatoes
4 eggs, slightly beaten
1 can (13 ounce) evaporated milk
1 teaspoon salt
1/2 teaspoon pepper

Cook bacon in heavy skillet until done, but not crisp. Remove from skillet; place in 13 x 9-inch pan. Sauté one finely diced onion in drippings. Mix onion with bacon and 1 tablespoon drippings. Grate pared potatoes and remaining onions very fine; mix with eggs, milk, and seasonings. Pour mixture over bacon and onion. Bake 30 minutes at 375 degrees, then bake at 350 degrees for 30 minutes longer or until golden brown.

Kit Rollins, Cedarburg, Wis.

STUFFED POTATOES

Makes 4 potato shells

2 medium baking potatoes
1/4 cup skim milk
2 eggs
2 tablespoons Parmesan cheese
2 teaspoons Dijon-style mustard
1 cup frozen chopped broccoli, thawed, drained, and finely chopped
1 green onion, finely chopped
1 teaspoon thyme leaves
Salt and pepper to taste

Scrub potatoes and prick with a fork. Bake potatoes at 400 degrees for 1 hour or until tender when squeezed. Cut each potato in half, lengthwise. Scoop out pulp, leaving about a 1/4 inch shell. Arrange potato shells in a baking dish.

Beat pulp with skim milk, eggs, Parmesan cheese, and mustard until smooth. Stir in remaining ingredients. Mound filling into shells. Return potatoes to oven and bake for 20 minutes or until hot. Serve two potatoes as an entree, or four potatoes as side dish.

Ruby Goreoki, Albany, OR

10-MINUTE PECAN SQUASH
Serves 4-6

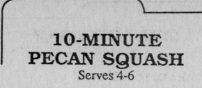

2 (12-ounce) packages frozen cooked squash
2 tablespoons butter
4 teaspoons instant breakfast drink (Tang)
1 teaspoon salt, if desired
Dash of pepper
6 tablespoons chopped pecans

Combine squash, butter, instant breakfast drink, salt, and pepper; cook as directed on package. Stir in pecans.
Karin Shea Fedders, Dameron, Md.

STUFFED PATTY-PAN SQUASH

4 patty-pan squash
4 slices bacon, cooked crisp
1/2 cup onion, chopped
3/4 cup bread crumbs
1/2 cup milk

Cook squash in boiling salted water for 15 minutes. Drain and cool. From the stem end cut a small slice; scoop out center, leaving 1/2-inch rim. Chop the squash which has been removed very finely. Sprinkle the squash cups lightly with salt. Sauté onion in bacon drippings; add crumbs, milk, and reserved squash. Fill cups; sprinkle crisp bacon on top. Place in flat casserole; bake at 350 degrees for 35 minutes.
Gwen Campbell, Sterling, Va.

SCALLOPED EGGPLANT
Serves 6

2 cups cooked eggplant
1/2 cup coarse cracker crumbs
4 tablespoons onion, minced
3 ounces cheese, grated
1 egg, beaten
1/2 cup milk
2 tablespoons margarine or butter

Peel eggplant and cut in 1-inch cubes. Cook in boiling salted water until tender, 8 minutes. Drain. Put eggplant, half of cracker crumbs, onion, and cheese in layers in buttered casserole. Combine egg and milk; pour over other ingredients. Dot with margarine and sprinkle with remaining cracker crumbs. Bake at 350 degrees for 30 minutes.
Suzan L. Wiener, Spring Hill, Fla.

FRENCH FRIED EGGPLANT

1 medium eggplant, peeled and sliced into 1/2 x 2-inch strips
1 cup pancake flour
1 egg
1/4 cup water
1/2 cup Parmesan cheese, grated
Salt
Vegetable oil

Beat egg and water together. Dip eggplant strips into egg mixture; then roll in pancake flour. Drop into hot oil and cook until golden brown, about 2 - 3 minutes. Drain on paper toweling and sprinkle lightly with salt and Parmesan cheese. Serve hot!!
Margean Gilger, Akron, OH

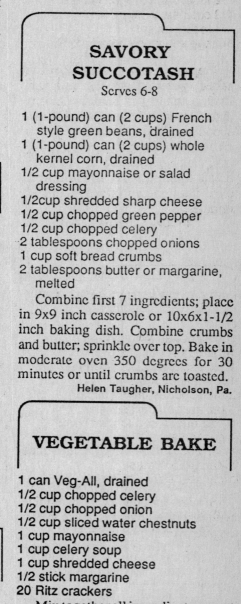

SAUCY ASPARAGUS

2 cans drained asparagus
1 cup cream of mushroom soup
1 can broken pieces mushrooms
1/4 pound squared American cheese
1-1/4 cups bread crumbs
1/2 stick butter

Grease a long flat casserole dish with butter. Place drained asparagus over bottom. Add cream of mushroom soup. Then add mushroom pieces and juice. Cover with American can cheese squares. Put bread crumbs over cheese and thinly sliced butter over top. Bake 25 minutes in 350 degree oven or until it bubbles up through and crumbs are browned. Can use 2 chopped hard cooked eggs, if desired, for garnish.
Virginia Beachler, Logansport, Ind.

SAVORY SUCCOTASH
Serves 6-8

1 (1-pound) can (2 cups) French style green beans, drained
1 (1-pound) can (2 cups) whole kernel corn, drained
1/2 cup mayonnaise or salad dressing
1/2 cup shredded sharp cheese
1/2 cup chopped green pepper
1/2 cup chopped celery
2 tablespoons chopped onions
1 cup soft bread crumbs
2 tablespoons butter or margarine, melted

Combine first 7 ingredients; place in 9x9 inch casserole or 10x6x1-1/2 inch baking dish. Combine crumbs and butter; sprinkle over top. Bake in moderate oven 350 degrees for 30 minutes or until crumbs are toasted.
Helen Taugher, Nicholson, Pa.

VEGETABLE BAKE

1 can Veg-All, drained
1/2 cup chopped celery
1/2 cup chopped onion
1/2 cup sliced water chestnuts
1 cup mayonnaise
1 cup celery soup
1 cup shredded cheese
1/2 stick margarine
20 Ritz crackers

Mix together all ingredients except margarine and crackers in a 2-quart casserole. Bake for 45 minutes at 300 degrees. Melt margarine. Mix with crushed Ritz crackers. Sprinkle over the top. Bake 15 additional minutes.

This is truly a super vegetable casserole, a crowd pleaser for church potluck suppers and one which carries and travels well.
Mary Lou Allaman, Kirkwood, Ill.

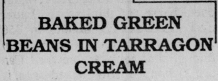

BAKED GREEN BEANS IN TARRAGON CREAM

1-1/2 pounds green beans
1 tablespoon butter
1/2 teaspoon tarragon leaves
1/2 cup heavy cream
1/4 teaspoon salt
1/4 cup seasoned bread crumbs

Prepare green beans; cook in salted water about 12 minutes. Drain; arrange in shallow baking dish. Dot with butter. Mix 1/4 teaspoon tarragon leaves with heavy cream. Pour tarragon/cream mixture over all; sprinkle with seasoned bread crumbs. Bake in 350 degree oven until golden brown, about 12 minutes.

Mrs. Gwen Campbell, Sterling, VA

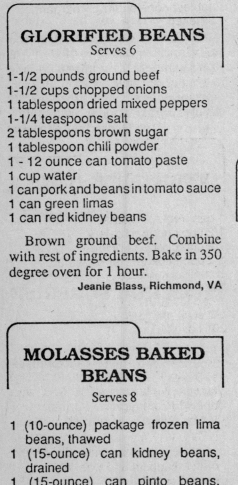

GLORIFIED BEANS
Serves 6

1-1/2 pounds ground beef
1-1/2 cups chopped onions
1 tablespoon dried mixed peppers
1-1/4 teaspoons salt
2 tablespoons brown sugar
1 tablespoon chili powder
1 - 12 ounce can tomato paste
1 cup water
1 can pork and beans in tomato sauce
1 can green limas
1 can red kidney beans

Brown ground beef. Combine with rest of ingredients. Bake in 350 degree oven for 1 hour.

Jeanie Blass, Richmond, VA

MOLASSES BAKED BEANS
Serves 8

1 (10-ounce) package frozen lima beans, thawed
1 (15-ounce) can kidney beans, drained
1 (15-ounce) can pinto beans, drained

1 (15-ounce) can baked beans, undrained
6 slices crispy fried bacon, crumbled
1/2 cup chopped onion
1/2 cup dark molasses
1/4 cup light brown sugar, packed
2 teaspoons dry mustard

Mix all ingredients in 2-1/2-quart casserole. Bake, uncovered, at 350 degrees for 1 hour, stirring occasionally.

Agnes Ward, Erie, PA

BAKED CREAMED SPINACH
Serves 6

1 cup heavy cream
3/4 cup grated Parmesan cheese
3 cups cooked, chopped spinach
1/2 teaspoon salt
Pepper
Nutmeg

Whip cream until stiff. Fold in 1/2 cup grated cheese. Then fold mixture into spinach and blend well. Season with salt; sprinkle pepper and nutmeg to taste. Put into buttered ovenproof pie plate. Sprinkle 1/4 cup grated cheese on top. Bake in 375 degree oven until slightly browned.

Mrs. Robert Combs, Fair Play, MO

SPECIAL SPINACH SQUARES
Serves 4

1 (10-ounce) package frozen chopped spinach
2 eggs
8 ounces sour cream
1 tablespoon onion, grated
1/2 cup Parmesan cheese, grated
1 tablespoon flour
2 tablespoons margarine
1/2 - 1 teaspoon salt
1/8 teaspoon pepper

Cook spinach as directed on package; drain well. Beat eggs; add to spinach. Blend in other ingredients. Place into greased 9 x 9-inch square dish. Bake, uncovered, at 350 degrees for 25–30 minutes. Cool slightly and cut into squares.

Mrs. George Franks, Millerton, Pa.

SPINACH LOAF
Serves 8-10

2 cups cooked spinach
1 cup soft bread crumbs
1 medium onion, minced
1/2 cup walnuts, chopped
1 teaspoon salt
1/8 teaspoon paprika
2 eggs, beaten
1/8 teaspoon pepper
1 tablespoon butter, melted
Milk or stock

Chop spinach; add crumbs, onions, nuts, seasonings and beaten eggs. Add enough milk or stock to form into a loaf. Place in a greased loaf pan and bake 30 minutes in a 375 degree oven.

Agnes Ward, Erie, PA

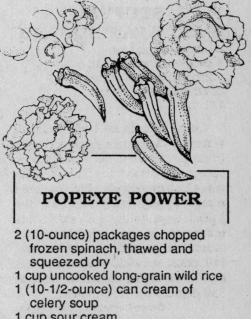

POPEYE POWER

2 (10-ounce) packages chopped frozen spinach, thawed and squeezed dry
1 cup uncooked long-grain wild rice
1 (10-1/2-ounce) can cream of celery soup
1 cup sour cream
1 medium onion, chopped
3/4 cup grated Monterey Jack cheese
1/2 cup grated mozzarella cheese
1/2 teaspoon oregano
1/2 teaspoon salt
1/2 teaspoon lemon juice
1/4 teaspoon garlic powder
1/4 teaspoon pepper

Mix all ingredients together well. Pour into a baking dish and bake at 350 degrees for 30-35 minutes or until it starts to bubble and browns around the outer edges.

Laura Hicks, Newport, Wash.

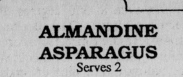

ALMANDINE ASPARAGUS
Serves 2

8 asparagus spears, shaved, cooked halfway and well drained
2-1/2 tablespoons mayonnaise
2-1/4 tablespoons sweet relish
2 pieces of fillet of sole (about 1/2 - 3/4 pounds of sole) wipe dry
1/2 tablespoon chili sauce
1/2 teaspoon margarine
2 tablespoons slivered almonds, toasted

Preheat oven to 350 degrees. In a lightly buttered baking dish lay the asparagus down gently. Mix the mayonnaise and relish; spoon over the asparagus. Place the fish fillets on top over the asparagus. Spoon the 1/2 tablespoon chili sauce over all and top with almonds. Dot with margarine. Bake for 35 minutes or until the fish flakes easily with a fork.

Marie Fusaro, Manasquan, NJ

GLORIFIED CABBAGE

1 small head cabbage, shredded
1 large onion, finely chopped
1 green pepper, finely chopped
1/4 cup green onion, chopped
2 ribs celery, sliced 1/8 inch think
2 tablespoons margarine
2 tablespoons vegetable oil
2 cloves garlic, minced
1/2 cup whipping cream
1 cup fresh bread crumbs (optional)
1-1/2 cups Cheddar cheese, shredded
2 tablespoons parsley, minced
1 teaspoon salt
1/2 teaspoon black pepper

Heat butter and oil in large saucepan; add onions, green pepper and celery; saute 5 minutes over low heat. Add cabbage and garlic; cook covered over low heat for 10 minutes or until cabbage is tender; stir in cream. Mix crumbs with 1/2 the cheese and the parsley; set aside. Add remaining cheese to cabbage mixture; stir in salt

and pepper. Turn into 1-1/2 quart buttered, shallow casserole. Top with crumbs-cheese mixture. Bake at 350 degrees for 20 minutes or until crumbs are golden and crisp.

Ella Evanicky, Fayetteville, TX

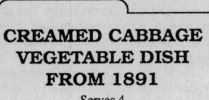

CREAMED CABBAGE VEGETABLE DISH FROM 1891
Serves 4

1 medium head cabbage
1 gill (1/2 cup) cream
1 ounce butter (walnut size)
Salt and pepper to taste
1 cup water

Slice cabbage as for slaw. Cook in 1 cup water until tender; drain. Return to saucepan. Add cream and salt and pepper. Simmer two to three minutes.
NOTE: Milk may be used by adding a little more butter.

Lou Henri Baker, Killbuck, OH

BAKED CREAM CABBAGE
Serves 6

1 medium head cabbage
1/2 cup boiling salted water
3 tablespoons flour
1/2 teaspoon salt
1-1/2 cups milk
1/4 cup bread crumbs
2 tablespoons butter

Shred cabbage very fine and cook 9 minutes in boiling, salted water. Remove cabbage; drain well. Place in buttered 1-1/2-quart casserole. Melt butter in saucepan; stir in flour and salt until smooth. Add milk gradually, continuing to stir until mixture thickens. Pour this sauce over cabbage and sprinkle breadcrumbs over top. Bake at 325 degrees for about 15 minutes or until crumbs are browned.

Karin Shea Fedders, Dameron, MD

ZUCCHINI FRITTERS
Makes 2 dozen

2 large zucchini squash
3 eggs
1/2 teaspoon salt
1/4 teaspoon pepper
1/2 teaspoon sugar
1 teaspoon dried dillweed or 1 tablespoon fresh dill
2 cloves garlic (finely diced)
5 tablespoons flour
1 onion (diced)
Salad oil and margarine

Wash zucchini, do not peel. Dice coarsely; cover with water. Add 1 teaspoon salt and bring to boil for eight minutes. Drain in colander (about 15 minutes). While draining zucchini, heat salad oil and saute onion until soft. Beat eggs; add next 7 ingredients. Stir in drained, mashed zucchini. Mix until well blended, adding sauteed onions.

Drop batter by tablespoon into skillet in which you have 2 tablespoons salad oil and 1 tablespoon margarine. Fry zucchini fritters, a few at a time, until light brown on both sides, turning once.

Place on platter with paper towel to absorb, adding more oil and margarine to skillet as needed and add more batter.

Serve plain or topped with dollop of sour cream or plain yogurt.

Carme Venella, Laurel Springs, NJ

ZUCCHINI SURPRISE
Serves 4
60 calories per serving

1 pound zucchini, sliced
8-ounce can mandarin oranges, drained
1/4 teaspoon nutmeg
Sprinkle cinnamon
1/4 cup pecans, chopped

Steam zucchini slices until tender. Add orange slices, nutmeg and cinnamon. Sprinkle with pecans; serve.

Marie Fusaro, Manasquan, NJ

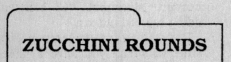

ZUCCHINI QUICHE

1 cup corn muffin mix
3 cups sliced small zucchini squash
1 medium onion, chopped
1/2 cup Parmesan cheese, grated
1/3 cup cooking oil
4 eggs, well beaten
Salt and pepper to taste
1 cup rich cream or half-and-half

Mix all ingredients together. Pour into a buttered 10" pie plate or quiche dish. Bake 45 minutes at 350 degrees. Can be frozen and baked when needed. If preferred, slice tomato or green pepper rings to place on top.

Nice served with relish plate of fresh vegetables and melon or other raw fruit for a luncheon.

Marjorie W. Baxla, Greenfield, OH

ZUCCHINI ROUNDS

1/3 cup commercial biscuit mix
1/4 cup grated Parmesan cheese
Salt and pepper to taste
2 eggs, slightly beaten
2 cups shredded, unpared zucchini
2 tablespoons butter or margarine, softened

In a bowl combine biscuit mix, cheese, salt, and pepper. Stir in eggs just until mixture is moistened; fold in zucchini. For each round, drop 2 tablespoons mixture in soft butter or margarine. Fry 2-3 minutes on each side until brown.

This is an excellent summer luncheon dish or for a brunch.

Alice McNamara, Eucha, OK

ZUCCHINI APPLESAUCE

Makes 2 cups

2 medium zucchini, peeled and diced
2 apples, peeled, cored, and diced
1/4 cup sugar
2 whole cloves
1/8 teaspoon nutmeg
1/2 teaspoon salt
1 tablespoon lemon juice

1/4 teaspoon cinnamon
1/2 teaspoon vanilla extract
Water

In a large saucepan, bring to a boil the zucchini, apples, sugar, cloves, nutmeg, salt, and 1/2 cup water. Reduce heat, cover, and simmer for 20 minutes; stir occasionally. Remove cover; continue cooking until all liquid has evaporated. Discard the cloves, then mash until smooth. Stir in the lemon juice and cinnamon. Cover and refrigerate until ready to use.

Marie Fusaro, Manasquan, NJ

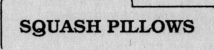

SQUASH PILLOWS

1 yeast cake
1/2 cup lukewarm water
2/3 cup shortening
1 teaspoon salt
1/2 cup sugar
1 cup mashed cooked squash
1 teaspoon grated lemon rind
1/8 teaspoon mace
1 cup scalded milk
2 eggs
6 to 8 cups sifted flour

Mash squash. Add sugar, shortening, salt, lemon rind, mace and eggs. Blend well. Dissolve yeast in water. Add yeast mixture to milk and add to the first mixture. Add sifted flour to make a stiff dough. Mix well. Cover and let rise in a warm place until doubled in bulk. Shape into rolls; place in greased pans. Let rise in warm place until double in bulk. Bake at 325 degrees for 25 minutes.

Mrs. Kit Rollins, Cedarburg, WI

STUFFED ACORN SQUASH

Serves 8-12

Water
4-6 acorn squash, halved crosswise and seeded
1 or 2 (6 ounce) boxes chicken-flavor stuffing mix, prepared according to package directions
Parsley sprigs (garnish)

Preheat oven to 350 degrees. Pour water into 1 large or 2 smaller baking pans to measure 1 inch deep. Arrange acorn squash in water with cut sides up, cutting a thin slice off ends so halves will stand upright. Bake, covered, for 45 minutes or until flesh is tender when pierced with fork. Fill each squash cavity with about 1/3 cup hot stuffing and garnish with parsley.

HOLIDAY STUFFED WINTER SQUASH

Serves 6

3 small acorn or butternut squash
3 green onions, chopped
1 tablespoon oil
1 cup finely-diced celery
1 bunch fresh spinach, coarsely chopped
3/4 cup whole wheat bread crumbs
1/4 teaspoon salt
1/4 cup almonds, finely ground
1 tablespoon butter

Halve and clean the squash. Bake in a 350 degree oven, for 35-40 minutes, or until tender. Sauté onions in oil until soft. Add diced celery. Cover and simmer on medium heat until just tender. Add spinach; stir to wilt. Combine bread crumbs with salt and ground almonds. Stuff the squashes with spinach; sprinkle crumb mixture on top. Dot with butter and return to oven for 10-15 minutes.

Gwen Campbell, Sterling, Va.

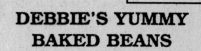

DEBBIE'S YUMMY BAKED BEANS

4 cans pork and beans, drained
1/2 cup minced onion
1/2 pound diced bacon
3/4 cup grape jelly
3/4 cup enchilada sauce

Fry onion and bacon; drain. Add jelly and enchilada sauce; mix well. Add beans; pour into casserole dish and bake, uncovered at 350 degrees for 1 hour. Serve hot.

Debbie Vlahovic, Mesa, AZ

SUNSHINE SWEET POTATO BALLS

Makes 18-20 balls

1/4 cup butter, melted
1/4 cup milk
2 tablespoons sugar
1/2 teaspoon salt
1/4 teaspoon pepper
4 cups cooked, mashed sweet potatoes
18-20 miniature marshmallows
3 cups coarsely crushed cornflakes

Beat butter, milk, sugar, salt, and pepper into mashed sweet potatoes. Form 2-inch balls with a center of a marshmallow. Roll in cornflakes. Place in greased 9-1/2x12-3/4-inch baking pan. Bake in moderate oven of 375 degrees for 25-35 minutes. May be frozen first, then baked without defrosting for 45 minutes at 375 degrees.

Audrey L. Reynolds, Lumberport, W.V.

POTATO 'N BROCCOLI SUPREME

Serves 8

3 cups hot mashed potatoes (5-6 medium)
1 (3-ounce) package cream cheese, softened
1/4 cup milk
1 egg
2 tablespoons margarine
1 (2.8-ounce) can Durkee French fried onions
2 (10-ounce) packages frozen broccoli spears, cooked and drained
1 cup (4 ounces) shredded American cheese

Whip together first 5 ingredients until smooth. Season to taste with salt and pepper. Fold in 1/2 can onions. Spread potato mixture over bottom and sides of a buttered 8x12-inch baking dish; form a shell. Bake, uncovered, at 350 degrees for 20-25 minutes. Arrange hot broccoli in potato shell. Sprinkle with cheese and remaining onions. Bake, uncovered, 5-10 additional minutes.

Lonetta Natale, Madison, N.J

BUBBLE AND SQUEAK (CABBAGE AND POTATOES)

3 cups unpeeled potatoes, boiled (approximately 3 large)
4 cups cabbage, chopped, par-boiled, and drained well
1 small onion, chopped
4 slices bacon, cut up and fried

With paring knife chop cooked, unpeeled potatoes. In large skillet, fry cut-up bacon; drain on paper towel. Add onion and sauté until golden brown; add chopped, cooked cabbage and chopped, cooked potatoes. Sprinkle bacon bits over top surface. Allow potatoes to become golden brown on bottom over medium heat, about 20 minutes or less. Invert skillet over large serving plate and serve. Garnish with parsley, if desired.

Donna Holter, West Middlesex, Pa.

SPINACH MASHED POTATOES

6-8 large potatoes
3/4 cup sour cream
1 teaspoon sugar
1 stick butter
2 teaspoons salt
1/4 teaspoon pepper
2 tablespoons chopped dried chives
1/4 teaspoon dill leaves
1 (10-ounce) package spinach (cooked)
1 cup shredded Cheddar cheese

Cook and mash potatoes; add sour cream, sugar, butter, salt, and pepper. Beat with mixer until light and fluffy. Add chives, dill, and drained spinach. Place in casserole and sprinkle with cheese. Bake at 400 degrees for 20 minutes. Delicious!!

Kristy Schemrich, Shreve, Ohio

CRUNCHY-TOP POTATOES

6 tablespoons butter or margarine
3 or 4 large potatoes
3/4 cup crushed cereal flakes (non-sweet)
1 cup shredded Cheddar cheese
1 teaspoon salt
1 teaspoon paprika

Place butter/margarine in casserole and put in oven that is pre-heated to 375 degrees. Peel potatoes and slice into 1/4 inch crosswise slices. Place slices in melted butter, coating well. Mix remaining ingredients; sprinkle over top of sliced potatoes. Bake 30 minutes, or until potatoes are done and tops are crisp

CREAMY CHIVE-STUFFED POTATOES

Serves 8

8 medium baking potatoes
Vegetable oil
1/2 cup butter or margarine, softened
1 (2-ounce) carton frozen chopped chives, thawed
2 tablespoons chopped onion
1 (16-ounce) carton commercial sour cream
1/2 teaspoon salt
1/4 teaspoon pepper
Paprika

Scrub potatoes thoroughly, and rub skins with oil; bake at 400 degrees for 1 hour or until done.

Allow potatoes to cool to touch. Slice skin away from top of each potato. Carefully scoop out pulp, leaving shells intact; mash pulp.

Combine potato pulp, butter, chives, onion, sour cream, salt, and pepper; mix well. Stuff shells with potato mixture; sprinkle with paprika. Wrap in heavy-duty aluminum foil; bake potatoes at 400 degrees for 10 minutes or until heated thoroughly.

Gloria Pedersen, Brandon, Miss.

CELERY CRUNCH
Serves 4

3 cups chopped celery
1 can cream of chicken soup
1 small can sliced water chestnuts, drained
1 stick margarine
36 (1 stack) butter-flavored crackers, crushed
1 cup sliced almonds

Preheat oven to 350 degrees. Melt margarine; add crushed crackers; set aside. Lightly butter 1-quart baking dish. Add chopped celery, and stir in can of cream of chicken soup, undiluted. Stir in drained water chestnuts. Spread cracker mixture over top of celery mixture. Top with sliced almonds. Bake at 350 degrees for 25-30 minutes. Great side dish for fish or chicken.
Marsha Miller, Hilliard, Ohio

RED CABBAGE

1 head red cabbage
4 tablespoons margarine
1/2 jar grape jelly
1 chopped onion
1 apple, sliced
1/2 teaspoon salt

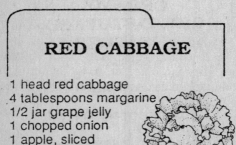

Shred cabbage and put in a colander; pour boiling water over cabbage two times and allow to thoroughly drain. Melt margarine in a large skillet. Place cabbage, apples, and onions in the skillet. Add grape jelly and salt; simmer to desired tenderness.

This vegetable is different and very good.

CUCUMBER AND ONION COMBO

3 medium-size cucumbers, peeled
1 small onion, thinly sliced
1 tablespoon salt

Dressing:
1/3 cup sour cream
2 tablespoons sugar
3 tablespoons white vinegar

Slice cucumbers; add salt. Toss and place in refrigerator for 1 hour. Rinse well and drain; add onion. Blend sour cream, sugar, and vinegar until smooth. Pour dressing over cucumbers and onion. Toss and chill 4 hours. Keeps well for several days.
Margaret Hamfeldt, Louisville, Ky.

CUCUMBER CINNAMON RINGS

15 large cucumbers, peeled, sliced, with seeds and centers removed
2 cups pickling lime
1 cup vinegar
1 small bottle red food coloring
8-1/2 quarts water
1 tablespoon alum

Put rings into lime water, and let stand for 24 hours. Drain and wash in cold water. Drain again. Soak rings for 3 hours with fresh, cold water; drain. Add vinegar, food coloring, alum, and water to cover rings. Heat and simmer for two hours. Drain.

Make a syrup of the following ingredients:

2 cups vinegar
8 sticks cinnamon
2 cups water
10 cups sugar
1 package red hot cinnamon candies

Bring to a boil; pour over rings. Keep lid on tight, and let stand overnight. Drain, reheat syrup, and pour over rings for three consecutive days. On third day, heat rings and syrup together.

Pack into sterilized pint jars and seal.

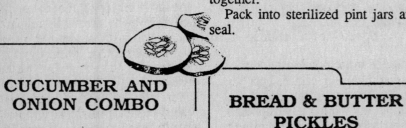

BREAD & BUTTER PICKLES

12 medium-sized cucumbers
1 cup sugar

1 teaspoon celery seed
1 pint vinegar
6 onions
1 teaspoon turmeric
1 teaspoon mustard seed

Slice cucumbers and onions about 1/4-inch thick. Sprinkle with salt. Let stand 5 to 10 minutes. Heat vinegar and other ingredients. Drain, then drop cucumbers and onions into warm vinegar mixture. Let boil 5 minutes only. Pack into sterilized pint jars and seal.

CORN PUDDING
Serves 6

3 slightly beaten eggs
2 cups canned corn
2 cups scalded milk
1/3 cup chopped onion
1 tablespoon melted margarine
1 teaspoon sugar
1 teaspoon salt

Combine ingredients. Place in greased 1-1/2 quart casserole. Set casserole in shallow pan; fill pan to 1 inch with hot water. Bake at 350 degrees for 40-45 minutes.
Kenneth McAdams, El Dorado, Ark.

SAVORY SOUTHERN FRIED CORN

4-6 ears fresh corn
5 slices bacon
3 tablespoons green pepper, minced
1/2 cup sweet milk
1 teaspoon salt
1/4 teaspoon pepper
Dash sugar

Cut corn kernels from cob; set aside. Cut bacon in half; fry in skillet until crisp; drain. Discard all but 4 tablespoons bacon drippings; reserve fried bacon strips for garnish later. Add corn and green pepper. Cook without stirring, until bottom is golden brown. Add milk and seasonings; stir until combined. Cover and cook over low heat 10 minutes longer. Arrange bacon over top when served.
Gwen Campbell, sterling, Va.

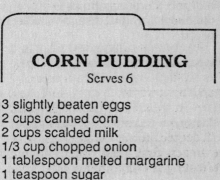
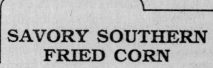

ITALIAN GREEN BEANS
Serves 4

1 (9-ounce) package frozen Italian green beans
1 (16-ounce) can onions, drained
1/2 teaspoon oregano leaves
1 tablespoon margarine
Salt and pepper to taste

Combine green beans, onions, and oregano. Cook according to package directions. Drain. Add butter, salt and pepper.

A 1/2-cup serving is 47 calories.
Helen Harlos, Ethel, Miss.

PIQUANT PICKLED GREEN BEANS
Serves 6

2 (1-pound) cans French-cut green beans, drained
1/2 cup onion, chopped
1/2 cup wine vinegar
1/4 cup salad oil
1 teaspoon prepared horseradish
1/4 teaspoon garlic salt
1 tablespoon sugar
1/4 teaspoon allspice
1/4 teaspoon dry mustard

In a large saucepan combine the beans with the onion. Mix together thoroughly vinegar, oil, horseradish, and seasonings. Pour over the beans; bring to a boil; simmer 5 minutes; stir occasionally. Refrigerate until serving time; serve ice-cold.
Gwen Campbell, Sterling, Va.

SWISS STYLE GREEN BEANS
Serves 6

1/4 cup butter, melted
2 tablespoons flour
1 teaspoon salt
1 teaspoon sugar
1/4 teaspoon pepper
1 teaspoon minced onion
1 cup sour cream
2 (16-ounce) cans French-style green beans
2 cups Swiss cheese, grated
1/2 cup Ritz crackers, crushed

Combine 2 tablespoons butter, flour, salt, sugar, pepper, and onion in large saucepan; mix well. Stir in sour cream. Over medium heat, cook until mixture thickens, stirring constantly. Stir in green beans. Spoon into greased 2-quart casserole. Top with cheese. Sprinkle crackers on top and drizzle remaining butter over crackers. Bake at 350 degrees for 30-35 minutes until bubbly.

CHUCKWAGON BAKED BEANS
Serves 6

4 strips bacon
1/2 medium onion, chopped
1/4 cup green pepper, chopped
1 (16-ounce) can pork and beans
4 tablespoons ketchup
2 tablespoons molasses
2 tablespoons brown sugar
1 teaspoon liquid smoke

In large skillet, fry 2 strips bacon until done. Remove from pan; reserve drippings. Sauté onion and green pepper in reserved drippings until tender. Place pork and beans in greased 1-quart baking dish. Add cooked bacon (crumbled), onion, green pepper, ketchup, molasses, brown sugar, and liquid smoke. Mix well and top with uncooked strips of bacon cut in halves. Bake in 350 degree oven 40-45 until bacon bubbles.

CROCKPOT BAKED BEANS

1/4 pound bacon, fried just until brown
1/4 cup chopped onion
1 (16-ounce) can pork and beans
1 (16-ounce) can kidney beans
1 (16-ounce) can butter beans
2 tablespoons vinegar
1/2 cup catsup
1/2 cup brown sugar

Break bacon into pieces. Place all ingredients in crockpot; mix well. Turn on high for 30-45 minutes and then on low for at least 4 hours or longer, if you wish.
Julie Habiger, Manhattan, Kan.

BRAISED CELERY AND POTATOES
Serves 4

3 medium potatoes, halved and thinly sliced
3 large ribs celery, cut in 1/4-inch slices
1/4 teaspoon diced thyme leaves
1/4 teaspoon minced garlic
Salt and pepper to taste
1 cup chicken broth

Preheat oven to 350 degrees. Lightly grease 9-inch square pan. Add all ingredients, except broth; stir and mix well. Add broth, cover tightly with aluminum foil. Bake 25 minutes until potatoes are tender. 75 calories per serving.
Donna Holter, West Middlesex, Pa.

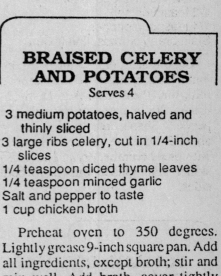

BAKED CELERY

4 cups chopped celery
1 (5-ounce) can water chestnuts, sliced
1/4 cup pimientos, chopped
1 can cream of celery soup
2 tablespoons melted butter
1/2 cup bread crumbs
1/2 cup toasted almonds

Cook celery 8 minutes in boiling water. Drain. Combine with water chestnuts, pimientos, and soup. Mix well. Pour into greased 1-1/2 quart baking dish. Top with mixture of butter, bread crumbs, and almonds. Bake in a 350 degree oven for 35 minutes.
Marcella Swigert, Monroe City, MO

MUSHROOM CUTLETS
Makes 10-12

2 cups drained canned mushrooms
1 cup chopped onion
2 tablespoons butter
2 cups stale bread cubes
1/2 cup milk
3 eggs, beaten
1 tablespoon chopped parsley
1/2 teaspoon salt
1/4 teaspoon pepper
Stale bread crumbs, fine texture

Chop mushrooms. Sauté with onion in butter. Soak bread crumbs in milk for 10 minutes. Add to mushrooms. Stir in eggs, parsley, salt, and pepper. Shape into patties, using about 3 tablespoons for each. Coat with bread crumbs. Fry in butter in a skillet until golden brown on both sides.

TOMATO-SQUASH-ZUCCHINI STIR-FRY
Serves 8

2 tablespoons vegetable oil (or non-stick spray)
2 medium onions, sliced or ringed
2 medium zucchini, sliced
2 medium yellow squash, sliced
1/2 pound fresh mushrooms, sliced
1/2 teaspoon salt
1/4 teaspoon pepper

Pour oil into preheated wok or large skillet; let heat for about 2 minutes. Add onions; stir-fry for 2 minutes. Add squashes and stir-fry about 5 more minutes. Add the remaining ingredients and stir-fry an additional 2 minutes. Serve over rice, if desired.

PEAS AND CAULIFLOWERETS
Serves 4-6

2 tablespoons salad oil

1-1/2 cups small cauliflowerets
1 (10-ounce) package frozen peas
1 pimiento, cut into 1/4-inch strips
1/2 teaspoon salt
1/2 teaspoon pepper

Heat oil in heavy skillet. Add cauliflowerets; cover and cook over low heat 10 minutes, shaking skillet occasionally to prevent sticking. Add peas, and increase heat to medium. Cover and cook 5-8 minutes or until vegetables are crisp-tender. Stir in pimiento, salt, and pepper.

Marcella Swigert, Monroe City, Mo.

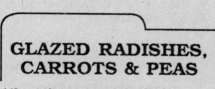

GLAZED RADISHES, CARROTS & PEAS

1/2 cup butter or margarine
1/4 cup water
1 tablespoon lemon juice
3 bunches radishes
3 (15-16 ounce) cans small whole carrots, drained
1 (20-ounce) bag frozen peas
1-1/2 teaspoons salt
3/4 teaspoon sugar
1/2 teaspoon pepper

Over medium heat, heat butter, water, lemon juice, and radishes to boiling. Reduce heat to low; cover; simmer 30 minutes. Add carrots and remaining ingredients; cook 10 minutes until heated thoroughly.

Laura Hicks, Troy, Mont.

GOLDEN FRIED SNOW PEAS
Serves 3

Juice, 1/2 lemon
1 pound pea pods
Salt and pepper to taste
1 egg
1/4 cup sweet milk
1/3 cup flour
1/2 teaspoon baking powder
Vegetable oil for deep frying

Heat amount of oil your skillet requires for deep frying. Squeeze lemon juice on snow peas; season with salt and pepper. Combine milk and egg in a shallow bowl. In another bowl, combine flour and baking powder. Dip snow peas in egg and milk mixture, then dip in flour mixture. Fry in medium-hot oil until golden brown. Drain on paper towels; serve immediately.

Gwen Campbell, Sterling, VA

SAUTERNE SAUERKRAUT
Serves 6

1 (1-pound, 12-ounce) can well-drained sauerkraut
1 medium-size onion, finely chopped
2 apples, peeled, cored and coarsely grated
1 cup dry sauterne or apple juice
1/2 teaspoon caraway seeds

Combine all ingredients in saucepan and heat slowly; stir occasionally for 20 minutes or until onions are tender. Will freeze. Try this with pork chops, too.

SPINACH STRATA
Serves 6-8

1 (10-ounce) package frozen chopped spinach
10 slices white bread, cut in 1-inch cubes
2 cups Cheddar cheese, shredded
1 (10-3/4-ounce) can condensed cream of chicken soup
1 cup water
4 eggs, slightly beaten
1/8 teaspoon ground nutmeg
1/8 teaspoon ground black pepper

Cook spinach according to package directions and drain well. In buttered 2-quart shallow baking dish (12x8x2 inches), arrange half of bread cubes. Spread spinach on bread evenly. Sprinkle with 1 cup Cheddar cheese. Top with remainder of bread and cheese. Combine soup, water, eggs, nutmeg, and pepper. Pour over bread mixture. Cover and refrigerate for 4 hours or more. Preheat oven to 350 degrees. Uncover. Bake 45 minutes or until set.

Home Cooking

INDEX

Appetizers

Cannoli Shells and Fillings 3
Macaroni Pizza 3
Shrimp Ball 3
Zucchini Appetizers 3

Beverages

Banana Breakfast 4
Breakfast Orange Nog 4
Chocolate Syrup Drink Mix 4
Chocolati 4
Coffee Punch 4
Thirst Quencher Punch 4

Breads To Make

Aloha Tea Bread 7
Apple Pastry 13
Apple-Streusel Coffee Bread 7
Applesauce Muffins 11
Apricot Bread 8
Bacon Cheese Nut Bread 12
Bacon Corn Bread 12
Banana Doughnuts 5
Banana Orange Nutmeg Bread 8
Banana-Chocolate Tea Bread 14
Boston Brown Bread 18
Buttermilk Biscuits 10
Butterscotch Treats 13
Calumet Prize Baking
Powder Biscuits 10
Cheese Caraway Batter Bread 6
Cheese Dilly Bread 12
Cheesy Drop Biscuits 12
Cornbread with Parmesan
Cheese 12
Cranberry Muffins 11
Croutons for Fruit Soups 13
E-Z Raisin Bread 8
English Muffin Bread 11
Fiesta Bread 6

French Bread Butter 5
Fresh Apple Bread 9
Fresh Carrot Bread 5
Fresh Strawberry Bread 14
Fruit and Bran Muffins 15
Fruit Bread 14
Garlic Bread 6
Garlic Cheese Bread 6
Golden Spike Bread 7
Hamburger Buns 10
Hawaiian Isle Carrot Bread 9
Hawaiian Sweet Bread 6
Honey Buns 10
Honey Pear Bread 14
Ice-Water Fudge Loaf 13
Josephine Hanel's Rhubarb Bread ...9
Lemon Bread 9
Low-Cal Gingerbread 13
Mashed Potato Biscuits 12
Oatmeal Apple Raisin Muffins 15
Olive Pizza Bread 7
Orange Apple Bread 9
Parsley Bread 6
Peanut Butter Bacon Bread 7
Pimiento Cheese Bread 12
Pineapple Oatmeal Muffins 11
Pineapple Pecan Bread 14
Popovers 5
Quick Yeast Buns 13
Sausage Biscuits 10
Spice Muffins 11
Spice Muffins 15
Strawberry Muffins 15
Super-Easy Delicious White Bread ...8
Swiss Cheese-Bacon Bread 7
Whole-Grain Apple Muffins 5
Whole-Grain English Muffins 11
Yum-Yum Buns 13
Zucchini Nut Muffins 15

Brunch Fare

Bacon Puffed Bancakes 20
Bacon Roll-Ups 18
Baked Western Omelet 16
Breakfast Egg Dish 19
Broccoli Oven Omelet 17
Brunch Pie 16
Buffet Rye Slices 20
Cheese, Ham 'N Olive Swirls 18
Cinnamon Raisin Batter Bread 16
Coconut Crunch Cereal 18
Corn Fritters 20
Egg 'N Chips 19
Elegant Quiche Lorraine 18
Foolproof Scrambled Eggs 19
Garden Medley 17
Granola Bars 16
Luncheon Tuna in Toast Cups 18
Maple Pancake Syrup 20
Oatmeal Pancakes 20
Old-Fashioned Bread Omelet 17
Omelet Supreme 17
Peach and Cottage
Cheese Salad 16
Potato Pancakes with Cheddar 20
Potato Pancakes 20
Quiche Lorraine 17
Quick and Easy Buckwheat
Pancakes 17
Scrambled Bagel Royale 19
Souffle Pancakes 20
Toledo Ham and Eggs 19
Tuna-Stuffed Eggs 19
Zucchini Quiche 18

Cakes To Bake

"500" Cake 23
"Pretty Posy" Easter Cake 36
$100 Chocolate Cake 24
14-Karat Cake 21

1917 War Cake 35
Almond Pound Cake 33
Apple Butter Cake 22
Apple Cake with Topping 23
Applesauce Cake 22
Applesauce Layer Cake 22
Applesauce Loaf Cake 21
Apricot Nectar Cake 25
Banana-Gingerbread Delight 21
Blue Ribbon Poppy Seed
Bundt Cake 35
Blueberry Coffee Cake 31
Buttermilk Coffee Cake 31
Buttermilk Nutmeg Cake 35
Butterscotch Spice Cake 34
Carrot Cake 26
Carrot-Cream Cheese Cake 28
Cherry Crumb Coffee Cake 32
Cherry Nut Brownie Cake 33
Chocolate Angel Food Cake 31
Chocolate Cherry Upside-
Down Cake 29
Chocolate Chip Cake 29
Chocolate Eclair Cake 29
Chocolate Sundae Cake 29
Chocolate Yogurt Cake 30
Cinnamon Pull-Apart
Coffee Cake 32
Coffee Can Cake 32
Cookies 'N Cream Cake 29
Cranberry Cake 25
Cream Cheese Topped
Pineapple Cake 27
Della Robia Cheesecake 28
Dutch Apple Cake 22
Dutch Hustle Cake 36
Easy Pumpkin Cheesecake 28
Edmonton Spice Cake 35
Elegant Apple Cheesecake............25
Favorite Spice Cake 35
Fourth of July Watermelon Cake 28
Fruit-Filled Sour Cream
Coffee Cake 32
Fudge Surprise Cake 30
German Chocolate Cake 30
Gooey Butter Cake 36
Grapefruit Chiffon Cake 26
Hawaiian Cake 26
Hazelnut Cheesecake 25
Heath Coffee Cake 32
Inside-Out Chocolate
Bundt Cake 30
Lemon Crackle Cake 27
No-Bake Peppermint Ice-
Cream Cake 24

No-Cook Frosting 22
No-Fuss Fruitcake 26
Nutty Pretzel Bundt Cake...............34
Oatmeal Cake 24
Old-Fashioned Triple
Fudge Cake 31
Orange Butterscotch
Coffee Cake 33
Orange Honey Cake 25
Orange Kiss Me Cake 24
Orange-Kiss Me Cake 27
Orange Peanut-Butter Cake 23
Oreo Cookie Cake 31
Pecan Cake with Praline Glaze 34
Peek-A-Boo Cake 36
Pineapple Upside-Down Cake 27
Poppy Seed Cake 23
Pound Cake 36
Praline Cheesecake 23
Quick Coffee-Chocolate Cake 33
Rejoice Cake 21
Rhubarb Dessert Cake 28
Saucy Apple Swirl Cake 22
Snickerdoodle Coffee Cake 33
Sour Cream Cake 23
Spicy Nut Sponge Cake 34
Sunshine Cake 24
Treasure Toffee Cake 36
Turtle Cake 31
Zucchini Pineapple Cake 25

Casseroles Creative

Baked Egg and Cheese
Casserole 37
Cheese Spaghetti Souffle 37
Easy Beef Goulash 38
German Potato Casserole 38
Indian Casserole 38
Lazy Beef Casserole 38
Mock Oyster Casserole..................38
Quick and Easy Chop Suey 37
Rice and Mushroom Casserole.......37
Rice Ole 38

Cookies & Bars

Almond Bars 50
American Flag Cookies 42
Angel Cookies 42
Apple Treasure Cookies 50
Aunt Minnie's Apple Butter Bars 50
Banana Oatmeal Honey
Nut Cookies 39
Butter Pecan Turtle Bars................48

Butterscotch Bars 45
Butterscotch Coconut Cookies 40
Butterscotch Coconut Cookies 48
Candied Orange Peel Cookies 49
Caramel O's Bar 45
Carrot Cheddar Cookies 46
Cherry Almond Snowball
Cookies 40
Cherry Twinks 39
Choco Date Balls 43
Chocolate Brandy Balls..................43
Chocolate Nut Cookies 49
Chocolate Pecan Pie Bars 45
Cloud Nine Cookies 46
Coconut Marshmallow Bars 45
Cookies (Diabetic) 39
Cranberry Cookie Bars 50
Cream Cheese Chocolate
Chip Cookies...............................48
Cream Cheese Lemon Bars 39
Cream Cheese Snowballs 43
Crunchy Oatmeal Cookies 50
Date and Almond Brownies 44
Date and Almond Brownies 47
Date Balls 46
Date Bars 39
Elegant Krispie Bars 44
Fruitcake Bars 44
Gold Rush Brownies 44
Halfway Bars 45
Hawaiian Oatmeal Cookies.............41
Iced Molasses Bars 48
Iced Peanut Butter Cookies 41
Italian Bow Knot Cookies 47
Jumbo Peanut Butter Apple
Cookies 49
Lemon Sugar Cookies 40
Macaroons 43
Milk Chocolate Almond Bars 44
Moist Oatmeal Cookies 41
Mrs. Field's Cookies 49
Oatmeal-Carrot Cookies 41
Old-Fashioned Raisin Bars 49
Orange Sugar Cookies 40
Orange Sugar Cookies 46
Peanut Butter Cookies 41
Pecan Balls 43
Pistachio Pudding Cookies 47
Poppy Seed Cookies 40
Quick and Easy Brownies 46
Sesame Macaroons 42
Simply Delicious, Easy Brownies 44
Sour Cream Coconut Cookies 50
Sour Cream Date Dreams 47
Special K Cookies 47

Starlight Mint Surprise Cookies 48
Sugar Golden Puffs 49
Sugarless Bar 44
Sweetheart Cookies 42
Toffee Cookies 43
Toffee Splinters 43
Walnut Bar Cookies 45
Walnut Clusters 46
Yule Logs or Wreaths 42
Zebra Cookies 42

Cooking For Two

Apple Brown Betty 51
Black Cherry Sparkle 62
Blueberry Cream Dessert 57
Blueberry Torte 59
Cherry Amaretto Cream 62
Cherry Cobbler 54
Chili Cheddar Omelet 53
Chocolate Sauce 53
Chocolate Torte 59
Chocolate-Pecan Frost 61
Coco-Nutty Bananas 62
Coconut Dessert Crust 57
Corn Pudding 53
Corn Pudding 58
Cream Cheese Tarts 60
Creamy Rice Pudding 58
Dessert Souffle 52
Deviled Eggs 51
Drumstick Treat 61
Easter Egg Twist 62
Easter Goodies 63
Easter Grunties 63
Easy Cheese Strudel 62
Easy Peach Crumble 64
Eclair Dessert 57
Eggnog Cream Puffs 64
Elegant Finale Torte 59
Frozen Refresher 64
Fruit Fritters 64
Fruit Sherbet 64
Glazed Parsnips 53
Golden Frost Peach Roll 63
Good Puffy Fritters 64
Grandma's Rice Pudding 58
Grapefruit in Raspberry Puree 51
Hawaiian Hash 64
Lemon Cake Dessert 57
Lemon Cheese Torte 60
Liberty Bell Cobbler 54
Marshmallow Pops 55
Midnight Mints 55
Millionaire Candy 55

Delicious Desserts

Mom's Apple Cobbler 54
Noodle Pudding 58
Orange-Flavored Apples 52
Oranges in Red Wine 51
Peach Delicious 63
Peanut Brittle 55
Peanut Butter Swirl Candy 55
Pearl Tapioca 60
Pink and White Aspic 62
Pralines 55
Pudding Pops 56
Puffy French Tost 53
Pumpkin Swirl Squares 63
Quick and Easy Strawberry
Parfait 61
Quick Glorious Rice Pudding 58
Rhubarb Meringue Dessert 57
Rich Buttermilk Waffles 52
Rocky Road Candy 56
Shaggy Dogs 56
Strawberry Cheesecake Tarts 60
Strawberry Chiffon Squares 61
Strawberry Parfait 61
Strawberry Refrigerator Torte 59
Strawberry Yum-Yum 61
Suet Pudding 58
Swedish Rosettes 56
Sweet Milk Waffles 52
Sweet Potato Pudding 59
Sweethearts 56
Thousand Island Salad 53
Tomato Pudding 58
Turtles 56
Valentine Heart Tarts 56

Foreign & Exotic

Buche De Noel (French
Yule Log) 67
Czechoslovakian Cookies 68
Dutch Apple Cake 67
Dutch Tea Cakes (Kletskoppen) 66
Enchiladas 67
Gareau Aux Poires (Pear Cake) ... 68
Gsusztatott Palacsinta (Walnut
Pancakes with Chocolate Cream)...65
Helado De Mango (Mango
Sherbet) 68
Oriental Cabbage Salad 68
Palacinky (Thin Pancakes) 67
Potato Dumplings (Germany) 66
Pressnako (Russian Cookie) 65
Puacki (Polish Doughnuts) 66

Risi Bisi (Rice and Peas) 65
Rumanian Apple Torte 66
Sleek Greek Salad 68
Swedish Toast 67
Viennese Poppy Seed Cake 66

Fruits Fantastic

Apricot Fool 69
Baked Bananas 69
Cherry Fritters 69
Country--Baked Apples 69
Gingered Baked Fruit 69
Peaches in Custard Sauce 69

Meat Dishes

Baked Chicken Reuben 77
Baked Chop Suey 78
Baked Halibut with
Cheese Sauce 72
Bandit Wings 76
Barbecued Spicy Shrimp 74
BBQ Pork Chops 79
Broiled Chicken Breast 82
Buffalo Chicken Wings 76
Cheesy Chicken Shortcakes 73
Cheesy Corned Beef Lasagna 80
Cherry Pork Chops 70
Chicken "N Noodles 72
Chicken and Dressing 78
Chicken and Rice 82
Chicken Breasts with Cheese 77
Chicken Cacciatore 76
Chicken Kiev 73
Chicken Livers 75
Chicken Pie 82
Chicken Shepherd's Pie 76
Chicken Skillet Ratatouille 77
Chicken-Asparagus-Cheese
Bake 77
Chicken-Fried Steak 81
Classic Swiss Steak 71
Corn Bread Chicken Bake 82
Corned Beef and Cabbage 70
Country-Fried Steak 81
Country Roast and Vegetables 70
Crab and Vegetable Frittata 72
Crab Barbecue and Rusks 74
Crab Rangoon 74
Cranberry Chops 79
Delicious Sloppy Joes
with Cheese 80
Deviled Chicken with Corn
Bread Topping 73
Easy Chicken Mushroom Bake 77

INDEX

Easy Pineapple Chicken 78
Gooey Chicken 76
Hamburger Chop Suey 80
Jeweled Chicken Squared 78
L'Orange Fillet of Sole 81
Lo-Cal Chicken Divan 77
Mandarin Chicken 78
Maple-Glazed Turkey Breast 71
Mexicali Chicken 75
Mock Chicken-Fried Steak 76
Oriental Rainbow Chicken 73
Oven-Fried Parmesan Chicken 82
Oven-Fried Chicken Parmesan 73
Patio Lickin' Chicken 70
Peachy Chicken 82
Pepper Steak 81
Pickled Chicken Gizzards 75
Pizza Meatballs 80
Pizza Porcupine Balls 80
Porcupine Meatballs 71
Pork Chop Bake 79
Pork Chops with Hawaiian Rice 79
Rich Salmon Romanoff 71
Salmon Circle Loaf 74
San Diego Ratatouille 72
Savory Spanish Tuna Loaf 72
Savory Swiss Steak 81
Shrimp Barcelona 74
Special Pork Chops 79
Spoonbread Chicken Pie 75
Stir-Fry Beef with Vegetables 81
Stuffed Pork Roast 79
Tender Meatballs in
Mushroom Gravy 70
Texas One-Dish Dinner 80
Tuna Bake Italian Style 74
Turkey Fried RIce 75
Turkey Meatballs 75
White Lasagna 71
Working Girl's Chicken 78
Yogurt-Marinated Chicken 73

Microwave Magic

Broccoli-Rice Quiche 83
Brussels Sprouts and
Carrots 'A La Slender 83
Cheesy Ham Scramble 84
Crab Canapes 85
Divine Mashed Potato Casserole.... 84
Herbed Chicken 84
Lemon Pudding Cake 85
Orange Zucchini Cake 85
Pork and Apple Casserole 84
Pumpkin Raisin Cake..................... 85

Pumpkin Spice Cake 85
Savory Brunch Casserole 84
Scrambled Sausage....................... 84
Spicy Pecans 83
Taco Rice Casserole 83

Party Fare

Caramel Apples 86
Cheese Wafers 86
Chicken Liver Pate` 86
Creamy Shrimp Mold 87
Dip Dip Hooray 86
English Toffee 87
Flowerpot Cupcakes 87
Fried Cheese 86
Ham Nibbles 87
Peanut Butter Fudge 87
Peanut Clusters 87
Popcorn Nut Log 87
Shrimp Deviled Eggs 87
Trick or Treaters' Taco-Bean
Dip Pie 86

Pies To Bake

"Breath of Spring" Parfait Pie 93
Amish Lemon Pie 94
Apple Butter Pumpkin Pie 90
Apple Butter Cinnamon Pie 96
Applesauce Cheese Pie 96
Bernice Wilson's Raisin Pie 91
Best-Ever Pumpkin Pie 95
Blueberry Bottom Pie 96
Brown Sugar Pie 93
Buttermilk Raisin Pie 95
Chilled Coconut-Peach
Chiffon Pie 89
Chocolate Butterscotch Pie 92
Chocolate Meringue Pie 92
Cranberry Apple Pie....................... 96
Cranberry Ice-Cream Pie 92
Creamy Lemon Meringue Pie 88
Date and Nut Pie........................... 96
Derby Pie 88
Double Decker Pumpkin
Ice-Cream Pie 92
Flaky No-Fail Pie Crust 88
Fresh Strawberry Pie 92
Frozen Crystal Lemon Pie 94
Fruit Cocktail Pie 96
Fruit Pizza Pie 94
Fruit Salad Pie 95
Gertrude Hungerford's Special
Rhubarb Pie 91

Grape Pie 95
Icebox Cherry Pie 95
Kahlua Pecan Pie 90
Lemon Chess Buttermilk Pie........... 94
Lemon Chiffon Pie 94
Luscious Peach Pie 88
Luscious Rhubarb
Marshmallow Pie........................... 91
Macaroon Pie............................... 94
Maple Pumpkin Pie 89
Maple Syrup Pie or Tarts 90
Melt-Away Pie 93
Mocha Sundae Pie 93
Mock Pecan Pie 90
Never-Fail Pie Crust...................... 88
No-Bake Peanut Ice-Cream Pie 93
Nutty Fudge Pie 90
Peanut Butter Ice Cream Pie 93
Pineapple Upside-Down Pie 91
Praline-Bottom Pumpkin Pie 89
Pumpkin Cheese Pie 89
Pumpkin Cream Pie 89
Pumpkin Ice-Cream Pie
with Pecan Topping 89
Raisin Pie 95
Sour Cream Raisin Pie 91
Vermont Maple Delight Pie 90

Salad Bowl

Apricot-Pineapple Salad 101
Bean Salad Toss........................... 101
Beautiful Cherry Salad 100
Bread Salad 100
Broccoli Aspic 98
Buttermilk Salad 98
Cabbage Patch Tomato Slaw 97
Calico Pasta Salad 97
Carrot Cole Slaw 101
Chilled Main-Dish Salad................. 102
Cider Waldorf Salad 99
Corn and Crab Salad 101
Corned Beef and Potato Salad 102
Country Slaw 101
Crab-Shell Salad 97
Cranberry Salad Mold 98
Creamy Coleslaw 101
Easy Fruit Waldorf 100
Egg Salad 100
Frozen Waldorf Salad 99
Ginger Pear Salad 99
Green Been Salad 99
Holiday Strawberry Gelatin 98
Italian Potato Salad 102
Macaroni Salad 102

INDEX

Mandarin Orange Salad 99
Marinated Salad 101
Orange Salad 100
Orange Sherbet Gelatin Salad 98
Orange Tapioca Salad 97
Raspberry Delight 100
Raspberry Salad 100
Sauerkraut Salad 101
Simple Salad Special 97
Sour Cream Potato Salad 102
Sparkle Salad 98
Special Fruit Salad 99
Special Potato Salad.....................102
Strawberry-Rhubarb Salad Mold.....98
Summer Fruit Fantasy 100
Taco Salad 102

Salad Dressing

All-Seasons Salad Dressing 103
French Salad Dressing 103
Fruit Salad Dressing 103
Low-Cal Dressing 103
Super Salad Seasoning Mix 103
Tarragon Dressing 103

Sauces & Toppings

Banana Butter 104
Corn Relish 104
Homemade Pancake Syrup 104
Piquant Raisin Sauce....................104
Seasoned Salt 104
White Sauce Mix 104

Soups & Stews

Chi Chi Chili 107
Chili...107
Chilly-Day Beef Hot Pot 105
Cock-A-Leekie Soup 106
Corned Beef Chowder 107
Country Soup 105
Cowboy Stew 105
Creamy Asparagus Soup 106
Creamy Tomato Soup....................106
Family Fare Chicken
Vegetable Soup 106
Fish Chowder 105
Golden Onion Soup 108
Great-Grandma's Old-
Fashioned Soup 108

Hearty Lentil Soup 108
Lumberjack Chili 107
Maine Corn Chowder 107
Meaty Split Pea Soup 108
Potato Broccoli Cheese Soup 108
Potato Ham Chowder 107
Potato Soup 108
Potato Soup 108
Taco Soup 106
Three-Bean Soup 105
Vegetable Beef Soup 106

Vegetables Delight

10-minute Pecan Squash..............114
Almondine Asparagus 116
Au Gratin Potatoes.......................113
Baked Celery 120
Baked Cream Cabbage 116
Baked Creamed Matchstick
Potatoes 112
Baked Creamed Spinach 115
Baked Green Beans in
Tarragon Cream 115
Braised Celery and Potatoes 120
Bread & Butter Pickles 119
Bubble and Squeak (Cabbage
and Potatoes)...............................118
Carrot Ring...................................110
Celery Crunch 119
Chuckwagon Baked Beans 120
Cinnamon Sweet Potatoes 111
Convenient Mashed Potatoes 112
Copper Pennies 110
Corn Pudding 119
Country-Style Fried Cabbage 109
Creamed Cabbage Vegetable
Dish From 1891 116
Creamy Chive-Stuffed Potatoes ...118
Crock-Style Barbecue Beans 109
Crockpot Baked Beans 120
Crumbed Julienne Carrots 109
Crunchy-Top Potatoes 118
Cucumber and Onion Combo 119
Cucumber Cinnamon Rings 119
Debbie's Yummy Baked Beans 117
Dietetic Scalloped Potatoes 113
Dilled Baby Carrots 110
Easy Potatoes 111
Foiled Potatoes 111
French-Fried Eggplant 114
Glazed Radishes, Carrots
and Peas 121

Glorified Beans 115
Glorified Cabbage 116
Golden Fried Snow Peas 121
Harvard Carrots 110
Hash Brown Delight 109
Hash Browns................................111
Hasselback Potatoes 112
Holiday Stuffed Winter Squash 117
Italian Green Beans 120
Mashed Potatoes and Turnips 112
Molasses Baked Beans 115
Mushroom Cutlets 121
Mushroom Fritters 110
Mustard Potato Patties 112
Peas and Caulifl owerets 121
Piquant Pickled Green Beans 120
Pizza Potatoes 112
Popeye Power...............................115
Potato 'n Broccoli Supreme 118
Potato Pie 111
Potato Pudding 113
Red Cabbage 119
Rice Pilaf with Fresh
Mushrooms 110
Roly-Poly Carrot Marbles 110
Saucy Asparagus 114
Sauterne Sauerkraut 121
Savory Southern-Fried Corn 119
Savory Succotash 114
Scalloped Eggplant 114
Special Spinach Squares 115
Spinach Loaf 115
Spinach Mashed Potatoes 118
Spinach Strata 121
Squash Pillows 117
Stuffed Acorn Squash 117
Stuffed Patty-Pan Squash 114
Stuffed Potatoes 113
Sunshine Sweet Potato Balls 118
Sweet Potato Balls 111
Swiss-Style Scalloped Potatoes ...113
Swiss-Style Green Beans 120
Tillie's Asparagus Scalloped
Potatoes......................................113
Tomato Souffle' 109
Tomato-Squash-Zucchini
Stir-Fry 121
Union Pacific Potatoes 112
Vegetable Bake............................114
White Potato Pie 111
Zucchini Applesauce 117
Zucchini Fritters 116
Zucchini Quiche 117
Zucchini Rounds 117
Zucchini Surprise 116

specialty cookbooks

✳ BREADS ✳ SOUPS ✳ MEATS ✳ FRUITS ✳ DESSERTS ✳ SALADS ✳

Recipes From the Old South
Over 100 Recipes! ✳ Creole Cooking ✳ Louisiana Gumbo ✳ Jambalaya ✳ Creole Swiss Steak ✳ Southern Fried Chicken ✳ Sweet Potato Pone ✳ Avocado-Shrimp Salad
$1.25 *(#SOUTH)*

Outdoor Cooking
Barbequed Sparerib Racks ✳ Summer Salads ✳ Steak Orientale ✳ Grilled Fish ✳ Rice Stuffed Fish ✳ Stuffed Pigs ✳ Tangy Grilled Lamb Patties ✳ Texas Chile ✳ Shish Kebob ✳ Barbecue Sauces
$1.10 *(#ODOR)*

Easter Cakes, Cookies & Confections
Easter Bunny Cake ✳ Ice-Cream Cake ✳ Orange Sponge Cake ✳ Whipped-Cream Cake With Fresh Fruit ✳ Frostings ✳ Hot Cross Wheat Germ Ring ✳ Easter Kolacky
$1.00 *(#EASTER)*

Breakfast Breads
Raisin and Bran Can Bread ✳ Mixed Fruit Loaf ✳ Grape Nut Bread ✳ Fruit Breads ✳ Sweet Potato Muffins ✳ Brioches ✳ Bagels ✳ Scones ✳ Popovers ✳ Biscuits ✳ Sweet Rolls ✳ Muffins
$1.25 *(#BREAD)*

Sumptuous Soups
137 Soup Recipes ✳ Hearty Meat Soups ✳ Chicken Winners ✳ Chilled Soups ✳ Soups from Foreign Lands ✳ Dumplings & Toppings ✳ Cheesy Soups ✳ Potato Soup ✳ Low Cal Soups
$1.10 *(#SOUP)*

Dessert Special #5
Over 60 Elegant Desserts ✳ Chocolate Mousse ✳ Butter Brickle Fruit Dessert ✳ Custard ✳ Date Pudding ✳ Creme De Menthe Brownies ✳ Hummingbird Cake ✳ Frozen Lemon Custard
$1.25 *(#DSRTSP)*

Collection of Chowders
Vegetable Chowders ✳ Corn Chowder ✳ Carrot Delight ✳ Ministra ✳ Egg & Cheese Chowder ✳ Cheesy Salmon Chowder ✳ Poultry Chowders ✳ Maine Fish Chowder
$1.25 *(#CHOWD)*

Cooking with Apples
200 Great Apple Recipes ✳ Hamburger Apple Casserole ✳ Sunday's Chicken Bake ✳ Gourmet Gravy ✳ Apple Crumb Stuffed Pork Chops ✳ Grammy's Apple Blossom Cake
$1.25 *(#APPLE)*

Barbequing & Summer Salads #1
Over 175 Exciting Recipes ✳ Blue Cheese Burgers ✳ Steak Kabobs ✳ New Mexican Barbeque Sauce ✳ Lamb on a Stick ✳ Sausage in Foil with Vegetables ✳ Jack Frost Salad ✳ Pina Colada
$1.25 *(BBQ)*

---

clip coupon and mail today

ORDER FORM

QTY	ORDER #	NAME / DESCRIPTION	PRICE

Please add $1 postage & handling
No charge when order is $10 or more

U.S. FUNDS ONLY. NO COD'S PLEASE.

TOTAL ENCLOSED

MAIL TODAY TO:

specialty cookbooks
House of White Birches
306 East Parr Road, Berne, IN 46711

NAME

ADDRESS

CITY / ST / ZIP

A198